foremother love

Marta Gonzalez Murphy, *Phillis Looking Forward*, 2024. Pencil on water-
color paper, 9 × 12 inches. Author's personal collection.

black feminism on the edge

A SERIES EDITED BY JENNIFER C. NASH AND SAMANTHA PINTO

foremother love

Phillis Wheatley and
Black Feminist Criticism

love

DANA MURPHY

DUKE UNIVERSITY PRESS DURHAM AND LONDON 2025

Printed in the United States of America on acid-free paper ∞
Project Editor: Ihsan Taylor
Designed by Matthew Tauch
Typeset in Garamond Premier Pro and ITC Avant Garde
Gothic by Westchester Publishing Services

Library of Congress Cataloging-in-Publication Data
Names: Murphy, Dana, [date] author.
Title: Foremother love : Phillis Wheatley and Black feminist criticism /
Dana Murphy.
Other titles: Black feminism on the edge.
Description: Durham : Duke University Press, 2025. | Series: Black
feminism on the edge | Includes bibliographical references and index.
Identifiers: LCCN 2024044825 (print)
LCCN 2024044826 (ebook)
ISBN 9781478031956 (paperback)
ISBN 9781478028734 (hardcover)
ISBN 9781478060925 (ebook)
Subjects: LCSH: Wheatley, Phillis, 1753–1784—Criticism and
interpretation. | American poetry—African American authors—
History and criticism. | American poetry—20th century—History
and criticism. | Feminist literary criticism—United States—History—
20th century. | Feminism and literature—United States. | Women and
literature—United States.
Classification: LCC PS866.W5 Z6665 2025 (print) | LCC PS866.W5
(ebook) | DDC 811/.2—dc23/eng/20250428
LC record available at https://lccn.loc.gov/2024044825
LC ebook record available at https://lccn.loc.gov/2024044826

Cover art: Billie Zangewa, *A Vivid Imagination*, 2021 (detail).
© Billie Zangewa. Courtesy of the artist and Lehmann Maupin,
New York, Seoul, and London. Photo by Jurie Potgieter.

For Mami and Mima

CONTENTS

Writing the preface to my book is an act of autonomy, yet it is one that connects me, inevitably, triumphantly, stickily, to the prefaces that precede my own. It is an act that harks back to works like the 1970 anthology *The Black Woman*, by Toni Cade (Bambara), in which her preface commences with this empowered call to action: "We are involved in a struggle for liberation." When Bambara proceeds to outline the various ways that traditional, long-established academic disciplines have ignored or obfuscated the study of Black women, she paves the way for "a beginning—a collection of poems, stories, essays, formal, informal, reminiscent, that seem best to reflect the preoccupations of the contemporary Black woman in this country." While understandings of Black feminisms (plural) increasingly both include and extend beyond Black women, I, along with Bambara, am hopeful about marking out another kind of "beginning." Across archive and genre, I gather the ensuing pages to clarify my own thoughts and to engage other scholars via citation and conversation—what otherwise would have evidenced itself in "a habit [of writing] letters to each other," "treadmilling the same ole ground."[1] Indeed, part of why I write is that the person I refer to within these pages as "Phillis" is both nowhere to be found within *The Black Woman* and yet is everywhere informed by and connected to the concerns of Bambara's pivotal anthology.[2]

Although Phillis herself is not individually featured in *The Black Woman*—among mentions of Sojourner Truth, Harriet Tubman, Mary McLeod Bethune, Ella Baker, and Fannie Lou Hamer—echoes of her story appear therein and across Bambara's work. In an interview with Claudia Tate, for instance, published in Tate's 1983 *Black Women Writers at Work*, Bambara describes how challenging it was to write her first novel, *The Salt Eaters* (1980), while she balanced academic and community work and the work of mothering her daughter as a single parent: "The short story, the article, the book review, after all, are short-term pieces," entailing "work for a few days," but a novel was "a way of life." A novel required time "to master the craft, to produce, to stick to it no matter how many committee meetings get missed," which resulted in "periods . . . when [Bambara was] just unavailable."[3] Tate's introduction to *Black Women Writers* presents Phillis and Bambara as part of a continuum. She emphasizes, "Black women writers did not suddenly begin to write in the 1970s," but there was "continuous literary activity among black American women ever since Phillis Wheatley in the eighteenth century." Many of these women, however, lacked the privilege of publication and flourished only in brief flashpoints garnered from their own resources, or their work was "hidden away from the world by both choice and fortune," complicating future scholars' efforts to study (with) them.[4] If we extend Tate's efforts by reading Phillis as a Black woman writer at work, we may recognize Phillis's attempts to make space for her craft and life in the same way we do for her future counterparts.

Rather than read Phillis and her poems as constrained by the historical context from which they emerged, a complex and often delimiting strategy for understanding Black writers who were enslaved, this book reads Phillis as a key participant in a longer transhistorical conversation within Black feminist thought. For example, the ways Phillis's work was once presented to the public has left a lasting—but, for me, unconvincing—impression. About two hundred years prior to *The Black Woman*, the publisher's preface to Phillis's 1773 book, *Poems on Various Subjects, Religious and Moral*, began thus: "The following Poems were written originally for the Amusement of the Author, as they were the Products of her leisure Moments. She had no Intention ever to have published them."[5] This "protest" may have been, as Julian D. Mason Jr. writes, "traditional" of the time, but the reasons it reads as a faux pas to readers today will also serve to preface my own book.[6] Today, few are likely to read with seriousness Phillis's 1773 *Poems* and its paratexts in total isolation given the many intervening histories and texts contextualizing the ascription of Phillis's literary prowess to "the Importunity of many of her best, and most generous Friends; to whom she considers herself, as under the greatest Obligations."[7] Indeed, one later tradition would preface Phillis quite differently, a specific movement—named a few years after the publication of Bambara's anthology—devoted to "writing about Black women writers from a feminist perspective."[8] In the 1970s and thereafter, a growing "Black feminist criticism" would validate readers' expertise in the subtext wrought through Black writers' lives and work.

The future-to-past application of Black feminist criticism to retroactively read Phillis and others also functions valuably in the inverse: past-to-future. As Farah Jasmine Griffin wrote in 2002, "*The Black Woman* is not a black feminist text as we have come to understand that term . . . [but it] paved the way for an emerging black feminism that came to flower in the late seventies and early eighties."[9] Phillis's poems and letters, Bambara's anthology, and other texts and materials indicative of Black feminisms from past to present continue to contribute to our increased understanding of its extensive parameters. In 1977, when Barbara Smith heralded Black feminist criticism as "a consistent feminist analysis" that "Black women writers and Black lesbian writers exist" and are not "beneath consideration, invisible, unknown," she built on shared knowledge of "the political, economic and social restrictions of slavery and racism [that] have historically stunted the creative lives of Black women."[10] This book also understands and works within the complexity of Black feminist criticism as both a late twentieth-century term arising from a unique period in literary history and an analytic that has broader historical influence and shape. This two-pronged approach enables us to understand why a writer like Phillis is invisible in works like *The Black Woman*, and yet be able to use works like *The Black Woman* to provide methods for understanding Phillis (and vice versa). As Black feminist criticism is taken up by future scholars and writers, it continues to challenge temporal-spatial restrictions in many directions, radically reconceiving our understanding of the when and where from which critical work originates.

Black feminist criticism is still often associated with literary critics publishing within academia or with writers working simultaneously as professors, but this perspective requires one to be mindful of the ways racial capitalism has structured, and still structures, academic halls. For example, Audre Lorde, who later worked as a critic and professor, began her career writing poems while working as a librarian and later explained in her 1984 book, *Sister Outsider*, that this was because poetry was "the most economical" form of art, having spent "the last few years . . . writing a novel on tight finances."[11] This should help us understand why writing individual poems (often addressed to prominent individuals) also worked well as a medium for Phillis to gain support and readers, while her commitment to crafting a *book* of poems was also a "struggle for liberation," in Bambara's sense, as its publication led to Phillis's manumission thereafter.[12] In other words, sometimes poetry functions as prefatory work to criticism, and sometimes it is the reverse. Sherley Anne Williams published her only critical book, *Give Birth to Brightness* (1972), while she was beginning work as a professor, and only later would be able to publish the books of poems and the novel she really wanted to write (while still teaching). For her own part, Bambara "chose not to enter completely into the academy," demonstrating that "the sites of intellectual work are always shifting."[13] Even when she was teaching in the university, her "mellowness scented the room like lavender."[14] Likewise, Black feminist criticism will be engaged in this book as it blurs into spaces in and beyond the academy, drawing Black feminists variously in and out. Whether Black feminist critics were removed by force or left teaching by choice to pursue better opportunities elsewhere, I explore each critic's leave-takings (or imaginations of leaving) in order to better understand their values and goals in their unique contexts.

Thus, while the above literary-historical moments of prefacing speak well to the scholarly questions I ask herein, they are offshoots of a larger expressive context that itself prefaces my work. In terms of how I found my way to this project, *Foremother Love*'s roots began long before I or, by extension, anyone in my family had any direct means of participating in this conversation in academia. I grew up in a multiracial family in a historically Black neighborhood on the northwest side of Altadena, California, and attended a private elementary school that prided itself on being interdenominational and multicultural—though what I remember most are the forms of secular expressive cultures that traveled through my group of friends in the form of dances, songs, and other modes of shared performance. In other words, outside of class, we were often left to our own devices to "study" what we wanted: ourselves and each other in a community often composed of our own celebration. I remember dance parties, where we made up our own dances to popular contemporary songs; "poem parties," where we recited works by famous poets and orators; and slumber parties, where we play-acted all manner of 1990s "girl power" imaginings. In many ways, this interdisciplinary environment would predict the scholarship I would do later in life. But I do not remember thinking too far ahead during childhood about what my college environment was going to be like. I just assumed it would be something like TLC's music video for their 1992 song "Baby-Baby-Baby"—an extension, in other words, of the kinds of Black feminist sociality and the safe space of the historically Black women's dormitory I already had access to, at least in part, in my elementary school and after-school program.[15] Unfortunately, this safe space all but disappeared when my parents moved my sister and me to public school a couple of cities away, only fifteen minutes west.

Gone were the affirmative parties of my earlier youth and the spaces where I and others like myself were celebrated. Middle and high school were largely replaced by a predominating culture of whiteness.[16] Yet select Black feminist expressions survived.[17] For example, 2007 is a pivotal year in this book, as it marks a shift in the concentrated moment, among the deaths of several originating theorizers, of the first generation of the tradition of literary and cultural thought first named thirty years prior, in 1977, Black feminist criticism.[18] The year 2007 is also when my mother, an administrative assistant then in her early fifties (working at the technology institute where I would later teach as the first assistant professor of Black studies and English in its history), came home one weekend afternoon during my last summer of high school and gave me a CD that she and her friend—both Black women who had immigrated to the United States as children from Cuba and Belize, respectively—had found earlier that day in a thrift store. Though she often gave me music I loved, I'm not sure why exactly my mother placed this album—released in the mid-1990s, with a Black woman singer looking off into the distance on its cover—in my hands. Nevertheless, I must have listened to Etta James and her musicians' interpretation of jazz standards across her 1995 album *Time After Time* hundreds of times in the coming months. It felt like I was listening to a version of myself. Hers was a music that signaled something to me far from our tiny unincorporated town on the northern edge of Los Angeles.[19] Something I could not yet articulate on my own.

Time After Time. The album my mother and her friend gifted me felt like it was my soul's own. An inheritance. I knew I had latched onto something that reminded me of my early Altadena years, something that was keeping me alive and that I couldn't let go. As I pondered the album's sound and meaning, I began to practice critical imagination and let the work help me think some things through. I now understand that listening to the album was an early act of resistance, and a preface to my later work as a Black feminist critic. But in 2007, as a student in a predominantly white public high school and town, I did not have much in the way of academic resources to learn more about the singer, her historical context, and what this album could have meant to a wider community of listeners. I had yet to discover that a criticism that could speak to the experiences of others like me had been taking shape across the institutions of literature, music, art, scholarship, and more, long before I was born. By listening re-iteratively, I was treating James like a "foremother," someone whose work I admired and connected to in an emotional sense but whom I could not yet—or struggled to—connect with across the broader textures of my everyday life. It was not until many years later that I read an autobiography by James and learned that although our lives had in several ways been different, we shared many similar experiences and ideas about Black women's expressive histories and about maternal lines of thought, survival, and rage.[20] The question was how to interlink my solitary practice of listening to Black women with a living practice of Black feminist criticism as an academic, teacher, and writer within, again, a larger community.

Along my journey toward the work of this book, I recognized Phillis's work as beautiful in the same way I recognized James's album. While I don't recall reciting Phillis's poems at the poem parties hosted by the multicultural private elementary school I once attended, I learned about and recited the work of other Black poets and writers from a young age. I first remember encountering Phillis in my early teens when I read my mother's copy of Dudley Randall's 1971 anthology *The Black Poets*.[21] Later, as a doctoral student in English at the University of California, Irvine, I returned to Phillis, or she returned to me—in coursework and across the texts in my qualifying examination reading lists. In the tradition of Black criticism, I saw how often she was read, how she defied exhaustivity. She was often (though not always) conferred honor by critics only because she was a foremother—the first or nearly the first—and often because her later readers were starved for choice in that matter. However, scholars and creative writers' differing accounts of their encounters with Phillis across a variety of archives and literary traditions—some positive, some glaringly vexed, and most deeply ambivalent—seemed to suggest the existence of a body of critical labor she helped generate, a criticism that was so often then richly applied to other writers. Accordingly, I argue herein that the critical energies that have gathered around Phillis in a way resembled my early survival strategy: listening to one beloved album over and over again in wait of, or perhaps in preparation for, a criticism that could do more.

In my doctoral dissertation, I wrote about how Phillis wrote poems that enabled her (future) readers to say what she could not. In this book, I take the opposite tack. Like Etta James in the jazz album my (fore)-mothers gifted me—who I later learned made the album because she wanted to sing songs made influential by her foremothers (including Etta Jones) as a way of returning to herself and what she wanted to sing[22]—I want to participate in a criticism that I believe Phillis began. I want to do criticism that feels like the party epistemology (knowing how to party) of my youth, like the feeling of study in the context of the dorm in TLC's "Baby-Baby-Baby" video—understanding that, in the absence of such critical attending, these practices become vulnerable to erasure. Rather than make any claims about her being silenced, which, in many ways I suppose she was, I want to celebrate Phillis by writing this, my own critical work, on the way to a poem. I want to celebrate her by writing a poetics based on reading her life, her work, and the Black feminist context that, in turn, has enabled me to understand her. What would happen if we listened not just to Phillis, her (abridged) poems, or her biography, but also to all the ways that critics have listened to her over the years, and especially to the ways that those crafting a Black feminist analysis have listened to her? In what follows, I aim to problematize before returning, possibly more lovingly, to the idea of the foremother, and to what it means to provide care for those prior members of our literary lineage. As it stands, this project is a lamentation for the free spirit that was Phillis as well as the version of myself I was at thirty-one (Phillis's estimated age when she passed away).[23] It is something of a praisesong. Something like foremother love.

—PALO ALTO, CALIFORNIA, JUNE 2024

naming ceremony

A legacy is not static. It is not suspended in the time frame of the birth and death of the person. Rather, it is like a poem. It imparts to each person who encounters it an affirmation, a confrontation, or an indulgence.
—MELBA JOYCE BOYD, *Discarded Legacy: Politics and Poetics in the Life of Frances E. W. Harper, 1825–1911*

I was born too late to have been able to take the Poetry for the People (P4P) course designed and taught by June Jordan (1936–2002) in the Department of African American Studies at the University of California, Berkeley (UC Berkeley), between 1991 and 2002. And I didn't get a chance, when I was a UC Berkeley undergraduate shortly thereafter, to take the version taught after Jordan's passing due to cancer and offered by Aya de León since 2006.[1] Nevertheless, all these years later it is one of my favorite courses to keep thinking about. In video recordings of Jordan's class meetings with her "student teacher poets," she looks so relaxed and often sits with her forearm rested on the back of the chair beside her—a deferral of her status as the professor and a sign of invitation to her students to become the teacher poets who would not only co-instruct their peers but also offer their knowledge and skills to communities in and beyond the Bay Area. It is not Jordan who asks, "Okay, so what are we doing today?" about fifteen minutes into class on February 13, 2001, but one of her students.[2] Indeed, much of the class is spent in cheerful student-facilitated discussion of, not so much the content of recent P4P lectures—how to understand a specific "poetic genre, history, or tradition," or close reading or workshopping students' weekly poem assignments—as how to navigate various pedagogy-related issues and questions: attendance, grading, and so on.[3] I can sense Jordan's interest in each and every turn in the conversation, how she often leans forward to listen to and laugh along with her students gathered around the table. In other words, the lesson was about learning to ask one another, "How are we going to be together?"[4]

I understand these questions to be part of a naming ceremony that centers a collaborative and continuously reflexive ethic when it comes to defining one's academic praxis. Indeed, I hope this book reads more like Jordan's "student teacher poet" classes than their lecture counterparts. As I've been thinking about this project in one form or another for over a decade now, earlier versions were composed of the groundwork studying that might be well suited to a lecture. Many previous scholars of the figure I refer to herein as "Phillis" (as part of a tradition of Black feminist naming I will unfurl in the coming pages) have already provided knowledge of her life and work within more traditional disciplinary formats.[5] What follows is not just my own contribution to the field of thinking about, as Tara Bynum writes, "what the poet Phillis Wheatley thought about as she brushed her teeth," but also what I thought about all the times I was brushing my teeth during the writing of this book.[6] Like other young scholars entering the profession during and after the end of the Obama era, my career began with mentors warning me of the precarity of the now profoundly adjunctified contemporary university.[7] My own transition from working in public land-grant universities to a private technology institute also meant going from having access to monumental research library systems to working with a single humanities librarian to build a collection in my field. Writing a book on Phillis that drew on a body of knowledge most of my technoscience students had never even heard of was a singular, albeit challenging, opportunity to think, teach, and write like I was reinventing the wheel. This impossible task gave me, at the very least, the breathing room to listen to the unruly student within who kept asking of herself as well as the university and the world, "What are we doing?"

This question is also an extension of the question Jordan asks multiple times across her 1985 essay "The Difficult Miracle of Black Poetry in America or Something like a Sonnet for Phillis Wheatley." Reflecting on Phillis's childhood survival of the Middle Passage and the moment she arrived to be auctioned in Boston, Jordan asks, "Was it a nice day?" The question's second instance appears after Jordan describes, or imagines, the Wheatley family eating breakfast, leaving home ("ordered the carriage brought 'round") to head to the auction, where they would then purchase and enslave Phillis. The question then becomes a refrain, always broken off onto its own line, repeated five more times across the essay, functioning like a skip in a record, a jolt in repetition that causes the reader to be confronted again and again with the fact that underlying Phillis's (vexed, according to Jordan) poetic output is her lived experience as enslaved. Reflecting on Phillis's most famous poem, "On Being Brought from Africa to America," and its "assertion" of a Black identity before slavery, Jordan asks, "Where did that thought come to Phillis Wheatley? / Was it a nice day? / Does it matter?"[8] Jordan never answers these questions outright in her essay, but they ring out and continue to demand response. On its face, and in its first mention, "Was it a nice day?" reads innocently enough, like a mere query on the weather, but with each subsequent repetition it becomes a clearly voiced critique. In forcing attention on the everyday factors surrounding Phillis's enslavement, Jordan connects readers to someone who might otherwise exist only at a historical remove. She also posits the argument (by asking "Does it matter?") that the material lived experience surrounding Phillis's poetry does indeed matter.

In this book, I present new research on Phillis's lived experience and how it shaped her poems while at the same time demonstrating how the lived experiences and labor of Black feminist critics of Jordan's generation have shaped that said research in generative ways. Altogether, it is a work rooted in archives, criticism, and poetics that reads the work, life, and afterlife of Phillis in the context of Black feminist criticism. Following Melba Joyce Boyd, I argue that Phillis's "legacy is not static. It is not suspended in the time frame of [her] birth and death." Indeed, throughout this book, I read Phillis's "legacy" like I would "a poem," as variously "an affirmation" of liberative thoughts, as "a confrontation" with power, or as "an indulgence"—as pure joy, pleasure, or peace.[9] As I follow new or revisited moments along the wide arc of Phillis's legacy, my analyses move temporally between the late eighteenth and twenty-first centuries, while tilting more toward the significance of reading Phillis alongside the articulation of "Black feminist criticism" starting in the 1970s. Thus, this term is alternatively used to describe, depending on the context, either a distinct body of work by late twentieth- and early twenty-first-century literary and cultural critics, following the earliest published articulation of Black feminist criticism as a term by Barbara Smith in 1977 in "Toward a Black Feminist Criticism," or a transhistorical criticism whenever critics or writers from earlier time periods evidence work that is suggestive of Black feminist critical values. Overall, it is important, to this critic, to define Black feminist criticism (a subset of Black feminist thought) with some looseness, celebrating the ways it is picked up and remixed by practitioners past or future, deepening our capacity to read in new, different, and flexible ways.[10]

Beginning with works like Alice Walker's 1974 essay "In Search of Our Mothers' Gardens" and culminating in Nellie Y. McKay's (1930–2006) passing and subsequent memorialization by her colleagues, Phillis is often present in key texts by and about Black feminist critics. When she is invoked, as in June Jordan's 1985 essay "The Difficult Miracle of Black Poetry in America," it is often with a combination of awe for her survival of the abject conditions of chattel slavery and a vacillating assessment of her poetry as at times "graceful and musical" and at other times, due to her fidelity to the conventions of her time, "awful, virtually absurd."[11] In McKay's 1998 essay "Naming the Problem That Led to the Question 'Who Shall Teach African American Literature?'; or, Are We Ready to Disband the Wheatley Court?" Phillis's literary success is curtailed by her having to prove her authorship, a concession that is indicative to McKay of the ongoing shortage of support for Black literary scholars.[12] Sometimes, however, Phillis is not invoked at all. Even so, I read her alongside the articulation of Black feminist criticism via its other corresponding works of literature and culture from many critics and writers hailing from diverse academic institutions and other intellectual sites.[13] For example, Phillis does not appear in some of the most famous extant Black feminist critical works, including Barbara Smith's 1977 essay "Toward a Black Feminist Criticism" as well as the 1977 Combahee River Collective "Statement," which is not a work of "literary analysis" but has "functioned," as Arlene R. Keizer writes, "as an empowering manifesto for black feminist literary critics."[14] Accordingly, this is not a book about Phillis's influence in a linear sense, but a theoretical meditation on the condition of her divine presence, and at times absence, as a shaping force within the Black feminist critical tradition in published as well as unpublished settings, including archives.

Archival work often demands long hours of labor, unexpected travel hiccups, and, ultimately, uncertain returns, but it is one of a few areas of contemporary academic life that provides the possibility of a kind of research that confounds traditional disciplinary constraints and tidy canons. Rather than uphold the authority and totality of the select works that have been published, it can be a radical way to dance in the aisles of history.[15] While the space between memory and record is often where Phillis found her groove as a poet, and many of her poems evidence a subtle choreography as they navigate the use of poetic language by an author who was enslaved, we know she did not have the leisure or luxury to preserve her own personal archive, and all its ephemera, in its entirety. What remains extant (letters, one volume of public-facing poems, a handful of additional public-facing poems, two proposals for a second volume, and maybe two copybooks) pales in comparison to what we would most certainly wish to find. We wait with bated breath in hope that someone discovers her diaries, her lost second volume of unpublished poems, "personal" poems (i.e., love poems for Obour), a lock of her hair—or, best of all, something so unexpected yet familiar we would not have recognized we had always longed for it until we suddenly chanced upon it.[16] Since we have not received such news and expect none, perhaps we may afford her something else: the ability to move freely in the possible space of the unrecorded. Such porous archival boundaries are traversed in the works, published and unpublished, of many future Black feminist critics, not limited to poems that have validated the importance of creative, as well as critical, speculation in our engagement with Phillis's life and work.[17]

Far from the distanced foremother or "progenitor" at the beginning of the canon, Phillis has lived on in the published works and unpublished archives that developed out of Black feminists' lives, work, and all too often untimely deaths.[18] Reading her as she appears within the wider archives of several future Black feminist critics and creative writers, especially those who often rejected "the politics of respectability" that predetermined the narrow pathways to power and privilege within their disciplines, opens alternate contexts for understanding Phillis's creative and critical work.[19] For her future counterparts, Black feminist criticism was a way to perform and practice an imperfect and messy love—both intrapersonal and interpersonal—that nevertheless proclaimed their determination, venturousness, and sense of a free self beyond others' attempts to further the opposite. Rather than embody an unrealistically optimistic rubric for solidarity, Black feminisms continue to navigate complex questions of affinity and difference. For example, while several works of Black feminist criticism praise Phillis and claim her as a foremother without hesitation, even more critique her quite severely, in what could also be read as instantiations of the darker side of foremother love, wherein critique does not mean a lack of love but does point out a thornier relation. This enables us to theorize Black feminisms beyond a solidarity rooted in cohesion and may help us better understand the perhaps more roughhewn work of Black feminists who have not been held in popular regard and who remain understudied by a criticism primarily focused on positive legacies. From unpublished letters and extant drafts of novels and poems that were never published, to the notes that laid the groundwork for works of criticism that were never attributed primarily to them, Black feminist critics demonstrated how much of their labor went unrecognized and unrewarded during their lifetimes. Their archives also provide insight into the roots of creative or critical success: constant strivings for due compensation, recognition, and resources—sometimes via unconventional academic channels as well as personal networks, a legacy shared by Phillis and by critics today.

Thus, in conjunction with acts of homage (or admonition), Black feminist critics have also indexed Phillis when they grappled with hardships like those that she experienced and when they asked questions that she also raised by virtue of being Black in times of ongoing white supremacy. Such works include but are not limited to Black feminist ephemera as survival work, writings on the state of Black people in academia, elegies and other genres of mourning (e.g., a growing archive of memorial essays and poems for Black feminist professors), and more. This book will not just tell Phillis's story in the way readers have heard it told countless times before, but it will evidence her significance for the development of a specific Black feminist critical practice that I term *foremother love*. In crafting this concept, I return to Barbara Christian's definition of Black feminist criticism as "a response to the writer to whom there is often no response, to folk who need the writing as much as they need anything."[20] I define *foremother love* as the Black feminist expression of the love (however complex) of a distantly related or even unrelated feminist ancestor as a legitimate relation in which to practice inheritance, mourning, celebration, and, if not friendship, collegiality. Foremother love is my description of a specific kind of Black feminist critical response; not all instances of Black feminist criticism are foremother love. As I will discuss in the following chapters, Phillis's own varying practices of fictive kinship with, and estrangement from, the figures in her poetry—as well as members of her community with whom she corresponded—predicted the many kinds of affective attachments future readers expressed for herself and others. Foremost among these will be their records of the academic, administrative, quotidian, and unexpected ways in which Phillis lives on, via foremother love, in Black feminist criticism and Black studies generally.

With regard to who might consider themselves a Black feminist critic who practices foremother love and who is the recipient of such scholarly study, some may assume that most accounts of Black feminisms privilege Black cis women at the expense of all other identities. However, my inheritance of this field is one that understands a long-standing intention to root the tradition in care for our society's most marginalized constituents and, others by equitable extension, a Black feminist foremotherhood that is written for LGBTQ+ people, such that "women," when used across this book, refers to both cis and trans women.[21] Contemporary Black feminist scholarship has been shaped by the theoretical contributions of gender-queer theorists and theorizing, enabling us to recognize that while several of the Black feminist critics studied in this book were cis women, they often practiced gender queerly by subverting gendered expectations and resisting legibility and visibility within cisheteropatriarchal critical lenses. Thus, I wish to reclaim the word *foremother*, which has so often been used to demarcate a distanced if not staid literary ancestor, as a term for someone who is, as Janet Mock writes, "celebrated" for being a "spiritual healer," "cultural bearer," "caretaker," and "instructor."[22] Whether one prefers to use *foremother* or the gender-inclusive term *foreother*, *foremother*—as I use it across this book—should be understood as blurring the gender binary, affirming gender nonconformity and diverse sexualities, and welcoming the possibilities that become available for study as a result. Further, while *foremother* might have once meant something narrow, *foremother love* is an extension of my study of a genderqueer Black feminist criticism and urges us to love all who understand themselves (and all whom we might understand) as fore(m)others.

It perhaps goes without saying that I was not alone while I wrote this book. Communicating what I know about Phillis and other Black feminist critics has also required bridging a variety of other disciplines. In addition to a selection of Black feminist critical works (and works about Black feminist criticism) that are engaged throughout, this book builds on criticism and theory on a variety of topics that have helped provide a model for my approach herein. In the 1980s–90s, select Black literary scholars reinvigorated the critical conversation on Phillis in various ways, which I aim to build on here.[23] In addition, works in Black poetry and poetics inclusive of or beyond Black feminisms of the period I focus on have been important models.[24] I have also been inspired by several works in white feminist or white women's historical poetry and poetics.[25] More recently, scholars of Black feminist literature and theory broadly have revisited the latter half of the twentieth century in ways that have been generative for this project.[26] And as previously noted, there are several recent extant biographies of Phillis (and recent creative reimaginings of her life), as well as many older versions of such works—and I try to cite from whichever is most definitive in order to ground what I can in the historical record. Everything else is my own, and at the time of this writing there are no other recent scholarly monographs on Phillis read as a single-author or defining figure via a literary critical theoretical perspective, though there are an increasing number of book chapters and works in academic journals.[27] *Foremother Love* is a scholarly monograph on Black feminist criticism generally as well as an intellectual reflection on Phillis—the first book to read Phillis as a Black feminist critic in concert with a collective of critics, my attempt to fulfill a wish to assuage the isolation she faced at the end of her life. Overall, to cite Nellie Y. McKay, the book aspires to the following practice: "If you found something, you let everybody else know what you found. You didn't keep it to yourself."[28]

From Foremother to Black Feminist Critic

As I approach the subject of naming, I invoke what Barbara Christian says toward the close of "The Race for Theory": "I can only speak for myself. But what I write and how I write is done in order to save my own life. And I mean that literally."[29] That being said, the following marks one way—my own—to think about Phillis's life and afterlives, how she saved her own life, mine, and many other lives in between, even while the conditions of those lives have shifted across time in various levels of proximity to the genres of social death. Thus, my approach to naming often differs from that of other contemporary scholars.[30] As you may have already noticed, I mainly use the name Phillis (as June Jordan did).[31] My writing about Phillis is attentive to her feminist selfhood, our fictive kinship, and the possibility of her embodied guiding voice, in the same vein that guides similar methodological acknowledgment by Black feminist scholars across diasporas. For example, in *Pedagogies of Crossing* (2005), M. Jacqui Alexander introduces "Kitsimba—not the [archive's] plantation name Thisbe," but the "true name" of "one of those captured and forced into the Crossing," whose very knowing "confront[s] the limits of . . . methodology."[32] Likewise, M. NourbeSe Philip's *Zong!* (2008) is coauthored, "as told to the author by Setaey Adamu Boateng," while the bottom-of-the-sea-like margin of each page of *Zong!* becomes a memorial to all the renamed, discursively transforming bone into being.[33] Similarly, I refer to her intentionally as Phillis, a name for the woman who existed in between the institutional documentation of slavery and marriage. While some have recently taken to calling Phillis "Wheatley Peters," which combines the names of her enslavers and her husband, I prefer not to use this approach, since I largely focus on Phillis's feminist and queer relationships with other Black feminist critics past and present in my book, including with her colleague-friend Obour.[34]

Of course, Phillis itself is also a vexed name, as it is the one ascribed by the Wheatleys in reference to the ship the *Phillis*, "her Christian name presaging her in its dark wet wood."[35] I retain it only to reclaim it, as I imagine she herself did, given that she retained this first name even as a freedwoman. Such a name also signifies in memoriam her counterparts in the African diaspora, who were connected via and forged into new subjectivities within the hold of such a vessel.[36] As Meta DuEwa Jones writes, "~~Phillis~~'s natal name is a keyword."[37] As I am also a Black diasporic subject, albeit now some generations from my ancestors' experiences of the Middle Passage, I have come to feel an intimacy with Phillis that is also a loss, as though I am both speaking to and about an ancestor of my own.[38] I also concur with Frances Smith Foster and Nellie Y. McKay, who experienced a sense of intimacy due to the experience of conducting long-term research together on their 2001 *Norton* critical edition of Harriet Jacobs's narrative, and referred to their project by her first name, Harriet.[39] In addition to its resonance within the contexts of Black feminist criticism, Phillis's name has several other ties. For example, "the given name Phillis, which means leaf or foliage, suggests a pastoral world and indeed recalls Virgil's Phyllis from the *Eclogues*."[40] In Latin, Phillis means "the name of the daughter of King Sithon of Thrace, who was changed into an almond tree, a stock female name in poetry"; "a pretty country girl; a female sweetheart"; and "a pretty or dexterous female servant."[41] As Phillis was an avid poet, I like to believe that her name combines the modern Black diasporic feminist as well as classical Latin poetic influences she embodied in her life and work. All this is to say that throughout this book I refer to Phillis using her first name as the best current expression of a number of my own scholarly investments. Further, if I could choose, my chosen full name for her would be Phillis Divine, taking up the word *divine* that she was so fond of in her poems as a term of endearment and a way to express my own foremother love for her.

The following story has been told before, and as readers of this book likely already know something of it, I'll not repeat too much of what has already been said. Typically, biographical or other scholarly accounts of Phillis's life begin with some version of the following: In 1761, a kidnapped Black African child (born ca. 1753) survived the Middle Passage and was renamed after the ship that bore her, the *Phillis*, and the Boston family of enslavers, surname Wheatley, who exchanged money for her flesh; a little over a decade later, the now young woman saw to the publication of her book of poems during a trip to London, ensuring that something of hers would transcend the violent conditions of her early life; however, she died of illness and poverty in 1784 (it is thought that her three young children died along with her). Stories about Phillis often begin this way due to an influential, though specious, memoir published by a distant member of the Wheatley family in 1834.[42] Thus, I devote the ensuing pages to a different telling, one that is more about how particular literary histories and texts have shaped our epistemological relationship to Phillis. While this book could have focused more on responses by early Black feminist critics and writers from the late nineteenth century, who tended to read Phillis positively, I've found they often also read the Wheatley family as benevolent in ways that are no longer supportable by the historical record.[43] Early twentieth-century Black male literary scholars tended to relegate Phillis to the eighteenth century, without having any particular aesthetic or political investments in that project.[44] Black Arts Movement or Black masculinist readings beginning in the 1960s decried that so few of her poems reference her enslavement.[45] More recently, scholars of "Wheatley studies" (now commonly called "Wheatley Peters studies") often emphasize reading her in her original eighteenth-century context.[46] Finally, those working on Phillis in the field of "historical poetics" privilege "the practice of reading [her poems] from the histories and theories of reading that mediate our ideas about poetry."[47] Overall, this book is grateful to the above methods of reading, even as it builds on them toward another analytic.

The task of Black feminist criticism of the late twentieth and early twenty-first centuries was how to adequately respond to issues of identity and lived experience (e.g., race, gender, sexuality) and issues of literary representation (e.g., history, poetics, theory). Phillis has long presented a barrier to this field because she is not, as previously noted, archivally transparent along all axes of her being or output. Thus, she became a "foremother," a term that functions as a placeholder, demarcating moments where Phillis continues to confound scholarly understanding.[48] Largely, ascriptions of Phillis as foremother are invoked with regard to her curious literary historical precedence, that is, her position as an early or even first figure in the timeline of Black access to the publication of "books" rather than Black "material culture" broadly.[49] Sometimes, or in conjunction with this, Phillis's foremotherhood is also understood primarily within discourses of pregnancy and childbirth (carrying and then bearing or "birthing" the Black literary tradition).[50] In many cases, when Phillis is introduced in either of these contexts, it is perfunctorily and without further interrogation of the ramifications of these claims—eliding a range of possible critical-affective relationships that readers have had or may have with Phillis. Meanwhile, Phillis's intensified foremother status has meant that she may be deeply unpopular and ubiquitous at the same time—all the while only perfunctorily critically engaged. Complicating ideas of literary output or childbirth as standalone or solely definitive events—a revision of Phillis as not merely a foremother who writes and/or gives birth but a foremother whom we love for doing these things and more—could widen the field of possibilities in which she is allowed to interact as a living participant across the Black feminist critical tradition. This would entail showing Phillis a different kind of foremother "love," and demonstrating care for and recovery of her as an extension of our flesh. It would entail engaging Phillis both as a foremother and as a Black feminist critic, as someone who is often held apart yet who is part of that history of holding.

To call Phillis a foremother as well as a Black feminist critic is to claim, I argue, that it is not her ubiquity but, rather, the uneven way she appears across Black feminist criticism that demands not merely our attention but also our love. For example, when figures like "Sojourner Truth, Harriet Tubman, Frances E. W. Harper, Ida B. Wells Barnett, and Mary Church Terrell" gain mention by name in the Combahee River Collective statement, it is in conjunction with the "thousands upon thousands unknown," whom readers are encouraged to recognize as "our mothers and sisters."[51] Similarly, in her introduction to the teaching guide to *Black Foremothers*, Barbara Christian writes that the biographies of Black women that do "exist are about women for whom there is readily available information," and she emphasizes the importance of the "ongoing effort to research, preserve, and write the history of black women."[52] While Phillis occupies a unique position as a historical figure in that she is, as of today, the subject of several biographies and scholarly works, she still remains difficult to encapsulate due to what Tara A. Bynum, Brigitte Fielder, and Cassander L. Smith discern as "a general politics of white supremacy that has for centuries made the study of Wheatley a vexed proposition."[53] Phillis's position as a freedwoman who wrote most of her literary output while she was enslaved has also led many scholars to throw up their hands. While Bynum, Fielder, and Smith root much of this trouble in white supremacy, this book will explore the ways in which various racialized and sexualized oppressive dynamics have impacted the attention given to recovering Phillis within Black feminist criticism specifically. As Samantha Pinto writes, "a black feminist epistemological orientation"—"a method of reading the political" in Phillis "through and with uncertainty" that "emphasizes vulnerability and interdependence as viable visions for black study"—enables us "to interpret generously and generatively through loss."[54] Indeed, as pre-2007 Black feminist critics' careers shifted and institutions changed, their analyses of Phillis have ebbed and flowed with varying levels of influence and power. Yet this is precisely why Phillis has remained an anomalous figure beyond any one person's influence and is far more legible within the discourse of what Black feminist criticism desires than some of its early proponents might have fathomed.

Accordingly, this book will read Phillis as a collaborator in the tradition of Black literature not only as someone whose poetry is invested in solicitations of response but also as someone whose work as a Black feminist critic—sustaining, sharing, explaining, and responding to her work and its wider contexts—suggests "there is still much more to Wheatley's story that we have not yet explored."[55] In fact, within the body of thought that has come to be known as Black feminist criticism, Phillis remains perpetually connected to several critical aspirations in quite complex ways, aspirations that include but are not limited to the desire for an overarchingly positive story of the tradition, a wish for synchrony between creative and critical work, and the maintenance of a shared idea of what constitutes Black feminist identity, friendship, and sisterhood. In terms of Phillis's own writing, again, most of her output was published while she was enslaved. Across this book, my close readings of her poems attend to their poetic effects and their historical contexts.[56] But because I am reading Phillis both as a poet and as a critic, I also read the ways her letters and other material surroundings respond to, and sometimes change, the original meanings of her poems. In this way, my readings of the poems look something like Elizabeth Catlett's 1946 linocut *In Phillis Wheatley I Proved Intellectual Equality in the Midst of Slavery*, wherein Phillis is depicted in an inverted version of her 1773 frontispiece image (this time she is facing the right), while the additional image of three enslaved women traverse—or join—the immediate background on which she is beginning to write.[57] Few works have imagined Phillis in an act of lived solidarity with other everyday Black people. Thus, *Foremother Love* seeks to change the stories we tell about Phillis and about Black feminisms—as they are theorized by her, her contemporaries, and other Black feminist critics past and future.

From Black Feminist Critic to Foremother

Barbara Christian (1943–2000), one of the early theorizers of Black feminist criticism, proclaimed in a 1982 speech at the Center for Research on Women at Stanford University that Phillis's "poetry reflects little of her identity either as a Black or a woman."[58] Christian then concurred with Alice Walker, another early theorizer of Black feminist criticism (especially a version she termed "womanism"), who had written in 1974 that "it [wasn't] so much what [Phillis] sang, as that [she] kept alive, in so many of our ancestors, *the notion of song*."[59] Christian's assessment of and agreement with Walker regarding Phillis's shortcomings arose during a pivotal moment in her career as a Black feminist critic and by then tenured professor of African American studies at UC Berkeley.[60] Having recently published her first book, the 1980 *Black Women Novelists*, and her 1980 *Teaching Guide to Accompany [Dorothy Sterling's] "Black Foremothers,"* it was just a few short years before Christian would publish her 1985 essay collection *Black Feminist Criticism*. Although Phillis would not feature extensively in any of these works, Christian's (dis)acknowledgment of Phillis in her 1982 speech, later published as an essay in *Black Feminist Criticism*, provides a useful rubric for understanding Phillis's position in the tradition of burgeoning literary criticism on Black women writers. Understandably, Phillis could not receive ample study in Christian's book on Black women novelists, nor in her teaching guide to Dorothy Sterling's *Black Foremothers* (which presents biographies of Ellen Craft, Ida B. Wells, and Mary Church Terrell).[61] Instead, it is in the expansion of authors and genres under study across Christian's *Black Feminist Criticism*, where Phillis makes a brief entrance as part of Christian's critical tradition, albeit only as a "curio."[62] Today, Christian's inability to fully interpret Phillis within her discipline's critical lexicon, from the foremother to the Black feminist critic, calls out for understanding and redress.

To foreground a better understanding of Christian's critical context as well as a call for redress is to acknowledge the conditions in which all Black feminist critics work. In other words, any foremother's vulnerability to mistake or misfortune, no matter how distanced they may seem from us, may one day be our own fate to share. Frustratingly, as will be discussed throughout this book, many Black feminist critics experienced systemic discrimination in their everyday and work lives in ways that paralleled the inequities Phillis experienced even after she was manumitted—often to the point of "premature death."[63] Just under two hundred years after Phillis passed away at the estimated age of thirty-one in 1784, Audre Lorde (1934–92) asked the readers of her 1980 book, *The Cancer Journals*, "What are the tyrannies you swallow day by day and attempt to make your own, until you will sicken and die of them, still in silence?"[64] Thus, I argue that one reason Phillis has not been the sole subject of any Black feminist critical book is the paucity of Black feminist critics to begin with. In response, I want to take this moment in my own career to break the silence that Lorde alludes to—the silence that stifled Phillis as well as many late twentieth-century Black feminist critics, and which still largely imperils my generation—while I have momentary capacity and the resources to do so. For to be a Black feminist critic today is to live in a somber reality. In addition to Lorde's untimely passing, several other major Black feminist critics renowned for reaching the pinnacle of academic stature and success have also passed away of cancer before their time, including Christian, McKay, Jordan, and Sherley Anne Williams (1944–99), truncating the first generation of official Black feminist criticism, which had begun to burgeon from the 1970s to the late 1990s and early 2000s.

Several scholars have also noted the prominence of this cancer cluster.[65] Ann duCille, in 2011, attributed the deaths of Christian, Jordan, McKay, Williams, as well as Sylvia Ardyn Boone (1940–93), VèVè A. Clark (1944–2007), Claudia Tate (1947–2002), and "too many others," to the "stress" of "our work environments."[66] Biographer Vincent Carretta also attributes Phillis's premature death to what was likely a combination of her being unable to find a publisher for her second volume of poems; the imprisonment of her husband, John Peters, for "debt"; and her ongoing vulnerability to the "asthmatic condition that had afflicted Phillis in previous winters."[67] Thus, this book will mourn the collective misfortune of the loss of recent Black feminist critics' lives alongside Phillis's own early death as a negative legacy that demands continued response. Contrary to academic disciplines that understand the critic as a solely professional role separate from one's subject position, this book will necessarily understand Black feminist critics' lives as intertwined with their work. Furthermore, I argue that the Black feminist critics under study herein were doing such a great deal of labor to recover the tradition of African American and Black literature generally that they likely did not have time to recover an archivally complex figure like Phillis, and even if they did, doing so would have required access to the Black feminist critical language that they were currently developing. Thus, I maintain that via the Black feminisms they practiced in their lives and in their critical work, Phillis's future Black feminist counterparts ensured that her story would not be forgotten. Indeed, the way contemporary Black feminist critics have written about each other has inspired the way I write about Phillis herein.

In 2000, when Christian passed away from lung cancer at the age of fifty-six, Ann duCille wrote a tribute essay memorializing her life and work. DuCille noted how quickly Christian had died (their colleague Sherley Anne Williams had passed away from cancer just the summer before), especially given that they had recently spoken on the phone about, among other things, "the health and well-being of black women in the academy."[68] In Christian's own tribute essay following Audre Lorde's passing in 1992 due to breast cancer, Christian wrote, "I am stunned, unprepared, though I should not be."[69] Indeed, as more and more Black feminist critics died prematurely in the 1990s and early 2000s, Black feminist memorial tribute works quickly became an elegiac tradition in their own right. Over and again, the authors of these elegiac remembrances have grappled with how to memorialize these mourned figures as they passed from the role of the living Black feminist critic to that of the foremother. Writing in tribute of these figures, these authors were establishing Black feminist criticism as a mode of cultural inheritance powerful enough to bestow "nothing less for its subjects than everlasting literary life."[70] DuCille noted Christian's discomfort with "generational metaphor[s]" like academic mothers and daughters, given "her own sense of marginalization" and concern about whether anyone "would freely choose a low-status mother and focus on intersections of race, class, gender in Afro-American women's literature."[71] The increasing prevalence of the Black feminist tribute essay demonstrates that several major academics indeed saw people like Christian as worthy of being foremothers.

Of course, *foremother* is not a term that Christian would likely have used to describe herself or her colleagues as modern-day scholars. In Christian's tribute to Lorde, she wrote that Lorde "refused to be limited to any one category, insisted on being all that she was: poet, black, mother, lesbian, feminist, warrior, activist, woman," imitating the elongated descriptions Lorde herself often used to self-identify and thus truly paying "tribute" to Lorde.[72] Christian also deferred the stricture of a single definition in terms of her own praxis and selfhood, writing in the introduction to *Black Feminist Criticism*, "What is a literary critic, a black woman critic, a black feminist literary critic, a black feminist social literary critic? The adjectives mount up, defining, qualifying, the activity. How does one distinguish them?" Similarly, while the word *foremother* and the phrase *Black feminist critic* predate my scholarship, my use of them here is idiosyncratic to my own critical propensities and desires. Nevertheless, I strive above all to remain true to the ethos of Christian's theorization of Black feminist criticism, including her mandate that "reading is itself an involved activity. It's a response to some person's thoughts, and language, even possibly their heart."[73] Christian's emphasis on the possibility of reading the "heart" of someone's writing underlines the significance of affective response within the body of responses that one might gather loosely under the title of Black feminist criticism. Christian could have easily demarcated the lines of what Black feminist criticism was and what it was not. Instead, she invited her readers into the tradition in ways that would require them to involve themselves in Black feminist criticism's definition, shifting the onus of responsibility away from Christian as the solitary expert and onto an array of Black feminist critics stewarding and extending its tenets and values.

Accordingly, this book will unfurl the history and status of the figure of the Black feminist critic with a similar attention to the ways it has, sometimes purposefully, sheltered a fair amount of definitional ambiguity. Rather than underpin a stable concept of Black feminist criticism, the archive often presents questions rather than clear answers and thereby encourages a model of the tradition that gathers around concepts such as difference rather than cohesion, and collective ethical study rather than the model of the singular expert. As a scholar, Christian remained skeptical of "prescriptiveness," preferring to remain open to different ways "of seeing the world and of playing with possibilities," especially the "difficult to control" instantiations of "multiplicity" and "eroticism" in literature.[74] Thus, in the following pages, I will use *foremother* less as a term for a stable role than as a gesture toward the critical practice of responding to one's (fictive) ancestors that I call "foremother love." While there is no one singular way to practice foremother love, one might recognize it as love rooted in, and an extension of, the theorizing of Black feminist critics as an ongoing affective-poetic practice. For example, some iterations of foremother love might lean heavily on Audre Lorde's concept of "the erotic," whereupon not only reading but even the act of "building a bookcase" alongside another is a practice of knowledge production.[75] I may never get to experience the act of building a bookcase with Lorde or Christian or Phillis, but this book—and those it joins in reading—functions as the next best thing. Others might take inspiration from a number of related concepts, from the joyful fictive kinship of Barbara Smith's "home girl" and Kevin Everod Quashie's "girlfriend" to the somber broken kinship of Rita Dove's "mother love" and Saidiya Hartman's account of "los[ing] your mother."[76] At its core, foremother love is about the people who came before us with whom we choose to feel close, and the lengths we go to bridge difference or distance between us.

Models for the foremother love practiced in this book do surface in various permutations across Christian's work. For example, Christian's infamous 1987 essay "The Race for Theory" has received ample attention for her critique of critical theory, or what she terms "New Philosophy," used specifically to describe a form of literary criticism informed exclusively by Western European philosophy.[77] Christian combatted the erasure inherent in this theory's tendency toward extreme abstraction by rooting her work as a critic in her identification with "the women I grew up around," women who "continuously speculated about the nature of life through pithy language that unmasked the power relations of their world," a language that Christian recognizes is also "celebrated, refined, critiqued" in Black women's writing.[78] These women are Christian's folk, and their vernacular oral literature forms the grounds of a language for written literature as well as for its criticism. In fact, key to Christian's argument is the importance of these women's lives to what she is able to do as a critic. Furthermore, for a critic to state explicitly that these women form a key part of their studies and livelihood means that what is tangible in their lives is not just acknowledged but also understood as actively shaping Black feminist criticism. While other versions of literary criticism may peremptorily disavow the writer for the text in accordance with a single theory, Christian instead emphasizes, "We need to read the works of our writers in our various ways and remain open to the intricacies of the intersection of language, class, race, and gender in the literature."[79] About two years before Kimberlé Crenshaw published her renowned articulation and definition of the Black feminist term *intersectionality* in her discussion of the erasure of Black women's identities in the discipline of law,[80] Christian posited the concept as a guidebook for practicing Black feminist criticism outside the prescriptiveness of one single-minded theory.

It is in, as Christian puts it, "the intricacies of the intersection of language, class, race, and gender" that Phillis indeed comes alive as a bellwether for the history of Black feminist criticism. Christian's conceptualization, what I will forthwith call "intricate reading," provides some guidance on how scholars might conduct intersectional criticism, or what Christian would call "the intersection of language, class, race, and gender" about two years before "intersectionality" was codified in scholarship under that name.[81] Again, Crenshaw's well-known articulation of the term *intersectionality* was first published in the 1989 essay "Demarginalizing the Intersection," in which she importantly explained that Black women live at the intersections, using the analogy of the traffic accident that occurs when two cars enter an intersection at the same time to describe a society that mainly caters to those whose identities travel within only certain intersecting lanes at the exclusion of others, so to speak.[82] While Crenshaw detailed the detrimental effects of an ignorance of intersectionality on Black women in a legal system that does not consider the ways they are excluded both on the basis of gender (since legal recourse might cater only to white women) and on the basis of race (since legal recourse might cater only to Black men), "Demarginalizing the Intersection" and the expansion of Crenshaw's research on intersectionality in 1991 in "Mapping the Margins" remind us that what often afflicts the law is troubling other disciplines as well. I propose that using Christian's concept of intricate reading in conjunction with other similar Black feminist formulations helps to continue to define a practice of Black feminist critique of literature as just as wide-ranging in its possible applications as Crenshaw's "intersectionality" was.

Following Christian's advice, I argue that intricate reading expands the possibilities of someone as seemingly archivally complex as Phillis. If, as Henry Louis Gates Jr. wrote in the 1988 introduction that appears at the beginning of each volume in the Schomburg Library of Nineteenth-Century Black Women Writers, "the history of the reception of Phillis Wheatley's poetry *is* the history of Afro-American literary criticism," then I would argue that the history of the reception of Phillis *herself*—read in conjunction with her work—is the history of Black feminist criticism.[83] Gates's introduction underlines the often negative ways Phillis is received within Black literary criticism, often by Black masculinist critics. Yet Gates's use of Phillis as the primary prefiguration for nineteenth-century Black women writers points to another critical tradition in which it is not enough to consider Phillis alongside other writers (or in critique by

Black writers) on the basis of their shared racialization or gender alone: It is important to consider Phillis alongside *Black feminist critics* actively living, working, and complicating the intersection of race, gender, and writing. If Black feminist criticism is an intellectual tradition in which the experiences of racialized gender transform, if not supersede, the experiences of being a writer, what does it mean to consider *Phillis* as not only a Black woman writer but as a Black feminist critic? In fact, the question of who Phillis was—or is—outside of, or in addition to, her identity as a poet mirrors a similar debate in the differentiation of the tradition of Black feminist criticism as distinct from others within literary criticism. Thus, in some of the earliest Black feminist critical readings of Phillis, she is engaged not just for her poetry, or just for her status as an enslaved woman, but for the complex ways she demands ongoing articulation of the complexity of her racialized and gendered writerly identity, requiring us to read what we can of her more intricately.

An Invitation

In this book, each chapter is as capacious as possible. I want them to feel not like folders in an archive after processing, but like the moments before papers are bequeathed to an institution. I want to linger in that time when everything is still (dis)organized in ways that made the most intrinsic sense to their author. To savor and protect the possibility of different critical interconnections. You, dear reader, may need to reorient yourself to this and work to follow my wavering thread of a through line rather than one stitched from a more traditional discipline of literary study (although I do my best to signpost navigational milestones along the way). *Foremother Love* is not an exhaustive account of all the legacies of affection for Phillis within the tradition of Black feminist criticism from the eighteenth century to today. Instead, it is an attempt to articulate in this moment what it might mean to be a practicing Black feminist critic despite all the difficulties of finding support for a life and work built on "foremother love" as read via Phillis and a selection of her future counterparts. Reflecting my research, teaching, and writing from the past ten years, this book is not organized hierarchically around any one critic; rather, each chapter conveys the interarticulations of several critics regarding a different conceptual aspect of Phillis's Black feminist critical legacy, and my own theorization of a selection of Black feminist critical moments as they index foremother love transhistorically. Again, the book's major intervention is in providing the first scholarly monograph on Phillis in conjunction with Black feminist criticism, theorizing her as a living participant in ongoing conversations in the discipline today. I hope you enjoy this book's transformative reading, its critical homage to previous and living critics, and its invitation to you to participate in the tradition going forward.

Chapter 1, "Obour Outsider," centers on how we might theorize one of the most archivally preserved Black relationships in Phillis's life: that of her friendship with Obour Tanner. Sometime shortly before she passed away in 1835, Obour, also an enslaved woman, bequeathed her personal collection of a first edition of Phillis's *Poems* and several letters Phillis wrote her between 1772 and 1779. While previous scholarship has often focused on the letters' cultivation of intimacy for intimacy's sake, I argue across this chapter that Phillis and Obour were not just friends but colleagues who communicated transactionally for the sake of their own respective goals. This chapter also navigates key ephemeral expressions (most glaringly, the loss of Obour's side of the correspondence) that complicate our ability to read friendship easily or transparently in the fragments that remain. To read these works has, for me, necessitated an analytic that gives language to the interstitial spaces between friendship acts, such that they may be studied without sacrificing acknowledgment of the real ways in which they were delayed, impeded, or erased. Further, while their correspondence has been studied before, I focus on the meaning of Obour's bequest and what it means that she harbored Phillis's letters and poems for over fifty years before bequeathing them—what it means that Obour was a key critic of Phillis's work and early practitioner of foremother love. Alluding to Audre Lorde's 1984 collection of essays, *Sister Outsider*, and applying Lorde's concepts of "the erotic" and "difference," terms central to her theorization of a Black feminist love that is radically interpersonal in the attempt to theorize queer solidarity between Black women and white women, Obour's choice to extend Phillis's work to the care of a young white woman provides a window onto nineteenth-century possibilities for feminist solidarity as well as challenges to such legacies today.

Chapter 2, "Their Eyes Were Watching Phillis," continues to interrelate Phillis and her future Black feminist counterparts. Therein, I describe how critics have reckoned with Phillis in the absence of definitive autobiography given that Black feminist criticism continues to grapple with the question of how critics may ethically talk about the silences in their research subjects' lives, especially the silences they purposefully cultivated, without compounding such silence with one's own acts of scholarly erasure. While no act of reading is ever completely neutral, this chapter traces a set of readings of Phillis that do not purport to be neutral at all, practicing foremother love with reckless abandon. Alluding to a period in the 1970s wherein Black feminist critics reimagined copyright to photocopy, share, and collectively read Zora Neale Hurston's 1937 novel *Their Eyes Were Watching God* when it was out of print, this chapter focuses on print and social engagements with Phillis that reckon, sometimes with great speculation, with the silences in her life and work in order to shed light on the histories behind their methodological practices. While several scholars, including Saidiya Hartman, have debated the extent to which speculative ascriptions of voice in some ways perpetuate and in other ways truncate historical violence, I describe why it is worth attending critically to these instances of projection, as doing so opens further inquiry into the ways in which moments of critical encountering reflect understudied historical dynamics. Phillis's critics inserted themselves not merely into what she wrote but also into what she did *not* write, and the long history of readers trying to rewrite Phillis's poems into the poems they would rather read indexes readers' own desires, fears, and grievances.

Chapter 3, "In Search of Our Foremothers' Gardens," moves to the most ephemeral threats to Phillis and her counterparts—their financial precarity, health issues, and deaths—while also making space for different, perhaps more nuanced understandings of ephemerality in the "garden" and in the elegiac poems critics never got to write for themselves. Overall, this chapter demonstrates that Black feminist critics are never working alone. From Phillis to her modern-day counterparts, they have engaged in transhistorical practices of collaboration, collection, preservation, and validation, not only for the subjects of their research but for themselves as members of the community they research. Presuming that Phillis wrote not just as a poet but as a critic to negotiate her manumission, this chapter contextualizes her letters and poems, especially elegies, within Black feminist criticism. Building on the theorization of mother love in Alice Walker's 1983 essay collection, *In Search of Our Mothers' Gardens*, this chapter asks how Black feminist critics may successfully recognize and thus research the work of their foremothers, especially the work of figures with whom they may have previously failed to find commonality. Beginning with the self-mourning inherent in Alice Walker's unexpected critique of Phillis, this chapter also reveals how Walker, Phillis, Williams, and Wanda Coleman practiced elegy not only in the poetry they wrote for others but also in genres of self-writing that retroactively expressed their own unmet professional desires. While these elegiac practices should have sustained both Phillis's and more recent Black feminist critics' careers, they alone were not enough to combat institutional forces that oppressed these critics. Thus, this chapter engages in a practice of restitutive criticism, wherein I retroactively lovingly mourn foremothers Phillis, Williams, and Coleman by constructing an elegiac criticism out of the archival fragments of their work.

Finally, while this book lingers long in the years between the 1970s and 2000s, I conclude with a brief chapter titled "We're Ready" that discusses the current life of Black feminist criticism, or, perhaps more accurately, my own intersection with Black feminist criticism in the latter half of my life, from the late 2000s to early 2020s. This chapter presents an overview of what an early practitioner of Black feminist criticism, Phillis, might say to the scholars of today—especially via a reading of her poem about Harvard, "To the University of Cambridge in New-England." I will join Phillis's expression of hopes, predictions, and notes of caution for the university first in 1767 and then in 1773 with June Jordan's own reflections on the university over two centuries later in the 1960s to '90s. Then this chapter closes with a meditation on the university today and my own set of recommendations for ensuring the future of the Black feminist critical tradition via my visit to Barbara Christian's papers at UC Berkeley in 2023. This chapter comes full circle by acknowledging that foremother love, the practice of Black feminist criticism for our foremothers, will only continue to exist insofar as present-day Black feminist critics and allies receive support going forward. In other words, remembrance, in all its complex manifestations, is not just a one-and-done but instead comprises an ongoing set of commitments that necessitate continued resources. For those of us who do have access to the power and resources required to re-member figures like Phillis, there is no telling what we may do for the future of our tradition specifically and for the transformation of criticism generally.

CHAPTER ONE

Obour outsider

When I first began this chapter, I wanted to explain the contemporary significance of Phillis's relationship to a woman named Obour Tanner by referencing an essay I read as a doctoral student (sometime in the mid- to late 2010s) about a Black woman undergraduate student, I believe at the University of California, Berkeley (UC Berkeley), but for some reason I could not locate the essay despite fondly remembering it.[1] It remains bookmarked in my mind because it was about the frequency with which Black women students were apparently not sharing greetings when they passed by one another on campus. One student noticed this phenomenon firsthand and was disappointed, interpreting the moments she walked past her peers without so much as a nod or smile of recognition as sign of a lack of Black sisterhood on campus—a symptom of the university's larger culture of actively not supporting Black community on campus in a variety of institutional ways.[2] In my memory of this essay, this student confided her sense of a lack of casual Black sisterly acknowledgment to her professor (perhaps it was Barbara Christian? or June Jordan?), and together they made it possible for the student to organize a listening circle for Black women students on campus to speak to each other and formally redress this culture of not acknowledging one another so that a community could begin to come into formation. The essay was a meaningful example of a Black feminist response to a painful intragroup experience. Although not being greeted socially might strike some as trivial, for students at a predominantly non-Black campus, it can be quite alienating, especially in the absence of a solid sense of perceived belonging. This student was able to respond to intragroup conflict in Black feminist fashion, not with resentment but with care, because there was already some kind of structure in place for this response to flourish. The question remains, however, whether this structure was part of the university or whether it was a natural outgrowth of this student's own experiences of Black feminisms stemming from her life beforehand.

Again, in my memory of this essay, not only was this student able to confide in her professor, but her professor also empowered her to convene a listening circle. This is not surprising as numerous examples of research cite the unique demands made on Black women professors. These "sister/colleagues" are subject to extra and unpaid labor in academia, including conducting additional forms of care, mentorship, and professionalization support for Black students and colleagues and other students and colleagues of color who are not otherwise given access to such on the campus at large.[3] Importantly, the essay did not specify that the professor laid down the book or essay she was writing, postponed preparing for the classes she was teaching, or put her family and friends on hold in order to find the time to help this student. The professor practiced radical self-care by encouraging the student to organize the event largely herself, offering to show up and show her support, and otherwise continuing with her general duties as a faculty member. Although I must confess, despite remembering reading this essay circa 2015, I seem to have never saved it anywhere, or it got lost in the shuffle between different universities as I transitioned between academic appointments in the intervening years. I fully anticipate and hope I will discover this essay again soon as this book meets more and more readers, but I have not found it at the time of this writing. Yet this essay has been crucial to my own professorial formation as well as my theorization of what it means to be a Black feminist colleague, friend, and mentor.

In her 2007 book, *Lose Your Mother*, Saidiya Hartman details a similar experience of a text being spirited away. When she was conducting her doctoral studies at Yale University, Hartman found a record of her maternal great-great-grandmother's enslavement "in a volume of slave testimony from Alabama" in the library while she was working on her dissertation research, what would eventually be published as her first book, *Scenes of Subjection*, in 1997.[4] For Hartman, the discovery compounded a deep sense of her personal relationship to the histories she engaged as a scholar. In *Lose Your Mother*, Hartman recounts how, years later, searching for her great-great-grandmother's testimony again, she could not locate the exact text containing evidence of her experiences of enslavement, despite still having her notes and memory of the exact passages. This leads Hartman to wonder whether she had truly encountered it in the first place or whether her deep desire to find her family's life reflected in the archive meant she only imagined doing so: "It was as if I had conjured her up." Rather than eliminate the experience from her scholarly work entirely,

Hartman theorizes the missing piece of otherwise formative evidence of what "the archive dictates" and what we as scholars bring to bear as we read across such archives instead.[5] Central to, rather than peripheral to, Black feminist scholarship, the archival slipperiness of even our most formative works—as our doctoral and early-career research often requires attention to more formally institutionalized archives—requires a different practice of attention and recuperation. Furthermore, the ways in which we reimagine the archive for our own purposes itself holds meaning.

As for myself, my incomplete memory of the essay, which I have imagined taking place at UC Berkeley likely because that is where I completed my own undergraduate education, has also taken a life of its own. I know this much: I did not encounter the essay as a seminar reading in my doctoral coursework or during a conference presentation or talk, which I would have been certain to remember if I had, but I first came across it as a primary source while doing my own dissertation research. Even though I remembered Christian or Jordan as potentially being the professor at the center of, and later the writer of, the essay, I could not find evidence that either of them had written it, and I do not wish to do disservice to the labor of the person who did experience this and write about it, especially if I am not remembering her name.[6] At the same time, I cannot disavow how formative it was to read this essay nor all the ways I have imaginatively filled in the gaps in intervening years. Not only did the professor in the essay validate her student's feelings, but she also validated my own feelings as well. At the same time, something about this UC Berkeley student's anxiety about a lack of intrinsic Black feminist sisterhood struck me as interesting for its potential to theorize more concertedly the power dynamics of how and why sisterhood is performed and to what ends. What does it truly mean to acknowledge and recognize someone as a *sister*? Indeed, this question is as significant and complex today as it was in Phillis's lifetime.

Obour and Phillis's Black Feminist Collegiality

Sometime before she passed away in 1835, Obour Tanner (born ca. 1750) bequeathed a small yet significant literary collection: at least seven manuscript letters from Phillis to herself between the years 1772–79, and one published volume of Phillis's 1773 *Poems*.[7] Although this collection may seem small, it contained the largest known number of letters that Phillis wrote to any one person, and these letters were also Phillis's only known correspondence with another Black person, let alone a Black woman. As this chapter will discuss, this collection has gone on to have a lengthy afterlife. Nevertheless, the exact date of Obour's bequest remains unknown, and one of its few historical records, a letter from Katherine Edes Beecher to Rev. Edward E. Hale dated October 23, 1863, states only that Obour gave the collection to her "ages since."[8] By the mid-nineteenth century, Phillis had long since passed away, but her celebrity status still retained some cultural currency. By contrast, Obour has never been read as a foremother in her own right. Outside of Obour's bequest, little is known about her—mainly that, like Phillis, she too was likely a Black enslaved "saltwater" woman,[9] plus other select fragments we learn about her through Phillis's letters to be discussed herein, and select other archival fragments.[10] For example, the first extant letter, written by Phillis and addressed to Obour on May 19, 1772, suggests that it may have been Obour, not Phillis, who initially commenced their correspondence.[11] The possibility of Obour's originative authorship disrupts long-standing assumptions about Phillis as one of the solitary "first" figures in Black literature and widens the circle of potential Black literary prowess in the eighteenth century.[12] Not merely a significant literary contribution, this chapter argues that Obour's bequest lives on as a significant early act of Black feminist critical foremother love.

Phillis typically took anywhere from days to months to reply to Obour's letters, often apologizing for her belated or incomplete replies with statements like "my being much indispos'd this winter past was the reason of my not answering yours before now"; "I have been very Busy ever since my arrival or should have, now wrote a more particular account of my voyage"; "Pray excuse my not writing to you so long before, for I have been so busy lately, that I could not find liezure"; "I have but half an hour's notice; and must apologize for this hasty scrawl"; and "tho' I have been Silent, I have not been unmindful of you but a variety of hindrances was the cause of my not writing to you."[13] The extant letters flicker vignette-like in and out of each woman's life. In fact, the letters do not even confirm whether Obour and Phillis "ever met in person."[14] Despite the prevalence of Phillis's apologies for her belated replies, the letters contain expressions of joy, too, as Phillis writes in her earliest known reply to Obour on May 19, 1772: "Dear Sister / I rec'd your favour of February 6.th for which I give you my sincere thanks"—"favour" indicating both the physical document of the letter as well as Phillis's signaling of appreciation for Obour's favorable literary attention.[15] Unfortunately, no manuscripts of Obour's letters have yet to surface in the archive, and they are unlikely to do so given that Phillis's manuscripts remain lost, including the manuscript for her second book of poems.[16] Nevertheless, Phillis's letters to Obour were quite reciprocal and responded often to aspects of Obour's previous letters such that readers may catch glimpses therein of what Obour might have had to say. Unlike Phillis, Obour was not a published poet. However, like Phillis, Obour was a Black woman who could initiate her own correspondence.

Textual evidence in the letters reminds readers that Obour and Phillis could not have presumed their correspondence to be private, yet the letters are not without a particular expression of codified intimate familiarity.[17] For some readers, however, the Phillis-Obour correspondence begets an even larger narrative of desire in which the letters become read solely as the women's "most intimate attempts to communicate with each other."[18] Throughout this chapter, I argue instead that in addition to interpersonal intimacy, Obour and Phillis's correspondence also displays evidence of their strivings for professional agency, an extension of a collection of strategies they would have had to hone to survive as Black saltwater enslaved subjects. However, the letters' lack of privacy reminds today's readers to negotiate questions of treading carefully and noting whenever the desire to read these letters as transparent diaries, or as transparent letters no less, might surge overly intensely, overpowering what is possible to corroborate with evidence. In other words, the correspondence necessarily complicates the kinds of reading expectations and desires for a transparent subject that modern-day readers may bring to Black enslaved women's writing generally and Phillis's writing specifically. As Tara Bynum writes, the correspondence "takes us out of the confines of the engraved room of the poetry collection's frontispiece into geographies of community, worship, friendship, acquaintance, and eighteenth-century urban living," a "correspondence that demands a reconsideration of the archive, what we expect to find inside it, and what terms we use to bear witness to the realities of black women—in particular, those who look for each other in the Word of God and on the words of the page."[19] I aim to build on and extend Bynum's demand for a "reconsideration of the archive" in the coming pages by asking what it may mean that Obour and Phillis had to speak across both languages—in other words, what it may mean if we consider the ways they looked for and looked out for each other not only "in the Word of God and on the words of the page" but also in the other kinds of geographies they could cultivate interstitially in between "the Word" and "the words of the page."

Again, in her final letter to Obour, Phillis wrote, "Tho' I have been Silent, I have not been unmindful of you but a variety of hindrances was the cause of my not writing to you."[20] While one could imagine those "hindrances" as any number of hardships entering Phillis's life after her manumission,[21] and while the letters themselves are always mediated by the threat of other readers and are never completely free in their disclosure of Phillis's feelings, I also want to consider here that she is acknowledging the presence of another set of "hindrances" to her letters: the many poems she had to spend time writing and performing in order to create the conditions for her publication, upon which success she could then write letters to Obour. Phillis never included a personal poem addressed to Obour in their correspondence, suggesting that her poems, while not necessarily personal expressions of her most intimate feelings, were bound up in professional power dynamics that dictated who was the beneficiary of her poems and who was not. Approaching Phillis's letters as self-aware of their positionality in the system of inequality that also barred Phillis from communicating transparently in her poems helps make Phillis's gloss on the mindfulness of her silence in her last letter to Obour a useful rubric for Black feminist criticism in the wake of Phillis. As her body of work remains saturated with such silences, preventing readers from ever fully accessing her, it becomes incumbent on her critics to voice what she could not say. Unsatisfying as this may be to many critics who expect Phillis's letters and poems to express her truth, it is also the case that her silence has guaranteed that critics may extend the afterlife of her work centuries after her death. One such critic who acted on Phillis's behalf, in being addressed through the silence that commenced with Phillis's 1779 letter, and lasted until her death in 1784, was Obour herself.

Phillis's "silence," perpetuated by a number of factors that led to her early death and the truncation of her writing career, is remediated by Obour, whose bequest of Phillis's correspondence along with a copy of her 1773 *Poems* successfully keeps these signs of Phillis's voice alive. Although the letters Phillis wrote to Obour were examples of her nonpoetic writing, Phillis's letters and poems were intricately connected as part of Phillis's social networking. As I will demonstrate in this chapter, it is clear that Phillis wrote to Obour, at least in part, in order to facilitate the distribution of her 1773 *Poems*. Any delays in Phillis's correspondence should signal the presence of impediments to Phillis's ability to continue to publish and distribute her poetry. In the wake of Phillis's early death in 1784, her 1772–79 letters to Obour become retroactive indictments of her worsening circumstances and, in their fragmentation, plead for the need for continued correspondence. Two centuries and several decades later, as the letters remain incomplete artifacts, their porosity and portability continue to invite readers to extend the promise of Phillis's still-unfolding commitment to Obour. Significantly, the first reader to do so was Obour herself. Closing her final letter to Obour, Phillis wrote, "In time to Come I hope our correspondence will revive—and revive in better times—pray write me soon, for I long to hear from you—you may depend on constant replies—I wish you much happiness, and am / D^r. Obour, your friend & sister."[22] Obour, picking up where Phillis's silence and deferred response left off, held on to Phillis's letters into her old age and, before she passed away, bequeathed them to a young white woman in her thirties, then the ultimate assurance of continuing the possibility of receiving Phillis's "constant replies."

In addition to Phillis's acknowledgment of Obour's likely commencement of their correspondence in 1772, two other characteristics stand out in Phillis's reciprocation of Obour's letters. First, readers learn therein that Obour was discursively fluent in the language of Christian religious beliefs and, just as Phillis was in her poems, overtly verbal about her belief in a heavenly afterlife.[23] As Phillis writes in her first letter, echoing Obour, "I greatly rejoice with you in that realizing view, and I hope experience, of the saving change which you so emphatically describe."[24] Second, readers learn through three of Phillis's letters that Obour participated in the sale and distribution of Phillis's volume of poems, and indeed received entreaties from Phillis to capitalize on her "interest to get Subscriptions," essentially to find buyers in advance, as stated in her October 30, 1773, letter.[25] While previous scholars have already noted the significance of these two separate qualities of the Obour-Phillis correspondence, I argue there is also meaning to be drawn from understanding them as intertwined, if not mutually constitutive. Bynum reads Obour and Phillis's epistolary religiosity as sincere: "These women pursue God. They cannot help but testify to the greatness that is a transforming and saving God."[26] My argument to follow, however, aligns more closely with Katherine Clay Bassard's interpretation that Obour and Phillis employ "the language of conversion as a common lexical, syntactic, and semantic domain."[27] Textual evidence in Phillis's letters indicates that she knew the sale of her volume of poems, following her change in status to freedwoman in 1773, could help ensure her economic independence as a freedwoman.[28]

I also wish to extend Joanna Brooks's argument that Phillis "grew an audience, developed a network of supporters, published a remarkable first book, and engineered her own manumission," but by locating these actions in both a Black and white feminist context. While Brooks debunks Phillis's reliance on a panel of white men deciding to authenticate her authorship by focusing instead on the "white women" who "ultimately . . . evade their responsibility to [her]," I focus largely herein on Phillis and Obour's responsibilities to each other.[29] Enlisting Obour as a facilitator of exchanges in the sale of her poems, and thus as a conductor on the tracks of Phillis's own journey on the Underground Railroad, so to speak, suggests it was not simply a heavenly afterlife that Obour was referring to as a "realizing view" or "saving change," but also the freedom of a manumission that is lived beyond the experience of being manumitted.[30] It is in this context that the Obour-Phillis correspondence enacts a dialogue in which both women provide each other the affirmation they could only otherwise seek from God. Yet what does it mean that Obour and Phillis's hopes for liberative life following Phillis's manumission, however well founded, did not come to be?[31] Were Obour and Phillis being sincere in their expressions of religiosity, or were their words code for another mode of being altogether? In the space between what Obour and Phillis theorized and the kinds of life that were impossible for them to access in eighteenth-century New England lies a poetics waiting for an alignment that will finally bring it into realization, a poetics that is not realized but passed down to future generations in the form of Obour's bequest.

Attendant to the argument that religion was a safe way of expressing activism, I also argue that religion would have been an appropriate vessel in which Obour and Phillis could encode their liberative labor as joy. In other words, the appropriation of the enjoyment of religious discourse for eighteenth-century Black women like Obour and Phillis could itself have been an articulation of a kind of abolitionism. The Obour-Phillis correspondence illuminates the importance of interpersonal relationships within religious spaces in providing alternative genres for the illegal discourse of freedom. For not everyone in Black enslaved communities participated in religious spaces in homogeneous ways, including Obour and Phillis. As I will argue here, enslaved women also used religion to empower themselves to have personal and professional relationships with each other both within and beyond the bounds of enslavement wherein they could be permitted to have complex, sometimes self-contradictory, views and could establish their own sets of boundaries based on ever-changing contexts and experiences of enslavement. Thus, when I read Obour and Phillis express-ing religious joy to each other, competing, if not testing the boundaries of each other's religious fidelity and knowledge, I recognize the same com-petitive yet respectful and safe dialogue I too have long practiced. With my own Black feminist colleagues-friends, I have had to establish trust and connection in predominantly white academic spaces, although this is not always an easy archive in which to transparently communicate, due, again, to its location in predominantly white spaces. These kinds of negotiations of context have continued to be an issue in the tradition beginning with scholars' studies of Black religion during slavery.

To illustrate, Albert J. Raboteau's 1978 book, *Slave Religion*, does much to correct facile understandings of Black diasporic religion in the US South and internationally, and it has been hailed for its relevance to Black feminist cultural criticism.[32] For example, Raboteau attends to a long-standing binaristic historical debate about whether or not Black people who were enslaved in the United States retained their "African" culture.[33] However, one of the examples Raboteau uses to showcase an instance in which someone did not retain their African culture involves a misquota-tion and misreading of Phillis's writing. Compare, for instance, the brief moments wherein Raboteau pits two of Phillis's writings, including her infamous poem "On Being Brought from Africa to America," against the words of "'Aunt' Adeline, former slave." We do not learn anything about Adeline other than the following epigraph at the beginning of Raboteau's second chapter, "Death of the Gods," which quotes Adeline ostensibly speaking these words: "I had always been told from the time I was a small child that I was a Negro of African stock. That it was no disgrace to be a Negro and had it not been for the white folks who brought us over here from Africa as slaves, we would never have been here and would have been much better off." Raboteau does not provide the source of this quotation, but reading Adeline's full narrative foregrounds more inconsistencies in her racial identity than Raboteau might have liked.[34] Of course, Adeline's expression of Black pride in this epigraph contrasts strikingly with Phillis's "On Being Brought," with which so many readers have grappled to unsat-isfying ends for the ways it retranslates and seems to justify the Middle Passage as a Christian conversion experience, thwarting many readers' creative close readings attempting to prove otherwise. Raboteau quotes the first three lines of Phillis's poem at the outset of his chapter "Death of the Gods": "'Twas mercy brought me from my *Pagan* land, / Taught my benighted soul to understand / That there's a God, that there's a

Saviour too" and lets them speak for themselves.[35] Again, while Adeline is described as a "former slave," Phillis (whose name is misspelled "Phyllis") receives no such acknowledgment despite her enslaved status.

In fact, the epigraph of Phillis's writing that Raboteau uses to contrast with Adeline's words is from none other than Phillis's first letter to Obour on May 19, 1772, written while both Phillis and Obour were enslaved— but this information is strangely absent from Raboteau's writing. Raboteau's epigraph reads,

> Let us rejoice in and adore the wonders of God's infinite love in bringing us from a land semblant of darkness itself, and where the divine light of revelation (being obscured) is as darkness. Here, the knowledge of the true God and eternal life are made manifest; but there was nothing in us to recommend us to God . . .
>
> PHYLLIS WHEATLEY[36]

By contrast, here is the opening paragraph of Phillis's May 19, 1772, letter to Obour using its original capitalization and spelling, and I have italicized the sections from which Raboteau draws his epigraph:

> I rec'd your favour of February 6.th for which I give you my sincere thanks. I greatly rejoice with you in that realizing view, and I hope experience, of the saving change which you so emphatically describe. Happy were it for us if we could arrive to that evangelical Repentance, and the true holiness of heart which you mention. Inexpressibly happy should we be could we have a due sense of Beauties and excellence of the Crucified Saviour. In his Crucifixion may be seen marvellous displays of Grace and Love, sufficient to draw and invite us to the rich and endless treasures of his mercy, *let us rejoice in and adore the wonders of God's infinite Love in bringing us from a land Semblant of darkness itself, and where the divine light of revelation (being obscur'd) is as darkness. Here, the knowledge of the true God and eternal life are made manifest; But* there, profound ignorance overshadows the Land, Your observation is true, namely, that *there was nothing in us to recommend us to God.* Many of our fellow creatures are pass'd by, when the bowels of divine love expanded towards us. May this goodness & long suffering of God lead us to unfeign'd repentance.[37]

Raboteau cites from the italicized section above without further contextualization that it derives from a letter from Phillis to Obour, a letter in which Phillis thrice refers to Obour's previous letter to which she is responding in clauses such as "the Saving change which you So emphatically describe," "the true holiness of heart which you mention," and "Your observation is true." In fact, while Raboteau's epigraph closes with an ellipsis, it does not use an ellipsis to acknowledge his abridgment of this letter either at its beginning or in the sentence that in the original text reads, "Your observation is true, namely, that there was nothing in us to recommend us to God." Absent its epistolary context, this epigraph indeed reads, as Raboteau intends, like a critique of Africa as the "*Pagan* land" which Phillis calls Africa in "On Being Brought."[38] Yet neither this poem nor the excerpt of the letter above should be read as a lyric poem or a transparent personal declaration of Phillis's true thoughts alone. What Raboteau excises, I argue, is this letter's most significant core, namely, its mirroring validation of Obour as Phillis echoes her in replying, "Your observation is true."

In fact, read in its original context, Phillis's letter to Obour is so highly reciprocal of Obour's letter, a text that has since been lost, that it seems impossible for us to fully understand it without its partner text. Was Obour (traumatized and overwhelmed at the prospect of corresponding with a fellow saltwater enslaved woman) speaking ill of Africa and her enslavement such that Phillis, to appease her, responded in overly veiled religious metaphor? Did both women feel pressured to pen such words out of precaution that their letters could be intercepted or read by others before delivery? Did they write such words out of expectation that their letters would one day be published in the wider literary marketplace? Were both using religious metaphor to describe, not Africa, but the mortal world at large as "semblant of darkness itself" barring Christian conversion? What we may say is that the stakes of this letter are apparently so high that Phillis jumps through many hoops to participate in the correspondence, showing a great deal of care not just for religion but also for the Black religious woman addressed on the page before her, evidence of care that Raboteau erases when, for the purposes of his counterargument, he erases all evidence of Obour from his citation of Phillis's words written expressly to Obour. While Aunt Adeline's words in her epigraph, "I had always been told . . . ," seem expressly to connect her to a larger conversation, it is clear in the unabridged Phillis epigraph that she too is participating in a wider conversation.

While Adeline conveys pride in her African heritage (without any explicit reference to religion), Raboteau frames Phillis's religious writing as denying her Blackness, without contextualizing her writing as a response to her Black saltwater enslaved woman correspondent. As Sherley Anne Williams might say, "How could one work for a black revolution in which so many casualties were black?"[39] Again, to be fair, Adeline's writings are not contextualized or cited to their original, complex source either.[40] That these women hover unmoored in the same space of the epigraph suggests that there are more possible concordances across their remarks than differences. Nevertheless, their contrast is the basis of Raboteau's argument that, in Phillis's case, the memory of "African religious heritage was lost" and that some, like Phillis, were left unable to express their religion in the lexicon of "African beliefs or patterns of worship."[41] Read differently, Phillis and Obour appear not as disconnected from their ancestral culture by virtue of their fluency in Anglo-Christian religious discourse, but as reciprocating an investment in religion as a way of addressing its extradiscursive power dynamics in ways their African forebears and Black diasporic colleagues recognized before and alongside them. Phillis often reads differently from formerly enslaved writers because most of her extant writing was written while she was enslaved. She reads differently because she was not seeking freedom as a fugitive; rather, she was seeking manumission while remaining, albeit temporarily, within the spatial strictures of enslavement. But she is completely illegible as an enslaved foremother, insofar as Raboteau suggests she is in *Slave Religion*, only if we continue to abridge and decontextualize her work. Instead, it is possible to read Phillis via the generosity Raboteau applies to the study of other Black subjects in *Slave Religion*, in "a way that requires greater specificity and subtlety."[42]

Thus, Obour and Phillis's correspondence becomes legible as part of a diasporic tradition of Black discourse whose critics may read the strategies of enslaved women as not disjointed from but in concordance with those of formerly enslaved women. For instance, Sojourner Truth's own practices of religion following her escape from slavery are not merely replicas of her Dutch American enslavers' religious practices but extensions of her mother's teachings and style of delivery in combination with Truth's Dutch American context. In her 1850 *Narrative of Sojourner Truth*, in the early chapter "Her Religious Instruction," Truth recounts to her amanuensis how her mother would also engage in oral history. Her mother would often tell a younger Truth about her siblings, those had been sold elsewhere, going into great detail, although the narrative does not recapitulate this word for word. Her mother also engaged in regular evening teaching sessions with all her present children gathered together, understanding her missing children as equally and spiritually present. This, along with Truth's mother's insistent belief in a divine leader "who hears and sees you" and who responds in kind, deeply informed Truth's inner world. Truth later recounts how she commenced her own prayers independently, beginning with "'Our Father in heaven,' in her Low Dutch, as taught by her mother, after that, all was from the suggestions of her own rude mind," an example of Truth using religion as a springboard for her own purposes. All of this takes place, interestingly, within a "sanctum" that Truth herself weaves out of "willow" branches:

> She talked to God as familiarly as if he had been a creature like herself; and a thousand times more so, than if she had been in the presence of some earthly potentate. She demanded, with little expenditure of reverence or fear, a supply of all her more pressing wants, and at times her demands approached very near to commands. She felt as if God was under obligation to her, much more than she was to him. He seemed to her benighted vision in some manner bound to do her bidding.[43]

It was not the words themselves that mattered, neither the exact language used nor the precise religion practiced, but the crafting of a "sanctum" and its reactivation of an inherited Black feminist poetics that allows Truth to "[demand], with little expenditure of reverence or fear, a supply of all her more pressing wants."[44]

In fact, just as such spiritually inflected conversations about Black women's liberation precede the twentieth century, they extend into the future as well. Truth's spiritual conversations and experience of subsequent validation supplemented her growing sense of agency and eventual abolitionism and continued activism, which would be taken up by future Black feminist critics. This discourse on a freely expressed Black women's spiritual empowerment is alive in later Black feminist theoretical writing. For example, I concur with Bynum's recognition of Obour and Phillis's relationship as a precursor to Audre Lorde's "the erotic," although to different ends.[45] Bynum reads Obour and Phillis's correspondence as "decidedly ordinary glimpses into a friendship between women," and evidence of "what pleasure and friendship might look like to two enslaved women in New England," using, among the works of other Black feminists, Lorde's concept of the erotic—imbued by Bynum with what womanist theology cannot encompass.[46] Bynum thus recasts Lorde's definition of the erotic as a combination of Lordean Black feminism and theology: "the sense of satisfaction that comes from a profound faith and from sharing deeply this faith as friends."[47] My argument herein hinges a bit less on Obour and Phillis's spirituality in a faithful religious sense, however, and a bit less on the interpretation of their friendship for friendship's sake, and more toward understanding these letters as discursive performances that are a means to a political end. Although Lorde might argue that this desire for friendship is an important prelude to organizing, I will argue instead that the cultivation of the erotic between Obour and Phillis should also be read as one of the mediums in which they practiced something more along the lines of Black feminist collegiality rather than friendship alone, a collegiality that was a bit more calculated than friendship for its own sake in order to facilitate their print culture participation and transactions in the literary marketplace. What is especially helpful here is that similar practices of print culture transactions are in fact integral to Lorde's own definition of the erotic in its early formulation and ongoing recitations.

Audre Lorde and "the Erotic" as Solidarity

Lorde relishes in the process of defining and sharing "the erotic" in her 1978 essay "Uses of the Erotic: The Erotic as Power," later published in her collection *Sister Outsider* (1984), beginning with establishing it as "a resource" and "a considered source of power and information."[48] While the erotic has often been celebrated within feminist and queer contexts for its contributions to the discourse of empowerment and self-love, I argue that Lorde was also stretching toward an erotic "excellence" that she knew not everyone could attain or understand. Her own careful efforts to define the erotic across epistemological, physical, and spiritual planes evidence her attempts to describe a Black feminism still in process.[49] While some of Lorde's definitions of the erotic (note the use of the definite article *the* before *erotic*, denoting a specific understanding of the word within Lorde's unique context) hinge on personal experience ("It is an internal sense of satisfaction to which, once we have experienced it, we know we can aspire"), others hinge on etymology: "*Erotic* comes from the Greek word *eros*, the personification of love in all its aspects—born of Chaos, and personifying creative power and harmony." Far from just a word for sex in and of itself, Lorde's erotic would understand sex and sexuality in conjunction with other kinds of everyday feminist practices, which taken altogether could comprise a radical political shift in the world. As a multihyphenate figure, a poet as well as someone who took on a number of other personal and professional roles, I believe Lorde wanted to demonstrate through her own life that it was impossible to understand women's sexuality separately from all other aspects of women's lives and lived experiences. To honor the erotic was to honor herself and all the many ways she extended herself creatively and to others, starting with something as attainable as "moving into sunlight against the body of a woman I love," before perhaps "writing a poem."[50]

In fact, if readers are to understand the erotic, in Lorde's sense, as a lesson in understanding sexuality's wider context, they might apply its lessons to a better understanding of Lorde's own essay on the subject as well. For example, SaraEllen Strongman writes that Lorde's essay is usually discussed not as a literary text but as "an essential feminist text," especially in terms of "the intrapersonal aspect of the erotic that Lorde outlines"— "self-connection," "my capacity for feeling," and "it feels right to me."[51] Strongman reminds us, however, that "although 'Uses of the Erotic' is widely read and much cited, Lorde's argument that the erotic can bridge differences between individual women and encourage understanding and alliances is rarely discussed."[52] Strongman's social history of the relationships that Lorde navigated between the lines of her public writing draws special attention to the legibility of lesbian sexual intimacy across racial difference, an intimacy Lorde was alluding to when she described, in general terms, "dancing, building a bookcase, writing a poem, examining an idea."[53] Lorde's decision to cultivate a Black feminist definition of erotic power and harmony that was inherently lesbian and interracial in this essay thus links "depth of feeling" to reciprocal action, one that has the potential to be collective and coalitional across racial difference: "the power which comes from sharing deeply any pursuit with another person. The sharing of joy, whether physical, emotional, psychic, or intellectual, forms a bridge between the sharers which can be the basis for understanding much of what is not shared between them, and lessens the threat of their difference."[54] Even less known is this essay's historical context in the realm of Lorde's own interpersonal literary relationships and her experiences in Black and lesbian feminist publishing.

As Mecca Jamilah Sullivan writes, more than "sociopolitical specificity," Lorde's efforts toward generating "an effective language of black feminist difference" were rooted in her striving toward "a radical artistic and creative vision that can express experiences of multiplicity, complexity, and simultaneity in ways that normative English prose cannot reach."[55] While writers like Lorde are often hailed exclusively for their expressions of collectivity and positivity, it is important to situate these expressions of resolution within the interpersonal conflicts and creative differences that often preceded them. For example, Strongman notes that Lorde's conflicts with and attempts nevertheless to heal her friendship/collegial relationship with white feminist and lesbian poet Adrienne Rich was one significant backdrop to Lorde's writing of her essay "Uses of the Erotic."[56] Strongman's archival research on Lorde's letters to Rich evidence the difficult navigation of interpersonal relationships within literary institutional settings that had inspired Lorde's written theorizations.[57]

Lorde would include in her collection *Sister Outsider* a 1979 interview of her conducted by Rich in which Rich's use of the pronoun *our* to discuss shared curriculum—"our history," "our lives," "our dreams"—prompts this response from Lorde: "There are different choices facing Black and white women in life."[58] The interview continues with Rich affirming, "White women are constantly offered choices or the appearance of choices. But also real choices that are undeniable. We don't always perceive the difference between the two." Lorde rejoined, "Adrienne, in my journals I have a lot of pieces of conversations that I'm having with you in my head. I'll be having a conversation with you and I'll put it in my journal because stereotypically or symbolically these conversations occur in a space of Black woman/white woman."[59] Lorde and Rich's willingness to tackle this conversation with each other despite the "different choices facing Black and white women in life" demonstrates their understanding of and commitment to intersectionality and its possibilities. However, Lorde's use of her "journals" as intermediary spaces in which to bridge their conversations, becoming what would later be published as Black feminist writing like that of *Sister Outsider*, also suggests Lorde's awareness of the literary market, and how her alliance with Rich might also serve her other aims within Black feminist organizing. This includes moments wherein "the erotic has been used against us, even the word itself, so often, that we have been taught to suspect what is deepest in ourselves, and that is the way we learn to testify against ourselves. . . . A Black woman devaluating another Black woman's work . . . Black women testifying against ourselves." Black feminisms indeed require the presence of "sister outsiders" like Lorde and Rich who are willing, even amid difficulty, to attempt feminist solidarity across difference and work at "creating another whole structure."[60]

Across Lorde's archive, there are many moments that speak to this positive intention, and others, still, that demonstrate that Lorde was not perfect. Her theorizations of the erotic and other concepts continue to speak to the possibilities of Black feminist life and work, but it was not always possible or feasible, for a variety of reasons, for Lorde to embody an ideal instantiation of them at every moment in her life or scholarship.[61] Similarly, I would have thought that Lorde would have been a champion of Phillis's significance, but her archive offers no such easy evidence. I did find one explicit mention of Phillis in Lorde's papers: in a course Lorde was proposing, titled The Black Experience in Poetry (ca. 1973 or thereafter) wherein she asked, "Does Afro-American poetry begin with Phillis Wheatley or Leroi Jones [Amiri Baraka]?"[62] While this is an interesting question in and of itself, it is far from the kind of meditation I would expect or perhaps want Lorde to make. In other words, it is not a course proposal on the Black *feminist* experience in poetry. I relished other moments in the archive much more, such as Lorde's September 5, 1986, card to Barbara Christian (complete with a Sojourner Truth stamp on the envelope) in which Lorde expressed her gratitude to Christian over several sentences handwritten in purple ink (the ink begins to run out toward the end of the note). Lorde mentioned reading Christian's work and finding her work both "humbling" and the fulfillment of a long-standing dream and an ongoing hope to see such work continue to come into existence. Notably, she expresses her excitement that Christian writes and works "so beautifully!"[63] The card's cover design itself, with pressed flower and leaves, bespeaks the beauty Lorde felt in reading Christian. While such a correspondence could convey more intimacy than a course proposal, Lorde was still likely engaging in a professional project of networking. She closes the card with a reference to "Afrekete" before signing her own name—coauthoring her correspondence with the foremother she herself created from her practice of reading of African diasporic myths.[64]

This chapter goes on to explore the significance of Lorde's theorization of the erotic as a calculated solidarity within Obour and Phillis's relationship and for Obour's future relationship with the white woman to whom she bequeaths Phillis's writing. In the context of the Obour-Phillis correspondence, it is worth noting that only after having established Lorde-like solidarity with Obour three letters into their seven-letter correspondence does Phillis shift from overly religious (read: erotic) language to shorter letters that privilege news of and requests for

Cover of card from Audre Lorde to Barbara Christian, September 5, 1986, Barbara Christian Papers, BANC MSS 2003/199c, box 1, folder 32, Bancroft Library, University of California, Berkeley.

Obour's help with the sale of Phillis's 1773 *Poems*. Again, Joanna Brooks has already evidenced that Phillis "engineered her own manumission" and demonstrates via archival research the likelihood that Phillis organized white male Boston leaders to sign the attestation of authentic authorship that prefaces her volume of poems, albeit eventually falling prey to white women's "[in]attentions."[65] While it is possible that Obour and Phillis enjoyed a genuine friendship, all relationships must navigate difference and build favor. I argue that Phillis reciprocated Obour's discursive religiosity in order to build the foundation for a working relationship in which she could better market her poems to Obour and her Newport, Rhode Island, community. Today we read the Obour-Phillis correspondence largely as a series of letters; indeed, Phillis often refers to her and Obour's writing as such. However, early in their correspondence Phillis also refers to one of Obour's writings on May 19, 1772, specifically as a "favour" and others, on July 19, 1772, and October 30, 1773, as "Epistles."[66] This more formal language corresponds with Phillis's three most religious letters: again, her three earliest to Obour, on May 19, 1772; July 19, 1772; and October 30, 1773. The marker of Obour as a writer of formal epistles suggests that Phillis especially wanted to appeal to Obour's own literary mastery as well as her religiosity, placing her letters on the level of the apostle Paul's infamous epistles.

Phillis's understanding of her correspondence with Obour as highly formal genres suggests that they were more than documents of friendship alone. Following Phillis's October 30, 1773, letter to Obour, another highly religious letter, Phillis does not mention her volume of poems until the letter's postscript, as if to downplay her eagerness in sharing news of its impending publication: "I enclose Proposals for my Book, and beg you[d] use your interest to get Subscriptions as it is for my Benefit."[67] The subscription model—a once-popular publishing approach whereby authors required several patrons, "would-be buyers," in advance—existed to securely fund the printing of the proposed volume in advance.[68] Obour could have been a subscriber herself, but she also had connections to prominent white patrons via her membership in the Reverend Samuel Hopkins's First Congregational Church. Thus, earlier in her letter of October 30, 1773, Phillis reciprocates Obour's words:

> Your Reflections on the Sufferings of the Son of God, & the inestimable price of our immortal Souls, Plainly dem[on]strate the sensations of a Soul united to Jesus. What you observe of Esau is true of all mankind, who, (left to themselves) would sell their heavenly Birth Rights for a few moments of sensual pleasure, whose wages at last (dreadful wages!) is eternal condemnation. Dear Obour, let us not sell our Birth right for a thousand worlds, which indeed would be as dust upon the Ballance.

Here Phillis reciprocates Obour's language, which, far from espousing the happy religiosity of Phillis's first two responses to Obour, suggests a marker of difference within the two women's religious aims. Perhaps Obour was using religious language to assuage Phillis's fears of succumbing to her illness. Perhaps in Obour's "observations on our dependence on the Deity, & [her] hopes that [Phillis's] wants will be supply'd from his fulness which is in Christ Jesus," she was cautioning Phillis not to have excessive esteem for the white patrons she encountered on her brief London tour.[69] In either case, Phillis might also have been compelled to reciprocate her friend's religiosity to assuage any doubts that selling her volume of poems would be at odds with their shared Christian belief system.

Obour's bequest is first detailed in the November 1863 meeting proceedings for the Massachusetts Historical Society (MHS), then a literary society composed exclusively of white men, wherein Obour is described as Phillis's "negro friend," a term that views their relationship as wholly interpersonal even though it was also collegial.[70] The term *friend* assumes that discursive relationships between eighteenth-century Black women are happening predominantly in the private sphere, outside the realm of literary work. Or perhaps it is more accurate to say that it assumes that Black feminist friendship is not a front for a form of critical labor. Lacking Obour's letters, the MHS highlights Phillis's "beautiful hand" and "unusual intelligence" and makes ungainly assumptions about Phillis's enslavers' benevolence.[71] Obour is pushed to the margin, literally relegated largely to the footnote space of the proceedings. No longer part of an ensemble, Obour effectively becomes the mere purveyor of Phillis's literary genius. However, by understanding Obour as a literary participant in her own right, as something more than a "bestie,"[72] my reading of the Obour-Phillis correspondence positions Obour as, like Phillis, a calculated participant in the spheres within which she struggled to survive. Obour was an enslaved woman with burgeoning religious connections (one of her letters to Phillis arrives "enclosd, in [her] rev.ᵈ Pastor's" and is hand-delivered by his son) according to Phillis's letter in reply on March 21, 1774.[73] Phillis, a burgeoning religious poet whose 1773 *Poems on Various Subjects* would be marketed as *Religious and Moral*, needed Obour's favor and approval of her project as well as her finesse in garnering the subscribers and buyers that would eventuate in Phillis's manumission.

While understanding their relationship as a working relationship in addition to an affective one may dampen some readers' desires for an early model of a Black feminist friendship that transcended the workplace, this orientation helps elucidate the lengths Phillis would go in her writing to satisfy, not simply white readers, but Obour as her reader. For example, at face value, Phillis's March 21, 1774, letter to Obour reads like a loving eulogy for her enslaver Susanna Wheatley, whom Phillis calls her "mistress," a now-unsupported term, along with "master," on the grounds that each "transmits the aspirations and values of the enslaving class without naming the practices they engaged."[74] Phillis's letter reads as an expressly representative document of public writing by enslaved (not formerly enslaved) figures. If we understand the Obour-Phillis correspondence to be a series of letters sent between friends, then such a reading stands. As Vincent Carretta writes, Phillis's "21 March 1774 letter is the most reliable evidence we have of the familial relationship Phillis felt she had with the Wheatleys."[75] But if we understand the correspondence as a public document by an enslaved woman hoping to heighten her reputation as a religious poet, the letter skews away from the confessional and toward the rhetorical: The letter is less about Susanna Wheatley and more about proving to Obour that Phillis's morality supersedes the conditions of her enslavement. Phillis again mentions sales of her book to Obour in the letter's close, as if it is an afterthought, and not, perhaps, the letter's overarching aim.[76] In fact, I argue that the letter is merely a framing document designed to showcase the strength of Phillis's morality with the hope that it will be repeated by Obour to her network and thereby help sell more copies of Phillis's *Poems*. Thus, in addition to providing documentary evidence of Obour and Phillis's religious beliefs and their calculated expression, the Obour-Phillis letters evidence their participation in, and contributions to future iterations of, Black feminist collegial and scholarly practices that come to be known as Black feminist criticism.

Obour's Bequest

I continue by linking hands with one literary history of feminist recovery that gathers itself around the moment of posthumous literary discovery. As Virginia Jackson writes in the "Beforehand" of her 2005 book, *Dickinson's Misery: A Theory of Lyric Reading*,

> Suppose you are sorting through the effects of a woman who has just died and you find in her bedroom a locked wooden box. You open the box and discover hundreds of folded sheets of stationery stitched together with string. Other papers in the bureau drawer are loose, or torn into small pieces, occasionally pinned together; there is writing on a guarantee issued by the German Student Lamp Co., on memo paper advertising THE HOME INSURANCE CO. NEW YORK ("Cash Assets, over SIX MILLION DOLLARS"), on many split-open envelopes, on a single strip three-quarters of an inch wide by twenty-one inches long, on thin bits of butcher paper, on a page inscribed *"Specimen of Penmanship"* (which is then crossed out). There is writing clustered around a three-cent postage stamp of a steam engine turned on its side, which secures two magazine clippings bearing

the names "GEORGE SAND" and "Mauprat." Suppose that you recognize the twined pages as sets of *poems*; you decide that the other pages may contain poems as well. Now you wish you had kept the bundles of letters you burned upon the poet's (for it *was* a poet's) death. What remains, you decide, must be published.[77]

In its restaging of a historical moment (Lavinia Dickinson's discovery of her older sister Emily Dickinson's poems), Jackson's criticism stages the scene of contemporary feminist literary critical possibility with aplomb: "Suppose you are sorting. . . . Suppose that you recognize . . ." resulting in the definitive, of course, "you decide." For Jackson, placing oneself as critic back into the scene of discovery now reframed as recovery (the immediate gut response to publish the poems runs counter to the history of Dickinson's obstructed paths to publication) is to "suppose"—that is, reimagine—what could be possible. While the act of supposition stems from assumption, the citation of hyperspecific details from Dickinson's idiosyncratic archive transforms mere supposition into literary criticism— that is, what Jackson understands as "the development of reading practices in the nineteenth and twentieth centuries that become the practice of literary criticism."[78] But supposition, what happens before criticism, requires that one place one's body in relation to the work in the present moment. Thus, Jackson's restaging of the discovery of Dickinson's poems models the ethos of what I would argue is feminist criticism broadly, whereupon one's suppositional insertion into the moment of posthumous discovery is understood as part and parcel of what is required to inquire into the history and authenticity of one's works under study.[79]

"Suppose you are sorting through the effects of a woman who has just died and you find in her bedroom a locked wooden box." Yet there was no locked wooden box left behind when Obour died. Locks, unlike suppositions, were not something she could exercise as an enslaved woman. Instead, what readers know about the scene of literary recovery as it relates to Obour may more easily map upon what we can imagine, because Obour did not have the luxury to leave much open to the imagination. Her archive was not hundreds of pages, only a handful.[80] The scene of feminist discovery would unfold not in the experience of finding essentially a lost treasure hidden away in a chest, but in the intimate exchange of a small collection of such treasure between women—one white, younger, and free, and the other Black, older, and enslaved. A discovery scene such as this one would require you to imagine yourself thus:

Suppose you are receiving a visit from an older Black woman in your commu-
nity, a pillar of religious fealty, who has just asked for your help in arrang-
ing beneficiaries for the few remaining items in her possession before she is
to pass away. You agree to help her, upon which she reaches for her bag and
removes from it a small parcel. This she holds out to you and says softly that
it is her most prized possession, the one she is most eager to see placed in the
right hands. You accept the parcel, proceed to untie its string, and open its
wrapping of cloth. Inside there is a stack of a half dozen or so sheets of folded
parchment tied together with a ribbon, the topmost is addressed in a bold
calligraphic cursive to "Arbour Tanner, in Newport." Underneath the letters
is a bound copy of Poems on Various Subjects, Religious and Moral, *by the*
poet Phillis Wheatley. Suppose you recognize the woman sitting before you,
Obour Collins, as not just an enslaved woman but a literary critic in her own
right. Suppose you recognize the sheets of parchment and the bound volume of
poems not merely as letters and poems *but as works of* criticism. *This radical*
collection, you decide, cannot be published, but must be safeguarded until the
day arrives when it may receive due recognition . . .

This act of supposition takes liberties in imagining whether its nineteenth-
century participants would have used the same critical language we use
today, and while we do know that such a scene took place, we cannot
know its full details, as its archival traces remain fragmented. This supposition nevertheless provides a language for the actions these participants
indeed took, and the actions they did not take, in ensuring the preservation of the Obour-Phillis collection. In the remaining pages of this chapter,
I test the possibilities of such a Black feminist criticism in order to provide
a ready gloss on what readers today, when asked to reembody the scene of
feminist discovery, may begin to dream is possible when reading Obour and
Phillis as well as the white woman to whom Obour bequeathed Phillis's
works.

Turning to the historical record of the bequest, the person to whom
Obour originally bequeathed her collection of Phillis's writings was a
young white woman, Katherine Edes Beecher (1802–70) (just Edes before her marriage to William Henry Beecher in 1830).[81] Edes Beecher later
penned a brief narrative describing Obour's bequest (whose exact date is
unknown, but likely after Edes is wed in 1830 and before Obour's death in
1835) in a letter to Rev. Edward E. Hale on October 23, 1863, which was
then given to Charles Deane, president of the Massachusetts Historical
Society.[82] A history of the seven-letter bequest and Obour's passing was

first published in the November meeting documented in the *Proceedings* of the MHS. Edes Beecher's letter (along with the bequeathed collection of the Obour-Phillis correspondence, which was transcribed in the main text) was then transcribed in the *Proceedings* as follows:

[The letters] were given to me ages since by the person to whom they were addressed. She was then a very little, very old, very infirm, very, *very* black woman, with a great shock of the whitest of wool all over her head,—a picture well photographed on my mind's eye. She died in the odor of sanctity, sometime in 1833 or '4, an uncommonly pious, sensible, and intelligent woman, respected and visited by every person in Newport who could appreciate excellence.

Obour gave me also one of Phillis Wheatley's books, which I read with pleasure, and almost wonder, quite through: but, to my lasting chagrin, it was soon lost,—either mislaid, or spirited away somehow; and it is long years since I have seen token of it. I have no doubt, however, that many copies of it are still extant among the old residents in Newport, as you will observe, from one of the letters, it was published by subscription.

You will notice, also, that Phillis speaks of "Mr. John Peters," "a complaisant and agreeable young man," "an acquaintance" of Obour's, &c. This was the man she married. . . . Obour informed me, pious soul as she was, with more than a gleam of that aristocracy of feeling, if not *hauteur*, which sits so curiously on those full-blooded creatures, that "poor Phillis let herself down by marrying: yes, ma'am." It is just possible, however, that this opinion might have originated in her own condition of single blessedness, but not probably so, as I heard the same thing expressed frequently by old people in Newport who remembered the circumstances. Phillis lived some twelve or fifteen years after her marriage; and died in 1794 or 5, a little more than forty years of age.

Perhaps more details, and letters and books as well, might be gleaned in Newport: but the old class who knew Phillis when I lived there a young woman must have greatly passed away; and I cannot, at this distance of time, designate any one who could assist such an investigation.[83]

Edes Beecher—whose physical appearance is not, of course, transcribed at any point in these extant texts—is described in the proceedings only as "Mrs. William Beecher, of Brookfield," as a "lady," and as erroneously relating the correct date of Phillis's death (and neglecting to remember that Obour herself had been married, too, becoming Obour Collins).[84]

Like Obour, Edes Beecher would have been an older woman nearing her final years at the time of her 1863 letter to Hale (she would pass away in 1870). Also, like Obour, she seems to have chosen this as a necessary time of relinquishing meaningful objects of her inheritance. Importantly, she did not bequeath the collection to her husband William Beecher or her children. However, no other information describes why Edes Beecher made her bequest at the time that she did. The MHS relegates it to a footnote, allowing for no discussion of her intentions. Whatever they may have been, they are subsidiary to the more important narrative of Phillis's poetry, the text of her letters to Obour, as well as the narrative of Phillis's 1761 sale to the Wheatley family, all of which appear in the main text (none of which are footnoted) in the proceedings. Without detailing the Black feminist and white feminist labor (however vexed) that brought the Obour-Phillis correspondence to the MHS, the MHS assumes a mode of benevolent passivity, as if the letters merely arrived on their doorstep with all their prior lineages largely irrelevant or at best tangential.

Although Phillis is often understood as distinct from traditions of eighteenth- and nineteenth-century Black autobiographical narrative writing, this example of a white woman's transcription of a scene concerning Phillis's letters to Obour as well as her 1773 *Poems* aligns both Obour and Phillis with other examples of narratives by enslaved and formerly enslaved people that feature complex authorship,[85] including those by Sojourner Truth (whose as-told-to *Narrative* was published in 1850) and Harriet Tubman (whose as-told-to *Scenes in the Life* was published in 1869). I read Edes Beecher's 1863 narration of Obour's early 1830s bequest within a history of transcription wherein white writers have served as complex amanuenses for Black narrators, following William L. Andrews's analysis that not everyone could tell their "story in an equally free manner."[86] Read within this tradition, Obour's narrative as told by Edes Beecher demonstrates that Phillis's own career is bookended with amanuensis-assisted texts that are connected to the MHS.[87] Following Erlene Stetson's suggestion of categorizing the Obour-Phillis correspondence as an enslaved persons' narrative,[88] I interpret Obour's literary labor in this vein by reading between the lines of her amanuensis. Like Sojourner Truth, who had been excluded from the circle of Black autobiography by virtue of her amanuensis-assisted text, Obour is otherwise treated with "invisibility in, and subordination to, an emerging African American abolitionist literary tradition." However, attention to Obour's participation in the text of her bequest, an understanding of authorship that Xiomara Santamarina describes as "conflicted collaboration," emphasizes the "narrating dynamics" of Obour's "labor" in and around the text of the bequest as indeed literary.[89] On Edes Beecher's part, there is also potential to try to read her role in the bequest as a manifestation of "white women's covert protest against their [own] subordination,"[90] although Edes Beecher's ultimate fidelity to a feminist position remains persistently unresolved.

As a complex amanuensis-like text, Edes Beecher's transcription led to further appropriation of the letters by the MHS.[91] For instance, seven of Phillis's letters to Obour paradoxically became, not part of a feminist community, but the property of the MHS when they were donated by Charles Deane, "an editor and critic of the English language," the latest inheritor of the letters. As may have been the case with the letters, Deane was in "the practice of offering unsolicited historical papers at stated meetings, other than the formal reports which were expected."[92] I include this information to note that while Edes Beecher's letter in the MHS is a transcription, it is unlikely that the MHS would lie as to its contents, as they were invested in a model of historical acquisition. At the same time, Edes Beecher's letter cannot be wholly understood as the expression of her private, transparently "true" thoughts, so perhaps she was masking a truer expression of her care for Obour. Charles Deane was a wealthy Boston merchant before retiring and becoming a member of the MHS in 1849 and the American Antiquarian Society a couple of years later.[93] Although Deane had possessed one of Phillis's letters for several years, he was inspired to inquire after and share a collection of a total of seven letters with the society after having recently heard one of her poems read from the manuscript by the MHS president. Deane valued the letters based on their scarcity, emphasizing that "but few letters of this remarkable person are extant" and "I have never met with any of her letters in print"; his response to remedy this gap is "to read some portion of them to the meeting," as though hearing them will surely convince members of their value.[94] With this, the MHS proceedings on Phillis conclude, providing an obscure script of a fractionally recorded performance that nevertheless enabled a large, albeit abridged, part of Phillis's corpus to survive her death. Nearly a century after she passed away, a wealthy white Boston man ventriloquized Phillis's correspondence (which could have never been private) and put himself in her position of address.

Yet what I still find more compelling is that long before this, following Phillis's final letter to Obour on May 10, 1779, Obour held on to her collection of Phillis's letters into old age and refused to let them die with her, passing them on before she herself passed away in 1835. While no extant letters document the sale of Phillis's volume of poems specifically to Obour, the resurfacing of Phillis's volume in the bequest suggests that Obour perhaps purchased her own personal copy, a significant purchase given that Phillis had not been in a financial position to freely gift copies of her works and also given that Obour, as an enslaved woman, would not have been in a financial position to buy volumes of poems at will. The collection accrued even more value as Obour held onto it for over an estimated fifty years, until she was an older woman. Obour's bequest also became even more valuable due to the fact that, following Phillis's early death in 1784, most of Phillis's manuscript archive has never been recovered. Did John Peters misplace her second manuscript of poems? How many of her manuscripts are moldering in old trunks in New England attics as I write?[95] Unfortunately, despite the increasing rarity of Phillis's works, the sanctity of Obour's bequest was not reciprocated in kind by the recipient to whom she entrusted carrying on the preservation of the collection. Again, according to the November 1863 meeting proceedings for the MHS, Obour bequeathed the collection to Mrs. William Beecher of Brookfield (Katherine Edes Beecher), who subsequently lost part of it.[96] Edes Beecher does not say, "I lost it." She says, "It was soon lost." But who bears responsibility for the loss of Phillis's volume of poems if not she?

Like many stories that attend to eighteenth- and nineteenth-century Black women's lives and their works, the story of Obour's bequest of her collection of Phillis's writings remains but a fragment. While only a few questions about the bequest are disciplinarily possible for me to answer here, the answers I am able to corroborate with evidence, including Edes Beecher's letter in the MHS proceedings and their information about Obour's bequest, allow us to conduct further research on other parts of Obour and Phillis's story in my partial uncovering of it. In the wake of what imagination cannot corroborate, I look to what other voices in the archive do say. I take particular inspiration from Melba Joyce Boyd's book *Discarded Legacy* (1994), on the poetry and poetics of Frances E. W. Harper, wherein Boyd quotes Harper's own "unedited thoughts and creative expression" across her book in italics. Boyd, herself a poet, frames herself not as an amanuensis in the antiquated sense but as a harmonious collaborator who is transparent about the aims of her methods:

A legacy is not static. It is not suspended in the time frame of the birth and death of the person. Rather, it is like a poem. It imparts to each person who encounters it an affirmation, a confrontation, or an indulgence. The conceptual framework of the book develops around the voice of Harper speaking directly to the reader, and my voice speaks over her shoulder in another verbal dimension. Like a voiceover in a documentary film, my writing is a commentary that supplies the information that fills the historical gaps and technical details about her work. My writing also formulates the transitions. The use of italic type provides a visual cue for the switching of voices and avoids the mechanical and disruptive interference of textual introductions, which makes the reading experience too stiff and staid.[97]

Boyd's description of this scene of writing evidences sensuality, in Barbara Christian's sense of the word, between her and Harper, rather than a purely institutional or forced scene of collaborative writing.[98] This scene has its echo in other works, including Saidiya Hartman's *Wayward Lives, Beautiful Experiments* (2019), that pursue collegial intimacy with their academic subjects.[99] These instances of choral and sensual criticism interrupt the conventional narration of single-author critical works by understanding their citational material as participants, too, in the utterance of the book. The italicized, or otherwise cited or marked, choral excerpts of such works remind readers there is a panoply of voices in the margins of disciplinary history's pages, and while some were invited, others risk interloping. These voices include ours, as critics.

Feminist Criticism after Katherine Edes Beecher

Edes Beecher's voice, for example, remains an important marker of interracial feminist limitations and possibilities. In one part of her archive, she ultimately adopts a rhetoric of passivity with relation to the correspondence and uses the passive verb tense to distance herself from the collection's partial loss. Again, as Edes Beecher writes in 1863 of receiving the copy of Phillis's volume of poems: "Obour gave me also one of Phillis Wheatley's books, which I read with pleasure, and almost wonder, quite through: but, to my lasting chagrin, it was soon lost—"[100] Whom do we as scholars hold accountable for an action, or perhaps a mistake, of casual literary neglect that took place almost two hundred years ago? Today Edes Beecher's assertion that it "was soon lost" suggests a linguistic distancing from verb tenses that would appoint her as steward of Obour's bequest and transforms Phillis's work, her volume of poems specifically, into a changeling, a faerie text that could easily be "spirited away." What would it look like to retroactively empower Edes Beecher to acknowledge the loss as the result of either her own actions or other extenuating circumstances? The manuscript of Phillis's second poetry volume is also often described in scholarly accounts as a failure to archive that haunts her extant oeuvre without a clear source of the fault. What would it look like for Black feminists and white feminists to collectively redress this failure today? One possible model would be to "call in," as Loretta J. Ross recommended in her 2021 TED talk: "A call-in is a call-out done with love."[101] Approaching Edes Beecher with a "call-out done with [foremother] love" might entail conducting more research to learn more about what exactly happened and bringing empathy as well as critique to the table.[102]

I will present my critique of Edes Beecher and will aim to provide as empathetic an interpretation of my findings as possible, especially toward the end. To begin, it bears mentioning that the seven letters that Edes Beecher bequeathed to Hale, and thereafter the MHS, did not comprise the full collection Obour originally entrusted to her. To illustrate, in 2005 the *New York Times* detailed the "discovery" of an additional eighth letter from Phillis to Obour dated February 14, 1776, and described the letter's path from Obour to Edes Beecher, who is characterized as an "abolitionist" and a "sister-in-law of Harriet Beecher Stowe."[103] This article also reported that "about 1860, Beecher gave the letter to the politician Amasa Walker because of his objection to slavery in the territories," a complex decision that denotes Edes Beecher's interests in abolitionism, although at the cost of splitting up the collection as Obour originally bequeathed it. That Edes Beecher gifted one of the letters to someone before she bequeathed the collection to the MHS even suggests there could be additional letters that have not surfaced yet. Remaining in private ownership, the letter discusses "the American Revolution," and Phillis apparently writes to Obour, "I doubt not that your present situation is extremely unhappy."[104] Another article reported that the letter also speaks "obliquely about slavery" and was eventually sold at auction to an anonymous buyer for "$253,000," "the highest ever paid at auction for a letter written by" a Black writer and "an auction record for a letter written by a woman."[105] The sale monetizes foremotherhood, as the private market sets the price on the value of its first enslaved Black woman poet and rewards Amasa's Walker descendant financially for their ancestor's abolitionism.

Suppose you are receiving a visit from an older Black woman in your commu-
nity, a pillar of religious fealty, who has just asked for your help in arranging
beneficiaries for the few remaining items in her possession before she is to pass
away . . .

Was this what Obour intended when she sought the young Katherine Edes Beecher's assistance in securing a new home for Phillis's remaining papers? As opposed to the logic of the capitalist auction, Obour's original bequest did not involve the exchange of any monies. Edes Beecher's narration of her exchange with Obour does not divulge any details about why Obour chose her as the recipient of her collection. Perhaps Obour thought that if the collection was safely ignored in a white religious family's trunk in an attic, it would survive to witness the nation's emancipation. Following Saidiya Hartman's caution about speculating into the presence of "the friendship that could have blossomed" amid the violent context of slavery,[106] I begin by sticking close to what the archive does tell us about Obour via Edes Beecher's extant words. By imparting the letters to a young white woman who ostensibly possessed the means of preserving them, Obour also preserves Edes Beecher in the amber of her bequest. While Edes Beecher was in a position of greater power relative to Obour in the moment of the early 1830s, that power today looks unappealing. Again, Edes Beecher writes that the letters "were given to me ages since by the person to whom they were addressed. She was then a very little, very old, very infirm, very, *very* black woman, with a great shock of the whitest of wool all over her head,—a picture well photographed on my mind's eye."[107] In relinquishing the letters, Obour widens the scope of their address but also exposes herself to near-photographic capture and caricature. Yet the caricature says more about Edes Beecher than it does about Obour. While the fullest expression of Phillis's poetic genius, Phillis's volume of poems, elicits only Edes Beecher's "pleasure" and subsequent forgetting, Obour herself is perfectly preserved "on [Edes Beecher's] mind's eye." At least, according to Edes Beecher.

Written around thirty years after Obour and Edes Beecher's physical exchange, Edes Beecher's remarks about Obour being well photographed in her mind speak to how greatly she attended to Obour's appearance and their moment of intimate proximity. Edes Beecher's compulsion to provide the MHS with a visual representation of Obour echoes some of the history of Phillis's frontispiece portrait—an engraving by a Black man artist, who was also enslaved, by the name of Scipio Moorhead.[108] Susanna

Wheatley, who bought and continued to enslave Phillis as a child, is purported to have received her own copy of the engraving, which she hung over a fireplace in the Wheatley home. During Phillis's visit to London, Susanna Wheatley reportedly once entertained a visit from a grandniece and "immediately directed her attention to a picture over the fire-place," whereupon Susanna said to her, "See! look at my Phillis! does she not seem as though she would speak to me!"[109] The anecdote's negative grammar highlights the fine line between Phillis's agency and subservience in relation to Susanna, her enslaver. Both Edes Beecher and Susanna Wheatley understand the Black subjects in their visual field as objects of their possession and consumption. For Edes Beecher, Obour's hypervisuality ("very little, very old, very infirm, very, *very* black") is internalized on and later recorporealized via her "mind's eye."[110] However, for Susanna Wheatley, as Phillis's enslaver for over a decade, Phillis's image is not just preserved in racialized remembrance but also as an extension of her enslaved status: subject to Wheatley's beck and call.

According to Edes Beecher's words, Obour seems to have aged into a position we might imagine Phillis would have occupied had she lived longer. Edes Beecher writes of Obour: "She died in the odor of sanctity . . . an uncommonly pious, sensible, and intelligent woman, respected and visited by every person in Newport who could appreciate excellence." What is curious, though, is Edes Beecher's contrasting descriptions of Obour as diminutive, "infirm," and having achieved a kind of saintly status, having been "visited by every person in Newport" and having passed away "in the odor of sanctity."[111] Was Obour a religious figure in historical terms we have not yet fully defined? How many others were there? Enslaved, subject to her community's definition of herself, Obour was sanctified. As Alice Walker writes in her 1974 essay "In Search of Our Mothers' Gardens," Obour could have been as incomprehensible to her contemporary white community as southern Black women were to Jean Toomer. Not legible as fully fledged persons, these were "black women whose spirituality was so intense, so deep, so *unconscious*, that they were themselves unaware of the richness they held . . . more even than mere women: they became 'Saints.' Instead of being perceived as whole persons, their bodies became shrines: what was thought to be their minds became temples suitable for worship." On the contrary, Obour was, in Walker's words, an "Artist," a "Creator," "rich in spirituality—which is the basis of Art."[112] Given Edes Beecher's ascription of Obour's extradisciplinarity, that she was "pious" and sanctified without the ability to serve formally as a church leader, it appears as though Obour was an early iteration of the open-ended terms in which Black feminists later described themselves while en route to better terminology.

Finally, apparently Obour also bequeathed to Edes Beecher her wry remarks about Phillis's husband John Peters, which are also recorded by the MHS in Edes Beecher's transcribed letter: "Obour informed me, pious soul as she was, with more than a gleam of that aristocracy of feeling, if not *hauteur*, which sits so curiously on those full-blooded creatures, that 'poor Phillis let herself down by marrying: yes, ma'am.'" Such a sentiment was not an uncommon opinion, as Edes Beecher "heard the same thing expressed frequently by old people in Newport who remembered the circumstances."[113] The assumption that Peters was not a compatible partner for Phillis, and that their marriage was ultimately a letdown, is taken up by the MHS in ways that echo long-voiced critiques of Black men's abilities to achieve financial solvency in the absence of any institutional and social support. Peters, not their white community or Phillis's specific community of white poetry subscribers, is blamed for their descent into dire financial straits. Edes Beecher highlights, via Obour, Phillis's marriage with Peters, however, I also read Obour's insistence on Phillis's marriage as a letdown as a queer feminist wish that Phillis could have had access to alternatives to marriage in her lifetime, queer in the way that "queerness" questions all forms of cisheteropatriarchy and "is that thing that lets us feel that this world is not enough."[114] While the historical record may emphasize her marriage to Peters and its subsequent letdown, I focus largely on the ways that Obour did not let Phillis down, including by holding on to her collection, and the ways she let Phillis down only by trusting others, like Edes Beecher, to do right by her. To be fair, Edes Beecher herself was not treated very kindly by the historical record or by her own marriage.[115]

Although Edes Beecher did not let on one bit in her letter detailing Obour's bequest, between her many moves due to her husband's transient work as an unpopular preacher and her responsibilities of raising six children, Edes Beecher ended up suffering some of the misfortunes of marriage that befell Phillis. Just as I lost track of the essay about Black sisterhood mentioned at the beginning of this chapter as I moved between universities, I can empathize with them both. Both Edes Beecher and Phillis lose—or, depending on how generous we feel, were subjected to the loss of—manuscripts and limited edition printed portions of Phillis's collection as a result of their precarious lives. Obour's bequest to (at the time) a young and potentially unmarried or newly married Edes (later Beecher), itself marks Obour's belief in a different future than that which befell Katherine as her marriage to William Beecher unfolded. Obour likely met Edes Beecher in Rhode Island just before their transient life commenced after her marriage in 1830, when William had "a parish at Newport, Rhode Island."[116] Excitingly, in her 2023 book, *Reading Pleasures*, Bynum published her discovery of a letter detailing that in 1809 Obour was "nearly sixty years old" and was one of the "founding members" and "president" of the "African Female Benevolent Society"— though after this Obour recedes once more from the archive.[117] By the time of the early 1830s, perhaps a future for Phillis's archive in the vein of Obour's society seemed possible, a future in which Phillis's collection could at least rest safely in a trunk in an attic for several generations, surviving until a historical moment in which Black women's writing could be understood and cherished in a loving and racially integrated context. Edes Beecher passed away in 1870, forty years after her marriage to William. She was a white woman who was unlucky in marriage, trying to make her way. I write so that Edes Beecher's story and Phillis's story do not become my story, too. I write with that Black feminist queer wish. What would it take for Edes Beecher to retroactively participate in a form of white feminist criticism that aligns with Black feminist criticism? It would have looked something like this:

> *Suppose you recognize the woman sitting before you as not just an enslaved woman but a literary critic in her own right. Suppose you recognize the sheets of parchment and the bound volume of poems not merely as letters and poems but as works of criticism. This radical collection, you decide, cannot be published, but must be safeguarded until the day arrives when it may receive due recognition. So you begin to draft a list of names, a manifest of feminists in your community who will each be told of the bequest and its significance. These will be its caretakers going forward. If one of us fails in our task to safeguard the collection, another may step in to carry it on in our stead.*

Mae Gwendolyn Henderson
Remembers Sherley Anne Williams

I am able to imagine what could have happened if Edes Beecher had been a practitioner of feminist criticism only because of my own inheritance of the creative works of Black feminists before me who have

reimagined the relationships between Black feminists and white feminists, works that have been published with increasing frequency since the
late twentieth century. Thus, I theorize Obour's bequest as an early example of Black feminist criticism as it would be formally termed in the 1970s.
Again, because we do not possess a narrative of Obour's bequest in her
own words, reading Obour in the context of later Black feminist criticism
provides a possible transcript of how Obour might have theorized her
bequest. In addition to peer-reviewed academic works of Black feminist
criticism, Obour's bequest resonates with the critical contexts that arise
and are explored within several works of memorial writing across a variety
of genres on the premature deaths of several prominent Black feminist
critics and creative writers. As I have mentioned throughout this book,
between 1979 and 2006, several such memorial works commemorated the
lives of Toni Cade Bambara, Barbara Christian, Sarah Webster Fabio, June
Jordan, Audre Lorde, Nellie McKay, and more. This chapter focuses on
Mae Gwendolyn Henderson's memorialization of Sherley Anne Williams
(1944–99) as a mirror image of the love espoused by Obour for Phillis to
imagine what their relationship could have been like in the future and
to reflect on how far we have yet to go.

Williams is well-known today for several works: *The Peacock Poems*
(1975); her second volume of poems, *Someone Sweet Angel Chile* (1982);
her novel, *Dessa Rose* (1986); a scholarly monograph published in 1972
that she later distanced herself from; several essays of criticism; and two
children's books.[118] Williams's novel *Dessa Rose* radically imagined the
friendship, and I would add collegiality, between a Black enslaved woman
and a white woman, characters who were each based on historical figures.[119] Williams was also a professor at the University of California, San
Diego, from 1973 until her passing in 1999.[120] Notably, she rose to the
professoriate after surviving her childhood and young adulthood "near
the subsistence level" and describes often in her poems her community
while growing up in a family of Black migrant workers in Bakersfield and
Fresno, California, her "early, early life when my father and mother were
alive and we followed the crops." When Williams was sixteen, her mother
passed away, and one of Williams's older sisters, Ruby ("Ruise"), a single
mother, became Williams's guardian (their father had passed away a few
years earlier). Ruise would become a formative figure in Williams's life
and work, and she wrote in 1980 that Ruise "worked as a maid/cook for a
white family five days a week," "attended night school four nights a week
to earn the high school diploma that pregnancy and marriage had forced

her to abandon," and "counseled and guided [Williams] through the shoals of adolescence." Ruise "paid for this schedule with ill-health which eventually forced her to quit work and go on welfare—but not before she had that high school diploma." Williams continues her praisesong:

> Ruise and her friends, young women much like herself, provided me with a community, with models, both real-life and literary. I was by that last year in high school more sophisticated in searching out black literature. But nowhere did I find stories of these heroic young women who despite all they had to do and endure laughed and loved, hoped and encouraged, supported each other with gifts of food and money and fought the country that was quite literally, we were convinced, trying to kill us. My first published story, "Tell Martha Not to Moan" (*Mass. Review*, 1967?, anthologized in *The Black Woman* and elsewhere), had its genesis in those years. Martha and her life are a composite of the women who made up that circle. Their courage and humor helped each other and me thru some very difficult years.[121]

In fact, Williams details her reasons for stopping at the receipt of her MA at Brown University and not pursuing the PhD in order to spend time not "poring over other people's work and trying to explain the world thru their eyes," but with "my life and my language," "my" being "used in the collective sense," as Ruise and her friends became the roots of her writing and scholarship.[122]

Sadly, Williams would join a generation of Black feminist professors who passed away due to cancer, most well before retiring age—an incalculable collective loss. Mae Gwendolyn Henderson reckons with this loss at the beginning of her 1999 memorial essay, "In Memory of Sherley Anne Williams," originally published in *Callaloo*, writing in remembrance of her late colleague and the relationship they shared:

> Like poets, critics may have muses. And it is fair to say that Sherley Anne Williams was my muse—my critical muse. Her immense creativity gave inspiration to my critical musings. Yet, at this moment, I can only ask, in the memorable words of Ralph Ellison, "when confronted by such an unexpected situation as this, what does one say?" Ellison's line resonates for me on the occasion of these reflections on the life and death of a muse, poet, novelist, critic, playwright, teacher, mother, and *sister-woman* whose life and death touch me personally and deeply.[123]

By nominating Williams as her "critical muse," Henderson elevates Williams to the status of muse and thereby elevates the work of criticism itself. Like poetry, according to Henderson, criticism is dependent on a muse to inspire the scene of writing as well as bestow her blessing on the eventual written product. Henderson adapts the model of the Ancient Greek poet's invocation of a muse to the Black feminist critical project, while specifying Williams, a fellow Black woman who was mortal, who lived and breathed among us, as a muse in her own right. Henderson's definition of muse is less a mythical goddess by birth and more a foremother, reminding us that for someone to be recognized as a muse or foremother in the future, she had to be recognized as such in her present-day life as well. Henderson also subverts the model of the critic as a solitary genius by positioning criticism as part of a literary tradition that also requires sources of inspiration to prosper. Again, Henderson also cites the opening question of Ralph Ellison's (1913–94) speech "Portrait of Inman Page," given in 1979, which further exemplifies Henderson's awareness of the multigenerational recognition by Black literary critics of the significance of elder Black figures (elders who were artists, creative writers, educators, etc.) to their work.[124] Henderson memorializes Ellison's own recent passing in 1994 and pays homage to Ellison's own speech honoring his former high school principal Inman Page (1853–1935), a speech wherein Ellison considers himself "a participant in [a] most incongruous juxtaposition."[125] Both Henderson and Ellison theorize a memorializing in which they, albeit unexpectedly, take upon themselves the crafting of ceremonial remembrance as an extension of their roles as Black critics.

Having to memorialize Williams changes Henderson's expectations and forces her into a new relation to Williams. Her essay lingers in this elegiac temporal dislocation—an intimate space in time of mourning. In fact, while "being called upon to play a role in a ceremony" inspires a kind of awe in Ellison, it is also codified for Henderson as an occasion to destabilize hierarchies within the tradition of Black feminist criticism. For instance, Henderson remembers Williams's own moment of atemporal tribute to Amiri Baraka (1934–2014) at the "*Reconstruction of Instruction* NEH Seminar held at Yale [University] in the late 1970s":

> Passionately, the younger woman poet gave both tribute and censure to her self-acknowledged model and precursor, Amiri Baraka *aka* LeRoi Jones. . . . Sherley took him to task on the woman's issue, importuning him to attend to the needs of the "sister" as well as the "brother." Afterwards . . .

they embraced—perhaps not an uncommon exchange between the brother and sister writers and activists during the 1970s, but, for me, a luminous and unforgettable moment![126]

Henderson remembers the moment as "not exactly a love feast," but one in which "a spirit of adoration and anguish, of veneration and rebuke" was fostered, such that normative academic hierarchies were loosened in the name of community. Also, unlike Ellison and Page, Henderson and Williams were similar in age, and Williams passed away quite young, just "three months" after receiving a cancer diagnosis, "six weeks shy of her fifty-fifth birthday."[127] Henderson's essay plays on normative elder-student relationships to demonstrate the ways her relationship with Williams worked to defy normative temporal bounds, given that they respected each other as elders even though they were both colleagues around the same age. Part of this involves Henderson's recognition of Williams as a creative writer with an older (blues woman) soul and their recognition of each other across disciplinary bounds. Since Henderson understands Williams to have been a multihyphenate figure, she is able to better propound their relationship in Black feminist (atemporal) terms.

In fact, one of the aftereffects of Black feminisms has been the ability to theorize in ways beyond single-axis sites of identification. Henderson's recontextualization of Ellison within Black feminist criticism highlights the centrality of atemporality to the theorization of Black feminist critical identity. For example, Barbara Christian recounts in her introduction to her 1985 collection, *Black Feminist Criticism*, titled "Black Feminist Process: In the Midst of . . . ," the astute questions that her ten-year-old daughter asks—as Christian works "surrounded by books and plants, a pad and pencil in front of me"—about the nature of her mother's work, valid questions that echo a larger tradition and prompt Christian to think citationally: "Not too long ago I'd read Marcelle Thiebaux's commentary on Foucault's 'Fantasia' in which she proposed replacing the male reader with a woman reader. She reminds us that her reader would occupy a different space; her reading would be seen as time away from her main work."[128] Christian writes that interruption is part of the experience of (Black) feminist criticism, especially if one is mothering at the same time—but also suggests in telling this story about her daughter that some temporal interruptions could also be welcomed as a healthy part of criticism broadly, since her daughter's questions indicate that even a Black feminist professor's daughter cannot simply absorb an understanding of criticism without active training—it must be taught and learned, given a welcoming, library-like environment for the student and given enough time. Christian's introduction emphasizes "process" and being "in the midst of" a conversation that is unfolding between her and her daughter simultaneous to Christian's academic teaching and writing—blurring the lines between mothering and academic work—"reinventing herself in the midst of patriarchal discourse, as to who she is supposed to be."[129]

What is more, like Christian, Henderson understands Black women creative writers' works to be an extension of a form of kinship and an extension of lived and personal kinship ties, as "our inheritance," and the mainspring of subsequent critical writing and teaching on Black literature.[130] Both Christian and Henderson resist "prescriptiveness" in criticism or theory, however, and instead indicate the ways in which relationships between Black creative writers and critics are dynamic and defy easy categorization.[131] As Henderson writes, "I've spent much of my intellectual and professional life teaching and writing about Sherley Anne Williams's superb work. I also knew her, although not so well, I imagine, as I might have. But on the rare occasions when we met, I found her observant, demure, somewhat mysterious, even enigmatic, yet always endowed with amazing grace." Henderson does not try to capture Williams in near-photographic visuality. In fact, Henderson does not claim the role of the exhaustive biographer. She instead theorizes her and Williams's several missed paths, and the gaps in time in between their meetings, as markers of the deep significance of the times they did meet, and that the significance of their relationship spanned the separations in which they each carried on their respective and mutually informed work. Henderson closes her own memorial thus: "Having taught and written about Sherley Anne Williams's work, I think it now perhaps fitting to *meditate*, as it were, not so much *on her history*, as on those small moments, seemingly so insignificant at the time, but which are now etched in memory."[132] Like the heretofore unrecorded body of knowledge and narratives that were lived by the women in Williams's early years and that Williams later fictionalized and made cogent as criticism, Henderson does the same for the "small moments" in which she encountered Williams with the special intimacy of the everyday. Henderson continues, "Our lives touched only tangentially, perhaps less than a half dozen times; yet her work and those few random encounters bear much meaning for me."[133]

Following Henderson's useful phrasing, I define the "tangential encounter" as any meaningful interaction between Black feminists that happens on the outskirts of their prescribed roles in academia or other institutions. The tangential encounter cannot be absorbed by or replicated within institutions—for it does not purport to result in increases in productivity for those institutions' own benefit. Instead, the tangential encounter points to a possible, though not managed, network of like minds, one that in the meantime sustains ongoing underrecognized work on Black women's political, social, and sexual lives. The tangential encounter is what that student at UC Berkeley was hoping to rekindle. Like "the erotic" for Lorde, Henderson's formulation is another "resource."[134] Henderson does not call for programming, institutionalization, or even increased literary productivity—only recognition of another one of "those various sources of power within the culture of the oppressed that can provide energy for change."[135] The tangential encounter could lead to "a study group," "a retreat," "a Black feminist publication,"[136] or the like, but there are countless examples that, in the case of Henderson and Williams, do not point to a form of organization, or at least not formally. This, instead, is a space of "extraordinary" theorization that "emphasizes the very ordinariness of that extra-ordinariness."[137] The evidence of its significance is legible in works that stemmed from the everyday, like Henderson's memorial essay, her articulation that Williams's "achievements betoken the legacy this generation will pass on to its survivors," and I would also add Henderson's own later work in furthering Black queer studies.[138] The tangential encounter emphasizes the importance of cultivating a network of Black feminist critics when institutionalization in the same place or time is not possible, and of making strides toward creating a community of accountability and joy in order to sustain the work across such distance.

Finally, Henderson's memorialization also extends and revises Williams's own 1980 essay "From Meditations on History," a nearly fifty-page draft of Williams's 1986 novel *Dessa Rose* that was first published in Mary Helen Washington's 1980 anthology *Midnight Birds: Stories by Contemporary Black Women Writers*. Again, Williams pays homage to the women who inspire her writing, whose everyday actions are not recorded but are fictionalized later in Williams's work. Similarly, Washington's anthology itself highlighted the many possible interconnections between Black women's autobiography and creative writing; Washington referred to her own editing of the anthology as "an autobiographical act." Washington's anthologization was also a critical act. Washington writes of Williams in her 1990 anthology *Black-Eyed Susans and Midnight Birds*, "Until the [1986] publication of *Dessa Rose*, Sherley Anne Williams was known more for her critical contributions than for her creative writing," and "there are only two scholarly articles devoted to that novel": "(W)Riting the Work and Working the Rites," by Mae Gwendolyn Henderson, and "Negotiating Between Tenses: Witnessing Slavery After Freedom—*Dessa Rose*," by Deborah McDowell.[139] Washington reminds us not to take the work of critics, their shepherding of cultural and textual works to a wider readership, for granted. Early on, Henderson recognized and voiced the value of Williams's creative writing. As Henderson later writes in her memorial essay on Williams, "She wrote about her mother and her sisters and her girlfriends—and her work spoke to me about my mother and sister and girlfriends (Oh, why did I not tell her that we had more in common than she would ever know?). I suspect, however, that I am a better reader of her writing than I could ever be of her life; yet and still, hers was a life that shared notable parallels and intersections with my own." Not able to tell each other how they felt, their criticism and creative writing said it for them.

Henderson and Williams's tangential encountering was in part due to geographic distance and in part due to professional obligations that allowed them to travel to meet for conferences or the like. It is also a reminder that Black feminisms happen in the interstices, including in the moments in which one discovers, reads, and passes on another's writing. Taking Henderson and Williams at their word, this chapter has drawn focus to one kind of relationship, one in which Black feminists cherish the possibility in being in close collegial relationship with one another, but in a way that does not require (or that cannot hope to achieve) day-to-day cohabitation or close collaboration. In this relationship, not being able to speak together all the time, perhaps because of any number of unwanted "hindrances," transforms brief moments of exchange into a space of theorization. Indeed, contemporaneous relationships between Black creative writers and Black feminist literary critics have long been woven in various patterns across the axes of collegiality and friendship, but rarely do they remain static as merely one or the other, or in one pattern, forever. Rather, the spectrum of possible colleague-friend interactions creates spaciotemporal play, or what Henderson describes as the experience of being "*inspirited*"—the chance to be "carefree" when in each other's presence.[140] The ebb and flow of such relationships has roots in the Black diaspora and thus is also recognizable between foremothers, including Obour and Phillis, and even possibly Edes Beecher, not merely in their letters but in the body of Obour's bequest—only insofar as we provide the conditions for their feminist flowering today.

their eyes were
watching Phillis

In Nellie Y. McKay's landmark 1998 guest column in *PMLA*, McKay employed Phillis's story as an extended metaphor for the ongoing obstacles facing the future of doctoral professionalization in Black literary studies and cautioned that the dearth of Black faculty members teaching Black literature would threaten the ability of scholars of all identities to fully participate in Black literary criticism and the criticism of all literature in English generally. Foregrounding Phillis's oral examination and the authentication of her authorship as the twin specters that continue to haunt the conditions of Black literary criticism in the US university, McKay argues that "if we are ever willing to disband the Wheatley court once and for all, a black pipeline of eager young scholars will flow as it should, and the walls of African American scholarly resentment toward white academic interlopers and of the fears of those guarding white, black, and all other intellectual territories inside our common property will come tumbling down around us."[1] McKay echoed research published in 1995 which found that Black professors made up only "6 percent of the 979 full-time English department faculty at the 25 highest-ranked universities," a figure that pointed to the various ways they remained "underrepresented," including the fact that the number of Black recipients of doctorates in English had decreased since 1978–79 from around 4 percent to "less than 2 percent of all doctorates" awarded in English in 1993.[2] McKay argues that what Phillis experienced in the 1770s continues to characterize the state of the field of Black literary studies in the late 1990s. Counteracting this situation would require us to "make the hard but necessary changes" that would benefit not only Black critics and writers but also the entirety of the English literary tradition.[3]

In 2006, following McKay's passing due to cancer after over twenty-five years as a professor at the University of Wisconsin–Madison, over thirty of McKay's former colleagues and students collaborated to write a different kind of testimony of the state of the Black literary tradition. Together they praised McKay's ethos as a professor, how she navigated academia in ways beyond the trial court model that has conditioned how we have received and how we pass on literature since Phillis.[4] For example, former students of McKay's, like Kimberly Blockett, emphasized the great degree to which McKay facilitated collaboration and the creation of a "scholarly community" among her students around the seminar table and beyond. This ran parallel to her investment in teaching her students, as Faith Smith wrote, "to think about Black women's writing in terms of a *tradition*."[5] McKay's teaching praxis offers us tools for how to meet Phillis, not on the court steps, but in the academy and under very different terms. As early as 1983, as an assistant professor at Wisconsin, McKay wrote, "To be a black woman professor in a white university is difficult and challenging, but it is exciting and rewarding, and black women professors like it here. We aim to stay!"[6] Contrary to misconceptions that including select Black professors in institutions of higher learning would solve the problems attendant to the broken pipeline overnight, McKay stresses that while we may "like" being in the university, it remains "difficult and challenging." Thus, McKay not only sought to map how to recover Black writers within a sense of a tradition; she also understood that criticism is an enactment of one's material and social realities, including the current overarching lack of a community and tradition for ensuring parity in representation of Black scholars and other scholars of color in English and the resulting repercussions for all if this goes unsolved.

McKay's own personal efforts to bolster the Black English PhD pipeline by practicing the values of community, tradition, and listening also propose a model for how it might be possible to read Phillis anew as part of this context. McKay proposes a living criticism that endeavors to build on even the work of its most misunderstood or simply understudied forebears. Significantly, this is not something that McKay learned from her formal graduate training. McKay recalls to her former student Shanna Greene Benjamin her "difficult and challenging" doctoral experience at Harvard University and all that she navigated before taking a leave of absence and eventually receiving her PhD in 1977:

> Harvard was very hard for me. It was a place where I felt out of place within the vast sea of whiteness and New England culture. It was alienating. There was this feeling that if you didn't come from there, you didn't

belong there. I don't think that the university did anything or went out of its way to make people feel miserable, but I don't think it knew what to do with women or with African Americans. And African American women, of course, found themselves in the double bind. In spite of the fact that I had some very good friends there, I was just terribly alienated. There were no African Americans on the faculty; there was no African American literature to study. I learned what I learned about black literature because many of my colleagues knew so much more than I did. We talked about this stuff all along and sort of tacitly agreed without agreeing that we were going to be the first people, the first cohort from Harvard, to do African American literature.[7]

Referring to the members of her graduate cohort as her "colleagues," McKay highlights how they charted the creation of a tradition despite their own professors' limited knowledge. Following her temporary withdrawal from Harvard's PhD program and transition to teaching at Simmons College, McKay recounts how she increasingly "learned from other women in the Boston community" across various institutions who began to gather for meetings in the early 1970s that led to the increased recovery of Black women writers. But since many such works were no longer in print, McKay explains, "we started copying everything and sharing."[8] In fact, this led to the expression of a Black feminist practice of copying as sharing: "There was no computerization or anything like that. You may have heard about something from somebody, or if you found something, you let everybody else know what you found. You didn't keep it to yourself. It was a very sharing community at that point."[9] In contrast to the culture of alienation at Harvard, McKay participates in a culture of sharing that she would later pass on as an integral part of her pedagogy during her tenure as a professor at Wisconsin.

For example, McKay, along with other Black feminist critics, specified the importance of photocopying the work of one author in particular during this time period: Zora Neale Hurston (1891–1960), and especially her novel *Their Eyes Were Watching God* (1937), which had long been out of print.[10] One famous early reviewer, writer Richard Wright, a Black man, wrote in 1937 that the novel was "cloaked in that facile sensuality that has dogged Negro expression since the days of Phillis Wheatley."[11] Yet for later Black feminist critics who did own their own bound copy of *Their Eyes*, it was considered a precious belonging in large part due to its "sensuality" as materially embodied via their communal efforts. McKay recalls trying to discuss the novel at a seminar at Yale University in 1973 or '74 and there not being a single copy in the surrounding city aside from one person's photocopy, which had to be shared among the group.[12] When Hurston was first rediscovered in the 1970s and became a touchstone for late twentieth-century Black feminist critics, she circulated, for a time, beyond the bounds of the book publishing world, and without the publishing house acting as central mediator between the writer and her readers. Instead, it was a much smaller operation that facilitated Hurston's circulation: the Black feminist critic and her photocopier.[13] Ann duCille called this "a form of illicit book-making."[14] While copyright restrictions prohibit uses of a work that could supplant a book's value on the market, Hurston's novel was no longer on the market. It was precisely such "illicit" critical practices that eventually boosted the novel's market value— demonstrating the extent to which critics' participation in making sure a work of writing is shared and read is indeed a form of "book-making" just as significant as the work of the writer who first creates it. In fact, I argue such forms of "illicit book-making" created two kinds of works: the original work and a fugitive work. In other words, the photocopies of the novel as fugitive works exist in a liminal space as being held and not held under the conditions of copyright. The illicit criticism that reproduced the novel in fugitive copies had another outcome: the Black feminist community who claimed that novel as a map of their intentions.

Due to Black feminists' increasing demand for a copy of their own, *Their Eyes* was not only reissued but has also remained in print to this day. It is perhaps incredible that Hurston's novel remains in such high demand—when duCille Googled Hurston in 2011 she found "upward of 540,000 entries relating to her and her work,"[15] and when I Googled Hurston in 2022, the algorithm produced 2,640,000 results (although I remain ultimately skeptical of the ethos of companies like Google and remain more interested in the acts of foremother love that made this outcome possible in the first place). But when Alice Walker wrote the 1975 essay "In Search of Zora Neale Hurston," few copies of *Their Eyes* could be easily found, and Hurston's grave was even unmarked until Walker found it and marked it.[16] Alice Walker had first heard about Hurston while "auditing a black-literature class taught by the great poet *Margaret* Walker, at Jackson State College," although Hurston's work was not actually read in the course but was kept in circulation by Margaret Walker, who "appended, like verbal footnotes" their names due to the fact that Hurston's and several other Black women's writings remained out of print.[17] However, some critics who had a copy of the novel in their possession made photo-copies for their colleagues and students. As duCille wrote, "I had to Xerox copies of the novel by hand and distribute them to students."[18] This Black feminist critical labor, not just the insistence that the novel should be dis-cussed in scholarship but that it should be shared in the classroom and in the seminar room—shared with both colleagues and students alike—is what shepherded the novel back to the printing press. Whether telling students about the novel verbally or enabling them to read the work when it remained out of print, critics greatly extended the novel's original audi-ence and print run.

Nevertheless, returning Hurston's novel to the printing press was not the sum of Black feminist critical labor on the novel. As duCille writes, readers of the novel in the early 1970s were "without benefit of critical interpretations other than our own, since what little secondary material there was on Hurston at the time, with few exceptions, did not do justice to her or her oeuvre."[19] Similarly, in her 1990 foreword to *Their Eyes*, Mary Helen Washington describes how the novel was vulnerable to misreading even by Black critics when it was interpreted outside of a Black feminist context. Washington recounts how Alice Walker came to *Their Eyes* pro-tagonist Janie's defense when critic Robert Stepto, a Black man, critiqued her silence during the courtroom scene wherein Janie is asked by the white male judge whether she has anything to say with regard to her relation-ship to her recently deceased partner Tea Cake. In response to Stepto, "Alice Walker rose . . . insisting passionately that women did not have to speak when men thought they should, that they would choose when and where they wish to speak because while many women *had* found their own voices, they also knew when it was better not to use it." Washington hails this as "the earliest feminist reading of voice in *Their Eyes*," echoing depictions of the novel's investment instead in a "collective" voice embod-ied by Janie's later disclosure to her friend (read: colleague) Pheoby. Key to Walker's response is not only her insistence on an intersectional inter-pretation of this passage in the novel but also her willingness to enact the fact that, as Washington writes, this "was a shared text" that no one critic or reader could totally delineate on their own.[20]

Besides its unique print history and the useful narrative of its recov-ery, there are other possible reasons why Black feminist critics have par-ticularly enjoyed *Their Eyes* as a foundational work. The novel's stylistic complexity—of characterization, genre, and narration—have made it attractive to literary critics of many backgrounds, but Janie's complexity has been especially noteworthy to Black feminist critics. As figures who often occupy the isolated position as the select few members of their communities or their scholarly tradition at the institutions where they teach, Janie's interstitial identity as a newly middle-class Black woman who finds fulfillment in Black social life—yet is neither a public-facing activist nor an organizer—provides a poignant early model for the Black feminist critic. For example, as I mentioned earlier, some critics have failed to understand the closing scenes of the novel. In addition to misunderstanding Janie's silence in the space of the courtroom, Janie's return, singly, to her house in Eatonville, where she lets Pheoby hear her story so she may tell it to others, has also been maligned.[21] If such readers are unable to read her agency in these passages, it is unsurprising if they fail to cherish the novel's closing words. Nevertheless, Janie, far from feeling alone, finds her house, which used to be "so absent," now "full uh thoughts." When Janie ascends the stairs and enters her bedroom, Hurston writes, "she closed in and sat down. Combing road-dust out of her hair. Thinking. . . . She pulled in her horizon like a great fish-net. Pulled it from around the waist of the world and draped it over her shoulder. So much of life in its meshes! She called in her soul to come and see."[22] While living a lively Black social life with Tea Cake (albeit a life cut short) and ultimately telling her story to Pheoby comprise key parts of Janie's identity, Janie is also entitled to the novel's closing moments of radical self-care, which look much like the Black feminist critic's meditative turn to their own thoughts as the root of the tradition—as the soulful, inward-facing work that makes all other aspects of the job possible.

I believe that if Phillis's full story could be told, several elements would sound a lot like Janie's. For example, the bulk of Hurston's novel is devoted to telling the story of the rise and fall of Janie's partnership with Tea Cake, just as scholars such as Honorée Fanonne Jeffers have often focused on the disappointing ending to Phillis's marriage to John Peters. But while I do not discount the importance of these relationships and their various roles in these women's lives, they are less important to me than the relationship that Janie or Phillis would have had with her own self. That such a story is seldom the stuff of novels or poems is perhaps no surprise, but thankfully, it often falls to critics to spotlight the places where a story is lingering untold. Therefore, I argue that Black feminist critics' reclamation of *Their Eyes* is not only a footnote in the novel's history but also the collective narration of its sequel. By photocopying and sharing *Their Eyes*, Black feminist critics were not intent on recapitulating Hurston's novel word for word in their own lives or in the lives of their students. Rather, they were sharing one square in a patchwork quilt from which other kinds of narratives of Black women's and Black feminists' lives could be stitched. It would be unfair to ask any one person's life—fictional or otherwise—to represent the full theoretical possibilities of Black feminist life forevermore. Just as Black feminist critics intervened and transformed *Their Eyes* from one woman's story of early twentieth-century survival into a model for a late twentieth-century scholarly tradition, it is up to subsequent generations to preserve, extend, and transform this work as it befits our needs today.

Despite the triumphant narrative of early Black feminist critical photocopying that successfully secured *Their Eyes* almost a half century of in-print status as of today, the reciprocation of care and protection of the Black feminist critics who were making this possible was not always the top priority of academic institutions. For example, Ann duCille recounts how her first academic job in 1974 at Hamilton College in upstate New York, where she hand-photocopied *Their Eyes* for her students,[23] lasted only one year because of a conflict with the college administration wherein she was not permitted to teach a course titled The Black Presence in American Literature that she had designed for the following year. According to duCille, the conflict stemmed from the fact that "Hamilton's English Department would teach the traditional British and American canons," while their sister women's college "Kirkland's Humanities Division would host all things innovative, experimental, and modern." Rather than collaborate with duCille or offer to cohost the course, Kirkland "refused to approve," leading duCille to resign from her appointment rather than persist in such an environment, for which her "(pitiful) salary" was no justification. While duCille did not share this personal history in print until she included it in her papers in 2017, it "dramatically affected the course of [her] professional life," especially as it took "a long eleven years before [she] again landed a fulltime, tenure-track position."[24] While her previous depiction of her teaching focuses on the extra labor she performed to copy *Their Eyes* for her students, the administration at Hamilton-Kirkland did not reciprocate duCille's efforts in kind, resulting in an eleven-year gap in which she could not advance Black feminist criticism from the relative stability of a tenure-track appointment.

Therefore, it is this social-historical context of Black feminist critical practices of illicit and insistent making that led to the canonization of Hurston's novel that I wish to hold close in mind as we revisit iterations of

Phillis's works as they pass through critics' hands across centuries. Rather than insist only on Phillis's original intentions for her work, just as I would qualify the extent to which I read any author's intentions for their work as nevertheless open to the practice of criticism, this chapter engages with some of the most striking examples of critics' blurring the line between homage and copying in order to bring Phillis to new audiences and print projects as well as the many social barriers that impede such distribution. It is important to note that back in 1773, Phillis expressed her concern in a letter to David Wooster that someone would sell unauthorized copies of her work, depriving her of sales: "If any should be so ungenerous as to reprint them the Genuine Copy may be known, for it is sign'd in my own handwriting." As readers also witness in this letter, Phillis describes the works she buys at the behest of the Earl of Dartmouth, demonstrating her own financial commitment to her forebears' work and awareness of their respective material specificity.[25] Yet in the late twentieth and early twenty-first centuries, it was no longer the threat of counterfeit copies of her 1773 *Poems* that prevented positive engagement with Phillis's poems; rather, it was works of criticism that adapted her poems as examples of, as Alice Walker writes, "stiff, struggling, ambivalent lines" or, as June Jordan writes, "especially awful, virtually absurd" lines.[26] Thus, it became commonplace to engage not Phillis's 1773 *Poems* but, instead, other kinds of writing that surrounded it, including new potential discoveries of Phillis's writings, future poets' adaptations of her poems, and writing produced for festivals commemorating her life and work. Overall, this chapter focuses on print and social engagements with Phillis, some of which involve great speculation, that reckon with the gray areas and silences in her life and work in order to shed light on the histories behind their methodological practices.

Black feminist criticism continues to grapple with the question of how critics should talk about the silences in their research subjects' lives, especially the silences they purposefully cultivated, without compounding such silence with one's own acts of scholarly erasure. Since reading is never completely neutral, the work of the Black feminist critic must be not merely to read, as traditional conceptions of literary criticism may maintain, but to understand the larger historical implications of our methodological practices. In other words, more than just understanding the work at hand, this criticism requires a keen understanding of ourselves, our own biases and points of integrity, in relation to our works of study. It requires that we balance our criticism with that understanding of ourselves close in mind. Yet even recently, as will be discussed in this chapter, scholars have filled in the gaps in Phillis's biography in ways that reflect their own desires, especially in terms of speculating as to what extent Phillis participated in relationships with her enslavers, in her Black women's friendship with Obour, and in her marital relationship with John Peters. In some instances, these speculations may seem naive, as they so clearly index their authors' desires, or their critical Achilles' heels. While several scholars have recently debated the extent to which speculative ascriptions of care in some ways perpetuate and in other ways truncate historical violence,[27] I argue that in either case it is worth attending critically to the instances wherein readers have projected their own desires onto their work on Phillis. Doing so shines light on the ways in which all literary critical work is reflective of the larger societal power dynamics that spill over onto the creative work under study in particular moments of critical encountering. Nowhere is this more apparent than when critics have inserted themselves into, not merely what Phillis wrote, but what Phillis did not write.

(Not) Phillis's Copybooks

If the formerly enslaved abolitionist Frederick Douglass's (1817 or 1818–1895) act of writing between the lines of his former enslaver's old copybook was practice for what would eventually become "one of the founding texts of African American literature,"[28] then Phillis's copybooks would seem to constitute a rubric for another such foundational text. This text, however, could not be Phillis's 1773 volume *Poems on Various Subjects, Religious and Moral*, or her lost second manuscript of poems, or any extant writing that has been clearly corroborated as her own words. Rather, the project in question remains evanescent in what she did not write, in what her future readers wish she had written. The long-practiced desire to read what Phillis wrote between the lines of her published poems resurfaced again when two copybooks reentered the critical archive a little over two hundred years after her passing in 1784. In 1997, Emory University acquired two copybooks—one small, titled "Joining Copies," and one large, "Untitled"—each containing the contents of poems purportedly hand-copied by none other than Phillis herself. Purportedly, "Joining Copies" and "Untitled" quietly weathered her own passing, and her various posthumous interludes of celebrity and obscurity, until 1997, when they made their way into the archives of Black literature and culture at the Stuart A. Rose Manuscript, Archives, and Rare Book Library at Emory, where they lay on the periphery of scholarship on Phillis for several more years. This is probably because the precise authorship of the copybooks remains undetermined, as they are thought likely to be the work of "various hands."[29] The copybooks contain dozens of poems of seemingly indiscriminate poetic genres: abecedaria, acrostics, elegies, epigrams, epitaphs, hymns, odes, and more. Neither copybook has a table of contents, suggesting the poems were copied at random over an indeterminate period. Yet the copybooks' errancy with regard to corroborating Phillis's authorship has enabled readers to imagine their own version of Phillis outside the strictures of enslaved authorship that dictated the publication of her 1773 *Poems*.

While Phillis left behind a confounding and extraordinary body of work, with her second volume of poems lost and with new letters surfacing every few decades, every page bearing her handwriting seems a fragile blessing. Even so, few scholars have attended to the Emory copybooks even though they contain an abundance of writing that, if not Phillis's, overlaps with her historical context. For instance, Alexis Pauline Gumbs writes in her 2010 dissertation that the copybooks "have not been addressed in published literary or historical work on Wheatley that I can find." Knowing that the copybooks, lacking a definitive author as the recording of "poetry and axioms published by others," have not been and cannot be singularly addressed, Gumbs performs her own modulation of response and concludes that the copybooks are Phillis's, especially due to their occasional transcription of poems referencing metaphors of slavery: "Wheatley's unpublished copybooks . . . serve as a record of what she found relevant *to record*," including, according to Gumbs, "her examination of the published poetry of her lifetime which often employed slavery as a metaphor for conflict in the democratic process."[30] This, of course, would make the copybooks impossible for Phillis to safely write as an enslaved woman; the only way to protect her authorship would be to make it difficult for others to assert such authorship. Should a copybook communicate Gumbs's reading as readily to one of Phillis's enslavers or a member of their community, it would have to disperse the threat of easy address. Still, we cannot know whether the copybooks were actually authored even in part by Phillis (her first known poem was written in 1765, about four years after she was enslaved by the Wheatleys).[31] The only author whose work we can truly study as her own is Gumbs's own critical reading of the copybooks as coded critiques of transatlantic slavery, something that is very much in line with Gumbs's subsequent Black feminist poetic-critical output.

Yet the two copybooks were acquired and codified by Emory bibliographer Randall K. Burkett with the understanding that they were possibly
Phillis's. In a memo dated September 8, 1997, Burkett shared news of the
copybooks' provenance with the members of Emory's African American
Collections Advisory Committee: "Acquired from First Folio Rare Books,
1206 Brentwood, Paris TN 38242 . . . who said the two copy books came
out of the estate of Guy Richards, Jr., a journalist from Fishkill, NY, whose
mother was Elizabeth F. Ver Planck Richards. The Ver Plancks were an old
New York family associated with the Newlins, a Boston (?) family for whom
Phillis Wheatley worked." According to Burkett, the copybooks "were the
first manuscripts acquired by Emory, following its creation of the position

of African-American Studies Bibliographer, charged with building research collections in the field for Emory," although Burkett acknowledges that the facticity of Phillis's authorship "is yet to be determined."[32] Not only were the copybooks filled with the words of others—and not only were these words themselves thought to be likely copied down by Phillis *and* other members of her literary community—but the copybooks would also continue to have an afterlife bound up in the writing of such communities. Burkett spotlights the presence of a Phillis poem, "Hymn to Humanity," first published in her *Poems* in September 1773, which is copied into the "Untitled" copybook with the date December 12, 1773, and is significantly revised from its earlier version. In fact, this "Hymn" would be instrumental in securing Emory's Collections' early finances, a boon that later enabled my own research in the late 2010s on future Black women critics and writers, many of whose papers are collected at Emory today.

Although it is uncertain whether this version of "Hymn" was in fact authored and copied by Phillis, buyers suspended their disbelief. Ultimately, whether or not Phillis wrote this "Hymn" was sidestepped by the conferral of honor on the poem via handmade paper and hand-printed sheets, as its transformation into unbound broadside sheets then became the founding texts of Emory's collection in Black literature and culture. As Burkett writes,

> The full text of this revised version of "Hymn to Humanity" has been published in a limited and numbered edition by Thomas Dorn's Wisteria Press, Atlanta, designed and printed by Dwight Agner at Type High in Athens, Georgia. Twenty-six lettered copies on hand-made paper, and 300 numbered copies on fine paper, have been hand-printed in three colors on a broadside sheet. At a gala benefit for the African-American Collections Endowment Fund at Emory University, copy "A" was auctioned for $5,000 and copy "1" of the numbered set went, after spirited bidding, for $600. The remaining lettered and numbered copies are being presented as gifts to those who contribute, respectively, $1,000 or more; or $100 or more, to Emory University Libraries. All proceeds will be used to acquire rare books and manuscripts in African-American life and culture for Emory University.

Transformed into works of late twentieth-century philanthropy, this version of "Hymn," despite the presence of "more than forty textual variations" from its published version in Phillis's 1773 *Poems*, took on a life of its own.[33] In some ways, this could be attributed to the kinds of variations presented in the copybook version. As Vincent Carretta writes, "Either the newly discovered version is a very unusual instance of Wheatley's revising an already published poem, or it is a revision of Wheatley's poem by another poet."[34] The poem as it is printed in Phillis's 1773 *Poems* is dedicated to "S. P. G. Esq," while in the copybook version it is dedicated to "S. P. Gallowy who corrected some Poetic Essays of the Authoress."[35] Burkett speculates that this Gallowy figure (who remains thus far unidentified) tutored Phillis and others, as a list of scholars is written on the inside cover of the "Joining Copies" copybook.[36] Indeed, it seems plausible (though pure conjecture at this point) that Phillis originally penned this occasional poem for Gallowy to express gratitude for his instruction, that he later used this manuscript to teach students, and that they copied it into their own copybooks. If this is the case, then Phillis took care to not mention the fact that he "corrected" some of her poems when she published "Hymn" within her 1773 *Poems*. Nevertheless, in the late 1990s, when Emory was looking for benefactors to fund their library, such acknowledgments of gratitude in Phillis's own work would certainly have aligned with their own.

The erasure of Phillis's acknowledgment of Gallowy's "corrections" from its variant as an occasional poem to its published and public version likely stems from the fact that any acknowledgment of collaboration would have brought Phillis's authorship further into question and imperiled her best chances of successfully publishing her 1773 *Poems*. Beyond this, the differences between the two variants of "Hymn" are not drastic changes in content but subtle changes in diction and tone that perhaps prove just as important as changes in content would. Just as in several of her other poems, Phillis invokes the muses as legitimizing her poetic project. In "Hymn," however, she also ascribes to Gallowy a key role in first addressing the muses on her behalf to further her cause. For example, the penultimate stanza of the September 1773 published "Hymn" addresses not Gallowy but "G——" and reads,

> For when thy pitying eye did see
> The languid muse in low degree,
>   Then, then at thy desire
> Descended the celestial nine;
> O'er me methought they deign'd to shine,
>   And deign'd to string my lyre.[37]

Capitalizing on the alliteration across the words *desire, Descended,* and the repeated *deign'd,* Phillis compounds the idea that Gallowy's desire for the muse's empowerment was consented to, and that the muses deigned or condescended to "string [Phillis's] lyre." These lines, published for all to read, appropriately temper Phillis's audacious poetic figuration with the rhetoric of the enslaved, and present her as someone who is beneath the social status of the muses. But the version of this stanza that is later copied in December 1773 reads quite differently, this time addressing "Gallowy":

> For when thy pitying Eye did see
> The languid Muse in low Degree,
>   Then did thy bounteous Hand Command
> Command the all-inspiring Nine
> From bright Olympus' Height to shine
>   And ev'n my Song demand.[38]

Rather than responding to Gallowy's desire, these lines depict him commanding (doubly in the manuscript, if only owing to the use of "Command" as a manuscript catchword spanning a page break) the muses "to shine / And ev'n [Phillis's] Song demand." If this was indeed an occasional poem that Phillis penned and gifted to Gallowy before later revising it for publication, she later demonstrably softened its tone away from its original figuration of his demanding the muses to grant her "Song." However, we may never know for certain whether Phillis was indeed the original author of both poems.

From here, possible readings of the copybooks all depend on one's methodology. Like Burkett and Emory's early philanthropists of Black literature and culture, in order to further the mission of the private university one could operate partially, though significantly, on the belief that the copybooks could have been authored by Phillis. This, of course, is a darker side to foremother love: using Phillis's good name as a form of development, and knowing that doing so is lucrative for the university. Although my own research has benefited from Emory's collections, I must wonder if there could have been other ways to grow its holdings. Thus, holding off further marketing of the copybooks as inaugural works for future Black writers at bay, I ask what becomes possible when we linger in the uncertainty of whether or not these copybooks were authored by her. I wonder what other kinds of questions arise when we follow Phillis's traces in the archive but do not hold on to her so tightly. In other words, what becomes possible to say about Phillis when we encounter her not only as a poet but also as a critic? While previous responses to the copybooks have often focused on "Hymn," certainly because it offers the closest evidence of Phillis's authorship, I am interested rather in the possibilities as they extend beyond what Phillis wrote toward what she makes possible for thought. Overall, a reading of the copybooks that privileges their uncertain authorship has the potential to privilege not excellence but the theorization of incongruousness and inconclusiveness as issues that continue to shape the conditions of many Black women's literary archives.

Privileging uncertainty in Phillis's archive runs counter to how traditional literary criticism operates, with its focus on definitive readings and reliance on demonstrable facts of literary authorship. While the copybooks confound literary critical methods based on single authorship, they paradoxically become a work of liberative criticism: offering a model for better understanding other works of which Phillis was not the sole author. Rather than emphasize individuality, mastery, and celebrity, the copybooks necessitate a turn toward collectivity, collaboration, and even the partial anonymity of the individual transcriber. For Black feminist critics, such an unresolvable archive often marks a site of healing, summoning a geography that has not yet been mapped and thus cannot be destroyed by mapping. For example, Katherine McKittrick's attention in *Demonic Grounds* (2006) to the palimpsestic map of alternative Black women's diasporic geographies has given interpretive legitimacy to the life of erasures, shadows, and spirits. In doing so, McKittrick pays homage to Black feminist critic Sylvia Wynter (1928–), extending her work and defining "the [demonic] grounds" as a methodology of absence that gestures "*toward* a new epistemology."[39] Wynter's own essay on the demonic first appeared as an "After/Word," with a note from the editors that "this is the first section of a much longer manuscript which could not be included here in its entirety."[40] Similarly, this chapter will devote itself to imaginations of Phillis's writing that are illegible to some of our most sophisticated literary critical parameters, imaginations that are instead, to use Nadia Ellis's words, "at large in the world, possessed of its enchantments and alive to its temporal creases; audacious about the possibilities for attachments to multiple, far-flung sources of inspiration."[41] While attempts to codify Phillis as a fixed icon and as a rarity have persisted into today's contemporary criticism, this chapter celebrates her afterlife as a collection of loose ends pursuant to someone who remains ultimately unattainable.

Briefly, Phillis's "On Being Brought from Africa to America"

There is a long history of readers trying to rewrite Phillis's poems into the poems they would rather read.[42] While these poems cannot change either the circumstances of Phillis's life or the fact that she could not have written poems like these in her lifetime, they keep us wondering, and also enable those of us who are not poets (or are emerging poets) to ask what kinds of poems we would write if we could. This paradox explains why Phillis functions so well as a foremother, for what remains in the gap between what Phillis wrote and others' later responses to her work is the broken and vexed space where the practice of Black feminist criticism, a labor of impossible kinship and remembrance, thrives. While Robert Stepto has described the most important task of the forefather of Black literature, the masculine writer of the autobiographical narrative of enslavement, as "above all *remembering* his ordeal in bondage,"[43] Phillis as foremother, by contrast, embodies something quite different and instead recruits others to perform her remembrance. She is more akin to the "lost mother" Said-iya Hartman notes as the absent figuration for those who, like Hartman and those of us who emerged on the other side of the Middle Passage, became orphans whose history and kin lines were erased by transatlantic enslavement, and whose lost mother's words, "the words she refused to share," became "what I should remember."[44] Similarly, Phillis's deferral inspires the meticulousness with which readers search for evidence of her own memory in her poems. For example, despite promising a fragment of Phillis's autobiography, her most infamous poem, the 1773 "On Being Brought from Africa to America," has become an irresolvable riddle and thus a site of ongoing overdetermined readings. While Phillis commands remembrance in the poem's seventh line, "Remember, *Christians*, *Negros*, black as *Cain*," she modifies it such that the lines together read, "Remember, *Christians*, *Negros*, black as *Cain*, / May be refin'd, and join th' angelic train," introducing a future that depends on readers' own predispositions toward Christian kinship or estrangement and depends on their interpretation of "May be" as probability or mere possibility.[45]

With each new reader of "On Being Brought," the process of assembling one's own discursive approach to transatlantic memory begins anew. Prevailing understandings of the poem have often held that Phillis "was not sensitive enough to the needs of her own people to demonstrate a kinship" with them, leading some readers to consider it "the most reviled poem in African-American literature."[46] The poem as it is published in Phillis's 1773 *Poems* reads in full,

> 'Twas mercy brought me from my *Pagan* land.
> Taught my benighted soul to understand
> That there's a God, that there's a *Saviour* too:
> Once I redemption neither sought nor knew.
> Some view our sable race with scornful eye,
> "Their colour is a diabolic die."
> Remember, *Christians*, *Negros*, black as *Cain*,
> May be refin'd, and join th' angelic train.[47]

While the emphasis on Christianity is fraught for some readers, for others it offers interpretive clues, such as Sondra O'Neale's reading in 1985 that "Biblically, 'ransom,' like 'redeem,' applied to the purchase of freedom by one who was taken captive against his will," which transforms that very line "Once I redemption neither sought nor knew" into a memory of Phillis's African past before her enslavement.[48] Indeed, what reader could possibly find more to parse in this poem after this or after perusing O'Neale's even more astoundingly in-depth analysis in her 1986 essay "A Slave's Subtle War"? Nevertheless, criticism of the poem has continued and we have since inherited countless more readings of it, but has doing so restored Phillis's voice, or has it only continued in order to tell us what we want to hear? "On Being Brought" may participate in almost any interpretive tradition in which you place it, and it has survived all kinds of manipulation. Even though it is a poem Phillis wrote when she was only about fourteen years of age,[49] try telling this to the critics who have spent hours puzzling over it. Overall, the act of interpretation has gathered readers of all kinds into what would certainly look like the assembly of an otherworldly realm. Rather than what the poem itself says, we receive a full portrait of what a poem about the Middle Passage must ostensibly say based on its archive of subsequent readings.

For my own part, I would argue that much of the power of "On Being Brought" stems from its brevity. At only eight lines long and comprising four heroic couplets, it barely has enough formal characteristics to help the poem cohere into a clear generic shape. If the poem calls to mind the preparatory octave of the sonnet, then the closing remarks of its sestet are blatantly absent. Phillis's frugality, her mere fifty-eight words on this subject, are compounded by the ease with which she extolls incorporation into "th' angelic train" in her final line. Additionally, a quarter of the poem is devoted to what others say and is distinct for the subjectivity of the speech it contains: "Some view our sable race with scornful eye, / 'Their colour is a diabolic die.'"[50] By quoting these words and calling attention to their framed contingency, Phillis politely mitigates the force of their truthfulness. Phillis knew her poetic enterprise could be successful only if she could persuade readers that with very slight modification, predominantly white verse culture could speak a Black woman's poetic consciousness. The brevity of this poem suggests the inability of English poetry to adequately speak to this experience at all. Rather than innovate on an already established English genre form to encapsulate this subject in as many words as possible, "On Being Brought" represents a startling recoil from genre and tends more toward epigrammatic incompletion—especially when compared to the sincerity and the breadth with which the rest of the genres in *Poems* flourish, dutifully expressing their generic contents, histories, and forms. The only definitive reading I can muster about this poem is that, overall, it says very little, requiring you to say what it cannot. Yet this is a strategy that has characterized other moments in Phillis's extant work, and in lieu of lingering overly long in "On Being Brought," I hope to attend to the ways Phillis and others navigated this divine quiet.

Purposeful Nonauthorship in "Niobe"

"On Being Brought" is far from the only poem of Phillis's that hinges on the benevolence of a "good" reader to say what Phillis refuses to utter. Rather than continue to try to close-read that poem, I find that its disciplinary questions also remain alive in other areas of Phillis's oeuvre. Thus, from here, I draw attention to a different poem, one that Phillis most certainly did not write from scratch. In fact, Phillis's poem on Ovid's writing of the myth of Niobe allegorizes the perils of generic innovation and the risk of not paying heed to preexisting power dynamics within an ancient Western context. What is especially notable about Phillis's revision of this poem is that while she indeed adapts most of the poem to her own style, it does not contain obvious changes in content, and its final stanza is markedly *not* written by herself. In contrast to "On Being Brought," the poem "Niobe in Distress for Her Children Slain by Apollo, from Ovid's Metamorphoses, Book VI. and from a View of the Painting of Mr. Richard Wilson" is one of the longest selections in Phillis's 1773 *Poems* and thus the most extended treatment of the ancient Western tradition therein. The first thing that an avid reader on par with Phillis herself might notice about her version of the Niobe myth is that despite evidence that Phillis's contemporaries heavily revised the Ovid, Phillis remains mainly true to the original's plot.[51] Further, despite its originating male authors and painters, "Niobe in Distress" is overarchingly about the agency that women possess in transforming each other's lives, a topic that indeed is differently, even if subtly, portrayed in the words of a Black woman.[52] While "On Being Brought" draws to an untenable close with "*Christians*" and "*Negros*" ever poised in potential unification, "Niobe in Distress" does not predicate itself on a community uniting across power differentials, only the ever-possible threat of conflict.

"Niobe in Distress" is composed in Phillis's characteristic iambic pentameter lines and rhyming couplets, the formal markers of her 1773 elegies, and therefore shares the sound of the elegies that precede it in her *Poems*. While the sound of the iambic pentameter line connects the poem to the elegies that came before, it is notable for at least three other framing mechanisms. For example, Jennifer Thorn writes that despite Phillis's overt invocations of Ovid and Wilson, she likely read the collection of translations of Ovid's *Metamorphoses* edited by Samuel Garth in 1717, "Welsh Wilson's 1760 *The Destruction of Niobe's Children*," and she "probably saw one of the many prints of the 1761 engraving of [Richard] Wilson's *Niobe* made by William Woollett" rather than the original painting by Wilson.[53] Nevertheless, when halfway through the first stanza of "Niobe in Distress" Phillis performs the classical request for inspiration—to "Inspire with glowing energy of thought, / What *Wilson* painted, and what *Ovid* wrote"—she is not pretending that this work has not already passed before at least two layers of historical engagement before the task then reached her.[54] Instead, she is aiming for the highest literary forms of this prior engagement, those who made the translations and engravings and prints possible in the first place. In this way, Phillis does the opposite of what readers soon learn is Niobe's downfall: She is acknowledging the forebears whose antecedence allowed her to write this poem, even if she subtly deviates from their model.

Overall, Niobe functions in the poem as someone who has been blessed by divine fertility in keeping with her Titan ancestry, even though she is not herself an original goddess. At its outset, "Niobe in Distress" is an allegory about women's creation and the dangers of innovation without gratitude to those who made it possible. Niobe is someone who via her pedigree is framed by godlike ancestors: Her father, grandfathers, and husband are all noted for their mythological connections. Therefore, Phillis describes Niobe's children by using the language of poetic and painterly creation: "What if their charms exceed *Aurora's* teint, / No words could tell them, and no pencil paint." However, Niobe's vanity in thinking so, and by usurping her position as a woman who is simply a reproduction of her godlike roots, has violent consequences. Niobe "left the rights unpaid," was willing to cut off all her ties to her ancestors, and was ready to laud her achievements without giving proper thanks to those that made them possible—so her creations, her fourteen children, are summarily cut down by the prior order.[55] Phillis sets herself up as a foil to Niobe from her poem's onset as she wraps the poem in a meter that connects it to her prior elegies and uses its title to respectfully acknowledge the myth's origin in other poetic hands. In many ways, the poem is about Phillis's ability to acknowledge a foremother who may provide guidance on how to best write Niobe's story of failed acknowledgment. While Phillis tells the story of Niobe's hubris and failure to acknowledge her forebears, where she deviates from the Ovid is in her depiction of Niobe's response to her punishment.

Thus, in "Niobe in Distress," Phillis takes up a mythical figuration of a powerful woman and her trauma and redefines the meaning of Niobe's original myth by making slight changes to the poem's plot. For example, in a 1717 English translation of Ovid's *Metamorphoses*, believed to be the edition that Phillis would have read, the demigoddess Niobe had the nerve to question the repute of a famed goddess and was consequently depicted as "haughty," "vile," "obdurate," and "Insensible."[56] As in Phillis's 1773 version, Niobe chooses not to pay "Rites" to the goddess Latona, whom she describes as "A Goddess founded merely on Report."[57] Instead, Niobe touts her confidence in her familial lineage and offers her fourteen children as evidence of all that stands between herself and ignominy. Hearing this, Latona's children, Apollo (Phoebus) and Diana (Artemis), move to kill each of Niobe's seven sons, but even then Niobe does not relent. It is only after the subsequent murders of her seven daughters and husband that Niobe's "Tongue" "stands congeal'd within her frozen Lips." In both the 1717 and 1773 versions of the poem, even after Niobe is effectively turned into stone, silenced, and woebegone, she continues to protest her situation via her tears. However, the 1717 translation concludes, "Yet still she weeps, and whirl'd by stormy Winds, / Born thro' the Air, her native Country finds; / There fix'd, she stands upon a bleaky Hill, / There yet her marble Cheeks eternal Tears distil."[58] Returned to "her native Country" as though borne aloft by her woe alone, Niobe perpetually mourns. However, Phillis's version does not end with diasporic flight, and Niobe does not return. With some additional subtle changes, Phillis maintains the arc of Niobe's story in her own retelling but roots her in a different locale altogether.

First, what is different in Phillis's 1773 version of the poem is that Niobe is figured as graceful and honorable throughout the recounting of her tale: Phillis refers to Niobe as "an empress with a goddess join'd," a "Titaness," a "queen," and ultimately as "all beautiful in woe." Early in the poem, Phillis writes,

> *Niobe* comes with all her royal race,
> With charms unnumber'd, and superior grace:
> Her *Phrygian* garments of delightful hue,
> Inwove with gold, refulgent to the view,
> Beyond description beautiful she moves
> Like heav'nly *Venus*, 'midst her smiles and loves[59]

Well aware of her beauty, Niobe does not understand why she and her subjects must pay "tribute" to another goddess. Meanwhile, in the 1717 version of the poem, Apollo and Diana, Latona's children, are depicted as fair conveyors of justice, but according to Phillis, they are overarchingly cruel beyond any apt proportion of justice, although they often feel "pity" for Niobe. They quickly set off to "punish pride, and scourge the rebel mind."[60] In Phillis's poem, Apollo's (there is little mention of Diana's involvement in Phillis's version) assassinations of Niobe's entire family proceed slowly and in great detail across the poem, resulting in some of Phillis's most gruesome descriptions of bodily harm. Finally, in Phillis's version, there is also no mention of Niobe's return to "her native Country" at the close of the poem. Lacking any description of transport, Phillis's Niobe appears to suffer her unfortunate fate without the possibility of escape, remaining in the country where her punishment was dealt out. This means that Phillis's Niobe remains diasporic, transoceanic, and in continued geographic conversation with her adversaries. Continuing to proffer signs of expression, Niobe's tears and the story of sorrow preserved therein become the progeny of Niobe's landless legacy.

During the 1760s and '70s, Niobe would have resonated with American readers as a figure for liberty under threat. Those who protested Great Britain's "tyranny" and who saw themselves "within the context of their own rhetoric—as slaves" might have also questioned why a goddess like

Latona should be so inflexibly worshipped without the sanction of Niobe's own worth in a more democratic distribution of power.[61] For such readers, what in 1717 was interpreted as Niobe's "haughty," "vile," "obdurate" "Insensib[ility]" would have been viewed in 1773 as the requisite behavior of political persistence. Phillis transforms the poem from a cautionary tale into an elegy on a figure who died on the blade of testing her own political beliefs. However, "Niobe" was not a poem that Phillis included in her original proposal for Boston publication.[62] Rather, it appeared later among the final group of poems that eventually gained publication in the London volume. The overt neoclassicism of Niobe may have been Phillis's attempt to impress English readers. Further, despite Americans' investment in the rhetoric of their enslavement to Great Britain, "Niobe" enabled Phillis to write about liberty in a way that would not have been possible within the limits of American anti-Blackness. Mythic figurations of stymied liberation would continue to circulate in Phillis's poems, unfolding in later poems that dramatize the conflict between Britannia and Columbia. That Phillis, as an enslaved Black woman, would stage a dialogue between two feminized godheads of colonialism is a delicious irony and a subtle tip of the hand of her knowledge that slavery was indeed both nations' common denominator, the cruel axis on which they stole power.

In three poems published separately from Phillis's 1773 *Poems*—one written before and two written after she had gained her freedom, including "America" (written in 1768 and not included in the London-published *Poems*), "To His Excellency General Washington" (embedded in a 1775 letter and published in 1776), and "Liberty and Peace, a Poem" (published in 1784)—Phillis allegorizes America and Britain as classical goddesses to which questions may be addressed and grievances aired.[63] Between the poems "America" and the revision of the poem to George Washington that becomes "Liberty and Peace," America is transformed from Britannia's son into a *goddess* in her own right: Columbia. In much the same way that Niobe questions Latona, Phillis's America becomes divine on the basis of its challenging the structure—even the gender—into which it happened to be assigned at birth. In "America," again, written in 1768 before Phillis was freed, a boy child's tears become the figuration of resistance. As Phillis writes, famously, toward the beginning of the poem "Ethiopians speak / Sometimes by Simile." Depicted in figurative form as the son of "Brittania," "americus" did not openly rebel—instead, he cried, wept, and "Prostrate fell at [Brittania's] maternal feet."[64] Brittania is figured not necessarily as a tyrant but as an unkind mother—and "americus" responds the way any child would to undeserved reproach. As in "Niobe," tears are the uncontrolled excess of what cannot be reined in by power—familial or national. By the time Phillis wrote the poem "To His Excellency General Washington" in 1775, however, she was no longer enslaved, and America is no longer figured in her poems as a disconsolate child.

Demonstrating further that her poems, especially those written after her manumission, were written with political intent, Phillis wrote a letter to Washington in 1775 in order to express her investment in "all possible success in the great cause" for which he labored as commander of the Continental "armies of North America." Yet the poem enclosed in that letter would stipulate the exact terms of Phillis's enthusiasm. America, no longer the child "americus," is now named "Columbia." Her "cause" is "freedom," and she holds dominion over a "land of freedom's heaven-defended race." Phillis embeds Washington in a mythical tradition that precedes him and closes her poetic address to him by writing, "Proceed, great chief, with virtue on thy side, / Thy ev'ry action let the goddess guide."[65] Phillis would find room to say even more about her vision of a freedom-infused America when she revised her poem to Washington in the poem "Liberty and Peace," which was printed independently in broadside form in 1784. (One of a handful of Phillis's poems to be published on North American soil during her lifetime, it first appeared, sadly, in the same year that Phillis passed away.) The poem functions as a celebration of the close of the American Revolution, but by beginning her poem with the proclamation, "Lo! Freedom comes. Th' prescient Muse foretold, / All Eyes th' accomplish'd Prophecy behold,"[66] I also imagine Phillis was celebrating the recent abolition of slavery in Boston in 1783.

In 1974, Alice Walker described a selection of lines from Phillis's poem "To His Excellency General Washington" as "stiff, struggling, ambivalent lines [that] are forced on us" and concluded that Phillis was "not an idiot or a traitor"; she was "only a sickly little black girl, snatched from [her] home and country."[67] However, Walker did not contextualize the lines she condemns—"The goddess comes, she moves divinely fair, / Olive and laurel binds her golden hair: / Wherever shines this native of the skies, / Unnumber'd charms and recent graces rise"—as coming from the poem to Washington or their own history of revision across Phillis's subsequent body of work.[68] Walker's overarching definition of Phillis's legacy is that she "kept alive . . . *the notion of song*."[69] Yet there is also evidence that Phillis also—in these very lines—practiced her own language of liberty. For these lines are not the first in which Phillis described a goddess—goddesses populate the

1773 *Poems*—but these particular lines arise in two poems Phillis wrote after gaining her manumission. Read accordingly, it is less that Phillis is adhering to a specific vision of white femininity and more that she is revising the expectations and responsibilities of such a subjectivity by expressing a beauty that could command praise *only insofar as* it did not interfere with the conferral of freedom. In other words, the lines appear first in a poem addressed to George Washington (in a 1775 letter) that envisions a fully democratic America and later, too, in a 1784 poem that celebrates Boston's abolition of slavery. Therefore, in addition to preserving "*the notion of song,*" another way to conceive Phillis's legacy is to view her 1773 poems not as perfect instantiations of protest, but as the lifesaving practice for the kinds of poems she would endeavor to write after she became free.

The fact that "Niobe in Distress" ends with a refusal to finish the poem in her own words speaks to what Phillis could *not* write while she was enslaved. The final result of Niobe's reliance on the footing of her own innovation is that she is turned into stone, in eternal mourning, forced to exist in a much more restricted form than she would have experienced had she simply performed the acts of duty required of her. The final stanza of the poem reads,

> The queen of all her family bereft,
> Without or husband, son, or daughter left,
> Grew stupid at the shock. The passing air
> Made no impression on her stiff'ning hair.
> The blood forsook her face: amidst the flood
> Pour'd from her cheeks, quite fix'd her eye-balls stood.
> Her tongue, her palate both obdurate grew,
> Her curdled veins no longer motion knew;
> The use of neck, and arms, and feet was gone,
> And e'vn her bowels hard'ned into stone:
> A marble statue now the queen appears,
> But from the marble steal the silent tears.[70]

Niobe's perpetual tears, her transformation into "slavish" imitation at the hands of her own resistance,[71] become even more polemical given that Phillis did not write this final stanza of the poem. Eric Slauter notes that "this scene might have been both attractive and repulsive and why Wheatley may have desired 'another Hand' to translate Niobe's petrification."[72] Claudia N. Thomas writes that Phillis simply "may have lost interest in the poem."[73] However, I believe the choice to not write this stanza is much more intentional and significant. Not quite to say that, as James Edward Ford III says, someone misread Phillis here and they thus "added a final stanza," I do concur that the formatting forces readers to "carry on the tradition of resistance Wheatley's poetry enacts through ongoing study."[74] In the Carretta edition of Phillis's *Writings*, this note appears below the final stanza,[75] but in the original 1773 edition, the note bisected the poem (possibly just due to formatting) and actually appears between the lines of the preceding poem and the final stanza, highlighting the final stanza's distinctness from the rest of the poem: "*This Verse to the End is the Work of another Hand."[76] Phillis's inability to write this moment, her silence, calls attention to the fact that she may be using another's words—with its series of quotation marks down the left margin—to write about an experience she in fact shares with her poetic subject, making this moment in "Niobe in Distress" one of only a handful of moments in her *Poems* where she may be writing about herself, and therefore without her own words. What is striking about this ending, in comparison to the original myth in the Ovid, is that while Phillis ends her poem here, Ovid goes on: The poem remembers and praises Latona's history. Phillis, again, chose to do no such thing. Her choice to end the poem here is striking and compounds the effect of Niobe's transformation into weeping stone.

When read on her own, Phillis may appear more aligned with traditional British or American literary conventions, but when read alongside the history of Black feminist criticism, her decision to propose only conditional community in "On Being Brought" and to maintain her silence at the close of "Niobe in Distress" speaks volumes to the significance of a Black feminist critical lens. As aforementioned, proponents of Janie, protagonist of *Their Eyes*, and their interpretation of Janie's silence as an intentional withholding of her voice during the courtroom scene was a watershed moment for Black feminist criticism. Alice Walker's assertion in 1977 that "many women *had* found their own voices" but "also knew when it was better not to use it" provided a rubric for scholars to revisit literary history for moments in which writers even before Hurston practiced their own acts of intentional narrative silence.[77] A "radical rewriting of the present" might place Phillis, Hurston, and Walker in closer conversation that they might have imagined possible.[78] Taken together, Phillis's silence at the close of "Niobe in Distress" and willing substitution of another's writing as well as Janie's silence in the courtroom and subsequent disclosure to Pheoby point to a poetics in which Black women's voices are understood as highly contextual, and transparent only insofar as the set of circumstances in which they are uttered permits. Given that the circumstances that would allow transparency so rarely transpire, it is important to read intentional acts of silence with extra sensitivity. If we understand Phillis and Janie to be acting in these scenes not merely as Black women with voices, but as Black feminist critics, we might attend to similar works of creative writing with renewed understanding of their dual function as criticism.

Robert Hayden's Unuttered Love

Nearly two hundred years later, what Phillis could not say at the end of "Niobe in Distress" is finally uttered by poet Robert Hayden (1913–80). In a poem that mimics Phillis's own act of acknowledgment in her title, Hayden provides another possible figuration of Niobe and thus Phillis herself. Like Phillis's "Niobe in Distress for Her Children Slain by Apollo, from *Ovid*'s Metamorphoses, Book VI. and from a View of the Painting of Mr. *Richard Wilson*," Hayden's respective Ovidian poem, first published in 1972, is titled "Richard Hunt's 'Arachne,'"[79] alluding to a real work of art: sculptor Richard Hunt's 1956 welded steel sculpture *Arachne*. Hayden's ascription of the Arachne myth to Hunt's sculpture makes space for a lineage of Black men's creativity as a key interlocution of the original Arachne myth, which parallels Niobe's and appears in book 6 just prior to hers in Ovid's *Metamorphoses*. Both Phillis's final stanza of "Niobe in Distress" and Hayden's full poem "Arachne" are twelve lines long, but while Phillis's poem ends in "silent tears," Hayden's ends with Arachne's transformation in a much more positive sense. While it remains uncertain whether Hayden knowingly paid tribute to Phillis's "Niobe in Distress," I perform my own fictive kinship between the two poems and argue herein that Hayden transforms Phillis's silence into a form of telling as the poem's variegated indentations communicate Hayden's artful attention to Arachne's spatial-temporal flux. Both the Phillis stanza and the Hayden poem emphasize the terror of bodily metamorphosis, as innovation comes at the risk of eliminating who you once were. Hayden's poem, however, establishes in Phillis's unwritten stanza the creation of Black poetics. What Phillis could not freely express as an enslaved woman, the violence she faced as well as her grace in turning that constraint into expression, Hayden figures as the condition for Black poetry and its criticism and theory.

Arachne and Niobe's stories were both recounted in the 1717 translation of the *Metamorphoses* Phillis is thought to have adapted.[80] In later translations, Ovid's versions of Arachne and Niobe's stories are still often told in a progression, and the women even sometimes exist as figures in each other's worlds. For example, Niobe's story often begins where Arachne's ends, and Arachne's story still echoes in the air often as Niobe's own story starts. Nevertheless, Niobe does not perceive Arachne's transformation as a cautionary tale: She ignores her foremother/sister-colleague's story. Interestingly, Hayden himself chooses to ignore select aspects of Arachne's previous figuration. In translations in and around the 1960s, she was an artist, particularly a weaver, and her transformation is often rendered as an extension of such.[81] By contrast, Hayden's honorific poem pays homage to, not only a weaver, but a poetic ancestor whose transformation harbingers something beyond her previous artistry. While Ovid highlights Arachne's possession of little familial or societal standing beyond her role as an artist, Hayden's poem does not condemn or class-shame Arachne. Hayden emphasizes Arachne's lingering humanity amid her transformation by emphasizing not only the monstrosity of her transformation but also the affective violence as she experiences it. Arachne's transformation is extremely painful, yes, but even more so due to how dehumanizing it is. Nevertheless, Hayden's poem wonders into what Arachne is being transformed. He does not conform to the assumption that she is just a spider (though different translations vary as to whether something of Arachne's humanity remains in the original Ovid), and Hayden's acknowledgment of Arachne's inauguration of a third mode of being, something between human and spider, makes room for a creation beyond what is taken away from her.

Like his own figuration of Arachne-in-transition, Hayden himself identified in complex ways beyond mainstream prescriptions of Black (often masculinist) poetic identity in his time. For example, Hayden's "refusal of the primacy of race in poetic pursuits" during the 1966 Writers' Conference at Fisk University, where he was in conversation with Arna Bontemps, Gwendolyn Brooks, Dudley Randall, Melvin B. Tolson, and Margaret Walker, was not well received.[82] The event's acrimony and its fallout left a deep scar on Hayden's reputation, and even impacted his career trajectory.[83] However, as Derik Smith notes, what is less often recounted is that the conference also consisted of moments where Hayden was held in great esteem.[84] Similarly, Dudley Randall recalled in an interview with Melba Joyce Boyd, "That night, [Hayden] read his poems of the black experience. He read 'Runagate' and 'Middle Passage' and other power-ful pieces. Everybody was moved, even those who had attacked him. The whole audience spontaneously gave him a standing ovation. Offstage, he leaned against the wall exhausted. There were tears in his eyes."[85] Smith reads this moment as evidence that the conference culminated not just in reproach of Hayden but also in a "communal celebration of [Hayden's] poetry."[86] I am also struck by Randall's remembrance of Hayden's exhaus-tion.[87] Multivoiced and painstakingly researched, the poem "Middle Passage" is purposefully arduous and takes time to read aloud. While its content alone was certainly very painful for Hayden to perform at his readings, there is no evidence that he ever delegated and shared the labor of its telling. Perhaps Hayden's remarks at the writers' conference were merely an attempt to wonder aloud about a possible space where he could begin to shift some of this weight.

Hayden's complexity would be more legible to later poets less bound to the narrow prescriptions of the Black Arts Movement's definition of Blackness generally and Black masculine poetic identity specifically. For example, in 2013, poet Kyle Dargan (1980–) also took up the debate of the 1966 Writers' Conference, but concluded with words that were an echoic rearticulation, refinement, and expansion of Hayden's: "I was, and remain, a 'black' poet ('African American,' if we must be technically im-precise). It is just that now I've turned the 'blackness' in my person and my work into a bottomless pool protected only by a HUMANS ONLY sign on the gate."[88] Dargan's 2004 poem "Search for Robert Hayden" also pays tribute to Black poetry in an expansive sense, connecting Hayden to the tradition via the organic, pulp material of paper in Dargan's library-garage after a move.[89] In the poem, looking for Hayden leads to others' poetry collections, including Lucille Clifton's 1987 *Next: New Poems*, Yusef Ko-munyakaa's 1984 *Copacetic*, and Cornelius Eady's 1986 *Victims of the Lat-est Dance Craze*. Today these works by Eady and Komunyakaa are out of print, but they live on in Dargan's library-garage, this space for storing multiple means of transport. Dargan honors the poems' print materiality, even if they do not make it into collected editions. While Dargan's own poem's anthologization points back to its own book and works well in an anthology, many do not, especially those by poets who wrote (seemingly) alone, or not as part of any discernible movement. Thus, Dargan provides a framework for how to read Hayden, just as many of Phillis's poems did not reveal themselves to me until I read those written in her wake.

Research published after Hayden's passing in 1980 (due to an "apparent heart attack" at the too-early age of sixty-six)[90] has suggested other reasons that he might have been hesitant to identify as a Black poet within the hypermasculine and cisheteropatriarchal definitions of Blackness heralded by other Black Arts Movement–era poets. For example, in 2011, poet Eduardo C. Corral (1973–) paid tribute to Hayden's influence on Corral as both a poet and a queer man by writing a poem that was also published with a brief interview in which Corral says,

> Hayden never publicly acknowledged his struggles with his sexuality. Arnold Rampersad's introduction to the *Collected Poems* touches upon this reticence. The scholar Pontheolla T. Williams in *Robert Hayden: A Critical Analysis of His Poetry* mentions the "wracking trauma that Hayden suffered as a bisexual." I understand Hayden lived in a different time. Sometimes it was not possible to live as a gay/bisexual man. But Hayden also seemed to believe his sexuality was a sin. He believed the cancer that claimed his life was a punishment for his orientation. As an out-and-proud gay man, this saddens me. This sadness overwhelms me each time I read his work. To counter this sadness, to claim Hayden as one of my queer forefathers, I wrote a poem in which Hayden has an intimate encounter with another man. Not a stranger, but a man he already knows.[91]

As Corral writes, to read Hayden's work—in the hindsight of understanding the violence of his having to deny a major part of his identity for his entire life—is to read with an overwhelming grief. Hayden was the first Black poet to serve in the role that would later be known as US poet laureate (after he had been forced to decline the first offer of the position), and he was well-known for writing poems that centered on experiences of Blackness and reflections on Black history.[92] Yet Hayden was not afforded the right to live as an out Black bisexual man. Corral's forefather love for Hayden is one with the theorizations of foremother love practiced across this book. By writing a poem in which Hayden may live his sexuality, albeit still within a historical context of national institutionalized homophobia, Corral makes it possible to radically widen the possibilities of Hayden's extant work, such that poems that previously seemed innocuous retain a new sense of radical, albeit subtle, queer possibility. Thus, Corral's fictive queership with Hayden, his acknowledgment of and celebration of the sexuality that Hayden was never able to fully affirm, mirrors and makes it easier to discern the kinds of poetic possibility Hayden performed for others, including a broadened sense of possibilities for reading Phillis.

Perhaps due to Hayden's own experiences of close-minded critique mixed with tribute, he was careful to help Phillis avoid this same fate in his work as editor of the 1967 anthology *Kaleidoscope*. Hayden acknowledges Phillis's anachronistic reputation, writing, "The poetry of Phillis Wheatley and her fellow poet, Jupiter Hammon, has historical and not literary interest for us now." Yet only a few pages later, Hayden concedes that "recent scholarship reveals that she was not a mere imitator but an intellectual poet who consciously used the devices of neoclassicism because they suited her purpose."[93] Attention to Phillis's conscious decision-making seems to reach its limit when Hayden commits what he would probably consider a violation if enacted on his own poetry. Hayden anthologizes just three Phillis poems: a quite abridged version of "To the Right Honorable William, Earl of Dartmouth, His Majesty's Principal Secretary of State for North America, etc."; "His Excellency, General Washington (1775)"; and, of course, her infamous "On Being Brought."[94] The lines from "To the Right Honorable William" in which Phillis describes her abduction and her parents' grief are the only part of the poem readers receive:

> Should you, my lord, while you pursue my song,
> Wonder from whence my love of *Freedom* sprung,
> Whence flow these wishes for the common good,
> By feeling hearts alone best understood,
> I, young in life, by seeming cruel fate
> Was snatch'd from *Afric's* fancy'd happy seat:
> What pangs excruciating must molest,
> What sorrows labour in my parent's breast?
> Steel'd was the soul and by no misery mov'd
> That from a father seiz'd his babe belov'd:
> Such, such my case. And can I then but pray
> Others may never feel tyrannic sway?[95]

Abridgment is typically interpreted as a negative, but for all Black Arts Movement–era anthology editors, fitting Phillis neatly into the canon required making interpretive selections. While even the abridged version of this poem is not immune from Dartmouth's reference, as he still lords over its first line, the act of cutting most of the poem away to prioritize Phillis's sorrow is simultaneously an act of marking the parameters of what would enable Hayden to provide an alternative definition of Black poetry.

While Hayden commits an abridgment of Phillis's poetry, by contrast, he adds words to the extant biographical information on her life. In the four paragraphs of biography that preface the three Phillis poems featured in *Kaleidoscope*, Hayden gets several aspects of Phillis's known biography "correct" (as far as we know), but there are several details Hayden includes that I have not read anywhere else. For instance, Hayden writes with frankness that Phillis "was purchased by John Wheatley . . . as a gift for his wife," but he then contradicts himself in the span of a few sentences and writes that "Phillis had been a slave in name only."[96] Hayden is incorrect about one detail, though. Phillis visited London from June 17 to July 26, 1773, after what she described in a June 27, 1773, letter to the Countess of Huntingdon (to whom Phillis's *Poems* is dedicated) as "a fine passage of 5 weeks."[97] In contrast to what Hayden writes in his biographical sketch, Phillis was not quite "lionized by the Countess of Huntingdon and her circle,"[98] for she never had the chance to meet Huntingdon in person. As Vincent Carretta writes, Phillis "left England without ever having met her patron."[99] Apparently Phillis had to return to Boston because Susanna Wheatley had fallen ill.[100] That Phillis had to spend about two weeks on the water to and from America for every one week spent in England is a fair contradiction to the idea that she was a "slave in name only." Was Hayden, avid researcher that he was, and despite having read a recent collection of her poems and letters, so overwhelmed by the promise held in Phillis's five, almost six, fugitive weeks in London that he glossed over one of its most striking disappointments, one preserved in her two pleading letters to Huntingdon? Actually, in the edition of Phillis's letters that had been published at the time of Hayden's writing, none of her letters to Huntingdon were then extant in published form, so he would not have known they never met.[101]

It is in this (albeit unknown) lacuna that Hayden imbues Phillis's work with new possibility, becoming much like the way Corral recognized what Hayden could never openly do and therefore later transformed into a poem of fictive queership. Similarly, Hayden's poem "A Letter from Phillis Wheatley" stems from a desire to read a letter that, as far as we know, Phillis never wrote. To illustrate, on October 30, 1773, Phillis closed her real letter to fellow Black enslaved woman Obour Tanner by writing, "I have been very Busy ever since my arrival or should have, now wrote a more particular account of my voyage, But must submit that satisfaction to some other Opportunity."[102] Although Phillis and Obour's correspondence is discussed in more detail in chapter 1, such a letter detailing "a more particular account of my voyage" is not included among the collection of extant letters. However, Phillis did give "a more particular account" of what she saw during her time in London in her October 18, 1773, letter to David Worcester (Wooster):

> the Lions, Panthers, Tigers, &c. The Horse Armoury, Sma[ll] Armoury, the Crowns, Sceptres, Diadems, the Font for christineng the Royal Family. Saw Westminster Abbey, British Museum[,] Coxe's Museum, Saddler's wells, Greenwich Hospital, Park and Chapel, the royal Observatory at Greenwich, &c. &c. too many things and Places to trouble you with in a Letter.[103]

By contrast to this saturation of activity and display of Britain's wealth—of which, no doubt, Phillis was aware of its transatlantic sources—her silence on the subject in her October 30, 1773, letter to Obour is telling. Beyond this, we only know of two letters that Phillis sent during her June 17 to July 26, 1773, stay in London. Both the June 27, 1773, and July 17, 1773, letters were sent to the Countess of Huntingdon. In the first letter, Phillis announces her arrival and expresses her desire to meet Huntingdon, challenging her to live up to her role as patron;[104] we know that meeting never took place, as is evidenced by Phillis's early departure from London and in her July 17, 1773, letter announcing that news to Huntingdon.

In Hayden's "A Letter from Phillis Wheatley," he imagines what would have happened if Huntingdon had indeed acknowledged Phillis by hosting their meeting and becoming an active supporter of Phillis's future career. The version of the poem included in Hayden's 1985 *Collected Poems* is subtitled "London, 1773" and begins with an address to Obour.[105] It is important to note Hayden's decision to lineate this fictive letter for, as far as we know, Phillis never addressed a single poem to Obour—suggesting that her published elegies participated in an economy of performed mourning that she was perhaps happily exempt from in her relationship with Obour. By lineating this letter, Hayden enables readers to imagine what a poem for Obour might have looked like while respecting, within reason, the boundaries that must surround any imagination two hundred years later of what Phillis's epistolary voice sounded like in 1773. Tellingly, unlike with Phillis's poems, the heroic couplet does not dictate the arrangement of the content of Hayden's poem. Also, the poem's use of enjambment allows room to prompt readers to conjecture all that Phillis might have remembered in terms of how her voyage to London differed from her original Middle Passage. Like Phillis in her October 30, 1773, letter to Obour,[106] Hayden refrains from providing more details of Phillis's transatlantic traversal, perhaps because it could only be experienced in reference to her Middle Passage, which Hayden emphasizes that Phillis remembers at least in part.

By beginning his poem on Phillis with her remembrance of the horror of the Middle Passage—while her enjambed parenthetical confession of her remembrance conveys perhaps her hesitancy or inability to definitively write about it while she was enslaved—Hayden effectively quashes any contemporary readers' suspicions that Phillis's experience of slavery was any less violent due to her rare (at the time) entrée into the role of poet. While we know that Phillis chose her manumission over her continued enslavement long after she was brought to Boston, we also have evidence that the experience of the Middle Passage would have been horrific enough to make if difficult if not impossible to inure someone to the institution of slavery thereafter. Hayden had previously written of the Middle Passage in his 1962 eponymous poem on the subject, which was published first in 1945 (in the journal *Phylon*) and revised and published again in his 1962 volume of poems *A Ballad of Remembrance*. Hayden's long multipart poem "Middle Passage" prefigured a wave of Black creative writing and scholarship in Black studies on the Middle Passage and showed readers in graphic verisimilitude what really happened to the people who endured these voyages.[107] While Hayden's ends on the positive note of insurrection and healing after this trauma, others have questioned whether the voyage has had an end. As Toni Morrison depicts the thoughts of her character Beloved in her eponymous 1987 novel in a passage that is rendered with expanded spacing, "All of it is now it is always now there will never be a time when I am not crouching and watching others who are crouching too I am always crouching."[108]

Phillis sailed to London in 1773, but Britain's system of transatlantic slavery and trade would not begin to be abolished until 1807. This context makes the details of Phillis's truncated London visit especially heartbreaking. Importantly, Hayden's poetic imagination of the visit does not fill in a missing space in the manuscript evidence of documented correspondence. While past readers of the poem may have taken the historicity of Hayden's poem as fact, "A Letter from Phillis Wheatley" *alters* the history of what happened to Phillis in London. First, the poem disregards Phillis's July 17,

1773, letter to Huntingdon (due to its not being widely available to readers at that time), in which she writes, "[I am ex]tremely reluctant to go without having first Seen your Ladiship," demonstrating that they never met in person.[109] We may never know what such a meeting could have done for Phillis's poetic career or for the quality and longevity of her own life. As Carretta writes, "She very likely would have found a publisher for her second volume, financial success, and access to influential literary, political, and social circles."[110] However, Hayden's fictionalization instead suggests that Phillis's meeting with Huntingdon would have left something to be desired, as Huntingdon is figured in the poem as a melodramatic, ridiculous, and questionably well-meaning white woman who makes promises ensuring the publication of *Poems* but still is okay with Phillis sitting apart from the other guests at dinner. In other words, Hayden acknowledges the likelihood that such a meeting would only have left Phillis with more of the same. By both imagining and not imagining a different possible future for Phillis, Hayden presents her legacy as similarly legible across different potential permutations of her success. Hayden's method also encourages readers to work from the consensus that we have more than enough material at hand to become astute readers of Phillis's life and work.

This being the case, Hayden takes on Phillis's voice but refrains from giving readers any more information than she herself did. Indeed, there is no single plot that encompasses the entire poem, and her emotional expression runs in differing and unexpected directions. Much like Phillis's poems and real letters, Hayden's poem is marked by her inability to confess her own sorrows. The moment in which Phillis describes her performance of her elegies—the poems that overwhelmed her book volume, poems that mourned the deaths of prominent white Boston residents and their children—is quickly glossed over, relaying subtle information about the strict boundaries around Phillis's emotional life. The tears Phillis holds back after reading her elegies contrast with Huntingdon's outcry and Nathaniel Wheatley's tears as the poem becomes oversaturated with Phillis's unexpressed feelings.[111] The poem ends, however, neither with Huntingdon nor with Nathaniel. Hayden instead closes the poem with an anecdote about a child chimney sweep who wonders if Phillis's Blackness means they share a profession. Here, Hayden's subtlety is very easy to gloss over.[112] Nevertheless, the lines hark back to Phillis's infamous poem "On Being Brought" and acknowledge the absurdity of the skin-deep basis for Phillis's otherness. Hayden uses a white child's question to highlight both the absurdity of anti-Blackness and perhaps too the fact that Phillis's labor had its own occupational hazards. Overall, gone from the poem is any regret for not meeting Huntingdon.

Margaret Walker Remembers Herself

Again, two hundred years following the publication of her 1773 *Poems*, Hayden was not alone in reconceiving Phillis's legacy as having meaning beyond the lack of support she received from her white contemporaries. Between November 4–7, 1973, about 1,200 people gathered at Jackson State College (now University), a historically Black institution of higher learning in Mississippi, to celebrate Phillis's life and work and the bicentennial of her original publication date. Nearly two dozen Black woman poets and writers were invited to read original works, recontextualizing Phillis's value in ensuring cross-temporalities of Black women's writing. The event also showcased several other forms of Black expressive culture, from drama to music to sculpture, resulting in what I have previously argued was not just a poetry festival but a "praisesong" for Phillis,[113] a ritual that Barbara Christian describes as "recounting the essence of a life so that future generations may flourish."[114] Much scholarship on Phillis has relied on her tidy placement at the beginning of a literary tradition on which she has a direct influence, but for Black women at the festival Phillis functioned more as an agent of time travel. Rather than perform the flights of return needed to understand Phillis in her eighteenth-century context, they recuperated her as a living example of Black feminisms' abilities to subvert history and change the meaning of their fate. Phillis was not merely an influence; rather, her legacy was understood as somewhat malleable, open to a reshaping that would help future writers reimagine their own lives. Thus, it is no surprise that when the festival was brought to life largely through the efforts of writer Margaret Alexander Walker (1915–98), she made organizing the event look all too easy.

The festival was Walker's idea. She was now a beloved professor at Jackson State and a renowned novelist and poet. While en route to the Paul Laurence Dunbar Centennial Celebration at the University of Dayton in 1972, she realized that in just one year there would be another opportune moment for celebration. She recalls, "In October of 1972, I was on my way by train to Dayton, Ohio, for the centennial celebration of Paul Laurence Dunbar. I rode the train from Jackson to Effingham, Illinois, and would have to spend a day's layover before taking the 'Spur' to Dayton. There in the Holiday Inn, I conceived the idea of a Phillis Wheatley Poetry Festival."[115] I include these details to emphasize the importance of time away and travel to enable Walker to generate the idea for the festival. Walker's role at Jackson State was a strenuous one, and her journals detail countless ways she navigated building the college's research name while also serving as a caregiver for various family members. Nevertheless, Walker continued to devote time to her writing as well. A year after the festival's inception, Walker published her third volume of poems, *October Journey* (1973), and was at work on a sequel to her 1966 novel, *Jubilee*. Walker also knew the significance of holding the festival at Jackson State, especially, perhaps, for those who "had never been that far south before." She said in her remarks at the festival, "The horror is here [in Mississippi], the corruption is here . . . but also the love is here."[116] It is love that shines through the most in the overarching narrative of the festival, but Walker's own challenges in organizing the event should not be understated.

In writing about the festival not only as a beautiful and transcendent event but also as one that required Walker's time and sacrifice, I hope to counter any lingering misconceptions that Black feminist literary organizing results in seamlessly positive events in and of their own accord qua Black feminist. One need only look to Walker's labor in writing her novel *Jubilee* to understand the difficulties she faced in finding enough time for her literary pursuits. Walker grew up listening to her grandmother Elvira ("Minna") Ware Dozier pass down the stories of her own mother's life—while Walker's parents, a minister, and a musician, were both often ministering or teaching—which would become the groundwork of *Jubilee*. This oral history would prompt Walker to later write that "before *Jubilee* had a name, I was living with it."[117] After beginning to put the story to paper in 1934, Walker would work on her novel for over thirty years, a testament to how deeply she acknowledged the importance of its historical roots. What she was not told, Walker drew from archival sources. Her fealty to the story's ever-present life supplants erasure with re-embodiment, for *Jubilee* purports itself to be a story without gaps, one made whole. At a mighty five hundred pages long and divided almost equally into three parts ("The Ante-Bellum Years," "The Civil War Years," and "Reconstruction and Reaction"), the novel's impossible bid for verisimilitude mirrors Walker's characterization of her great-grandmother, Margaret ("Vyry") Duggans Ware Brown, who practices persistence with such ritual faith that she is poised as the catalyst that drives the novel's plot forward. A century later, Walker, Vyry's great-grandchild, would persist in writing her novel with similar fortitude, but it would take her many years to gain enough free time to complete it.

To help ensure that a new generation of Black women writers would not face the same barriers that she did, nor the barriers that her great-grandmother and Phillis did, Walker transformed Phillis into the rebirth of Black women's poetry, an extension of the concept of jubilee she had been refining since the 1930s. Phillis's spirit was ushered into this world again with the ascension of seventeen Black women poets who by the early 1970s were known as Marion Alexander, Linda Bragg, Margaret G. Bur-roughs, Carole Gregory Clemmons, Lucille Clifton, Margaret Danner, Mari Evans, Sarah Webster Fabio, Nikki Giovanni, June Jordan, Audre Lorde, Naomi Madgett, Gloria Oden, Carolyn Rodgers, Sonia Sanchez, Alice Walker, and Malaika Wangara.[118] Each answered a call and traveled to Jackson, Mississippi, to celebrate the Phillis Wheatley Poetry Festival on the bicentennial of the publication of Phillis's 1773 *Poems*. With their coming together, the festival became a reinterpretation of the "angelic train" envisioned at the end of Phillis's infamous poem "On Being Brought." But it was not "mercy" that "brought" them. It was fellow poet Margaret Walker. Walker retained Phillis's significance as event, but re-membered her significance within the craft of poetry in a way that would herald a contemporary Black feminist poetic tradition. Nevertheless, one must be careful of painting an overly rosy picture and risk a flattened account of the unevenly distributed labor and support that made such a tradition possible.

In my 2020 essay on the festival, I wrote that Walker's novel *Jubilee* and her organization of the festival in honor of Phillis (in conjunction with the history of Phillis's authorship) should be understood as having come to fruition despite a mainstream literary context in which Walker and Phillis were often othered and set apart from their wider contexts and deemed largely important only due to their status as originary "first" figures. By contrast, I argued, Walker's work understood the importance of the per-sistence of a fictitious imagining of "an eternal present of Black women's expression . . . that expects nothing less for its subjects than everlasting lit-erary life." Nevertheless, in doing so, I wanted to emphasize the mortal labor that has had made such extended literary life possible, drawing attention to "a concert of Black women's literary practices, including poems, novels, and sermons" as "they inform the lifelong investments at the core of *Jubilee* and the Phillis Wheatley Poetry Festival."[119] While my essay centered on Walker's work, my research also studied the extant literary archive of the festival more broadly, especially within the papers of Lucille Clifton and

Alice Walker at the Stuart A. Rose Library at Emory University, the papers of Audre Lorde at Spelman College, and more. As Kirsten Lee writes, to counter the fact that many instances of "Black women's writing and cultural productions are often unpreserved and eventually undervalued because unpreserved,"[120] the festival relied on and cultivated ephemeral practices and works wherein in-person Black feminist collaboration and sociality was valued alongside other forms of (more mainstream) memorialization. This is an archive that has been well preserved (paradoxically) in the (ephemeral) papers of several of the festival's attendees, including Margaret Walker herself.

Walker's extant journals record the months in which she planned the festival, beginning with her generating the idea for the festival in October 1972 during a trip she enjoyed while participating in a centennial celebration for Paul Laurence Dunbar ("The trip has been fabulous"),[121] and proceeding in spurts of activity recorded in her journals into the summer of 1973. In a journal entry on August 5, 1973, Walker wrote, "I am now hard at work planning a Phillis Wheatley Festival of Poetry to be held here November 4–7, 1973."[122] Walker's journal entries from September 1973 to March 1974 evidence that she herself thought out the festival's participants, the program, publicity, exhibits, music, hospitality, and more—before later assigning each element of the festival to a respective committee. Walker planned the festival across over fifty pages of this journal alone. In addition to organizing the names of the poets and when and with whom they would perform, Walker's journal entries demonstrate that she was also gathering each poet's biographical information and travel itineraries, and jotting down ideas for meals, including "pressed chicken," "pink candy-cake confection," and "Swedish meatballs in wine sauce."[123] Further, the journals evidence that Walker was brainstorming how to track down photographs of Phillis's manuscripts to present at the festival. Perhaps most importantly, her journal entries bear her repetition of her wish to host a book fair and autograph party for the invited writers. One journal entry even notes a possible anthology to be generated based on the poetry. While no such thing surfaced, Walker expressed an active investment in the success of contemporary Black women poets that was subjunctive and thus open to possibility.

Yet I would be remiss not to note the stressors that Walker encountered in 1973. In the months leading up to the festival, Walker continued to struggle with her family's caregiving demands, writing in her journal on March 8, 1973, "I once thought the problems I encountered with my children from Spring of 1969 one right after the other would kill me and although my problems have lessened and with them some of the tensions, I still feel washed out, drained, and all in a stupor. Everything under the sun has come against me except death itself and only God has seen me through."[124] By September 1973, an older family member was staying with Walker to recover from a recent stroke. Wondering how she was going to navigate the next few weeks with the term soon starting, Walker wrote on September 1, 1973, "I pray to God not to get evil and let the whole thing floor me."[125] The family member ended up passing away on the last day of the festival. It is clear that Walker used journaling to cope with the challenges she experienced. At least 133 journals are extant, spanning 1930–98, ages fourteen to her passing. In addition to diary entries (Walker did not write every day but often wrote multipage accounts of significant days), her journals also record her astrological readings, budgeting, doodles, letter drafts, prayers, recipes, speeches, teaching assignments, travel plans, and plans for future writing. In all, they record an alternative map of the life of Walker's dreams and all that could have been.

On November 11, 1973, Walker wrote in her journal, "The Festival is over. It was a tremendous success."[126] Over the next few pages, Walker gave a personal, firsthand account of what the festival was like through her own eyes. Immediately, she emphasized that Nikki Giovanni and a few other women came to stay a couple days before the festival at Walker's house, providing insight into the intimate experiences that exceeded the festival's formal bounds. As Walker goes on to reflect on each performance of the festival, she emphasizes all that went well and, crucially, elements that did not meet her expectations. For example, while I have previously noted that "Sarah Webster Fabio's essay 'The Poetic Craft and Art of Phillis Wheatley' was proposed in the festival's program but never actually read," Walker provides more insight in her journal into what possibly happened by writing a biting critique of Fabio, culminating in her disclosure that Fabio "failed to disrupt and sabotage the festival but she tried."[127] Walker does not go into great detail into what exactly Fabio did except to say that Fabio's poetry performance (accompanied by an otherwise great jazz band) was "lewd, coarse, vulgar" and that Fabio was "bad news!" By recording her immediate postfestival impressions, Walker disrupts a tidy narrative of the festival's Black feminist camaraderie. Based on Walker's journal entries alone, it sounds as though Fabio had recently been in a car accident and was likely still recovering. Walker writes that the accident had not "dampened [Fabio's] exhibitionism and inordinate ambition. She wants to be seen." The entries gesture toward the particulars the official narrative of the festival cannot hope to document: Black women writers' moments of disaccord, injury, and the ever-present specter of respectability politics.

Given Walker's months of labor in organizing the festival, it is understandable that she had little patience for another attendee's ostensibly disruptive presence at what was supposed to be a primarily honorific event. Although it is disappointing to hear that the conflict between her and Fabio could not be addressed while they were both in Jackson, it is exciting to learn that the festival, however unwittingly, bore witness to something that could not be encompassed by a tidy conception of the tradition of Black women's writing after Phillis. Fabio, who is fondly remembered as one of the early organizers for Black studies academic departments in the Bay Area, was a little over a decade younger than Walker, but she passed away exactly six years following the festival, at the age of fifty-one, following a diagnosis of colon cancer. Thus, Fabio, who was never appointed as a professor with tenure despite her organizing on behalf of Black studies, embodied what Stefano Harney and Fred Moten write of "the subversive intellectual": "Her labor is as necessary as it is unwelcome. The university needs what she bears but cannot bear what she brings."[128] Although Walker likely did not anticipate doing so, her journals memorialize Fabio's wish "to be seen" and provide a glimpse into an alternative reading of her poetry performance that was not captured in others' rhapsodic reporting on Fabio.[129] Walker could have neglected to write about Fabio at all, but Fabio's performance clearly communicated something to Walker that could have disturbed the festival, something potentially outside the bounds of Walker's version of Black feminism, something potentially so erotic or queer that it shattered the conception of Phillis that Walker's festival tried so hard to achieve.

In Maryemma Graham's 2022 biography of Walker, *The House Where My Soul Lives*, Graham notes that Walker was beholden to variously freeing and limiting "Victorian" values of womanhood while she navigated cultures of sexism across the institutions of academia and publishing, cultures that often delimited her own ability to pursue a career solely as a writer.[130] Walker did not often publicly disclose the professional conflicts she experienced (except when others infringed on the copyright of her novels), but they are manifest in her journals. In the case of published documents on the festival, an overarching narrative of Black feminist camaraderie often persists, but in Walker's journals, more complex dynamics are shown to have characterized the festival. Graham writes that after the festival Walker did not stay in touch with the other writers of the younger Black feminist poet generation.[131] Similarly, in Lucille Clifton's draft of a poem she wrote during the festival, another one of the extant ephemeral traces of the event, Clifton named several though not all of the other Black women poets who were present. Even more, Clifton's published version of the poem addresses Gwendolyn Brooks along with Margaret Walker as maternal poetic figures—even though Brooks did not in fact attend the festival.[132] This is a revision of the festival's true details, as well as the manuscript version of the poem extant in Clifton's papers, and demonstrates how deeply she felt that Brooks should be part of the festival's legacy despite her physical absence. Lucille was not so much witnessing Brooks's attendance, and she was certainly misremembering it. The moments where Black women do not adequately acknowledge each other (or overly acknowledge each other) tell us more perhaps about the critic or the writer herself than the festival itself.

To conclude, in the collection of interviews conducted by Claudia Tate and published in 1985 as *Black Women Writers at Work*, Margaret Walker, now retired from teaching at Jackson State, spoke candidly about her work on the festival: "The Phillis Wheatley Symposium. I'm not going to do any of that again. That phase of my life is over. I don't have energy for it anymore. I've got to write for the rest of my life, no matter how short or long it is. I've got to write."[133] It is tempting, perhaps, to feel disappointment at these words, but I read them as a quiet kind of triumph. In her late sixties, with her professorship completed and her children grown, Walker finally had time to write. With the stage of her life that the festival represented over, I wonder if Walker ever came to change her mind about what constituted a respectable form of praise. Based on her journals, Walker was someone who took the shape of her life quite seriously. Across countless entries, she recited key dates in her life, listed her publications over and again, and made plans to finish her autobiography. The last page of her extant journals depicts her writing out her plans to bequeath her papers to Jackson State, and her hope that her descendants understand the papers as "their real inheritance."[134] Like the many critics who have preceded her, and the many who would follow, Walker's conception of Phillis said more about her than it said about Phillis. Her journals indexed her desire for a respectable writer's life and all the accolades that came with it until she realized that her project all along may have been, not some other project, but the journals themselves. Herself.

in search of our foremothers' gardens

While writing this chapter in the spring of 2022, the ground-floor apartment I was renting had two exposed dirt plots on its western patio, one very small with a spigot and a hose and a larger L-shaped one that housed a large lemon tree and partly wrapped around the side of the building. As spring turned into summer, I planted several native pollinator bushes and started a small container garden. However, by summer's end, after increased water restrictions and a heat wave so intense we received emergency notifications on our cell phones to conserve power, it seemed my efforts to garden had all dried up. I took it as a sign to stay inside more and focus on the remaining chapters of my book. Unbeknownst to me, my plants had already extended their deep taproots, just like I had with my book. As Carole Boyce Davies cites Sylvia Wynter in 2013, doing scholarly work is connected to all the other things that sustain your being: "Caribbean people embrace and indigenize their landscapes, as Sylvia Wynter describes it: growing their 'ground provisions,' herbs, vegetables, and plants." Caribbean people are also, Davies continues, "populating the landscape also with their duppies, jumbies, and other spirits; carnivalizing all locations consistently, creating housing sometimes precariously on hilly terrain or in densely populated urban environments that later become desired locations overlooking seascapes; living on fault lines sometimes."[1] That summer and autumn, I read a variety of nature poems—including Phillis's "On Imagination," which is a nature poem, according to Camille T. Dungy—as well as other poems that inspired me to write as though I were gardening.[2] I was also, in other words, searching for poems that spoke to my unique predicament: poems about all the reasons I was indoors searching for poems that sounded like they were about home gardens, and yet weren't.

As I continued writing into the winter of 2023, California experienced thirty-one atmospheric river storms. Needless to say, most of the in-ground plants on my patio soon bloomed far beyond my expectations, even as I mourned this new aspect of climate change. The garden, drought-tolerant by now, took care of itself that spring into summer; I hardly needed to water at all. I marveled at a pink caterpillar eating the De La Mina verbena flowers, and again when I saw the blue elderberry tree begin to bloom. As Dungy writes, "Every person who finds herself constantly navigating political spaces—by which I mean every person who regularly finds herself demoralized and exhausted by the everyday patterns of life in America—should have access to a garden."[3] Moreover, looking for Phillis and other Black feminist critics' gardens has also meant looking for the ways they navigated a society in which they could have the resources to garden. Since this has involved a great deal of failure on the part of our society to provide such, I read in the ensuing pages a variety of transhistorical practices that run adjacent to gardening as a form of criticism. To illustrate, as I was completing my book in the following winter (2024), I hardly spent any time in my garden. I didn't even notice until my parents came by one day that a squirrel had built a giant nest in the lemon tree. It made me feel more at home. Another day, my partner pointed out to me an Anacapa Pink morning glory vine that had appeared on a construction fence on campus, just down the street from our apartment. It already had several flowers that looked just like the one on our patio. Here it was, I thought: proof that my work was materializing in academia, physically changing it, making it, perhaps, more beautiful and humane. I couldn't help but smile.

Flower Pit Feminism

Across Alice Walker's 1983 essay collection, *In Search of Our Mothers' Gardens*, its elegant titular theme emphasizes Black feminist critical inquiry as the search for our (fore)mothers' ever-living artistry. Underpinning this theme's beauty is Walker's awareness of the struggles, hardships, and poor treatment Black people have long endured, such that their artistry deserves to be carefully described. Walker's collection validates the importance of a personal connection and relationship to such research. Born in rural Eatonton, Georgia, Walker is able to theorize "our mothers' gardens" because of the gardening practice of her mother, Minnie Tallulah Grant: "She planted ambitious gardens—and still does—with over fifty different varieties of plants that bloom profusely from early March until late November."[4] Gardening was an art that Walker's mother could cultivate frugally, despite their family's disadvantaged status as sharecroppers, and while Walker remembers challenging moments during her childhood, she recalls how "even my memories of poverty are seen through a screen of blooms."[5] While "working in her flowers," her mother was "involved in work her soul must have."[6] However, even as Walker honors her mother's ingenuity, she wonders what she and other Black women could have created if they had greater respite from domestic, enslaved, and sharecropping labor.[7] Reading Walker's *Our Mothers' Gardens* as a window onto "the lives of women who might have been Poets, Novelists, Essayists, and Short-Story Writers" encourages continued scholarship on the other kinds of "gardens" these women created, once we are able to recognize them as such, as well as the gardens they might have created given the resources.[8]

A recent 2022 collection of Walker's selected journals, *Gathering Blossoms Under Fire*, sheds more light on why Walker chose gardening as an apt metaphor for Black women's artistry.[9] For example, the journal entries detail how Walker's mother's gardening involved a set of hyperspecific practices she invested with very intense personal meaning, practices that go far beyond the purview of basic gardening. Walker recalls in her journal entry dated August 1966,

> A remarkable memory: Today, walking with Eric, we saw a flower pit full of summer flowers all in bloom. I called it "a flower pit" and a memory, long buried, of where I got the expression, came alive. When I was a child at home—when we lived in the country—my mother kept her flowers in a flower pit during the winter. This pit was like an outdoor cellar, rather shallow—I imagine four to six feet deep, and built close against the house for added protection from the wind. Sometimes the pit would get a lot of water in it and for fear of freezing or rotting the flower roots my mother would throw open the doors, or take away the tin or whatever and let the sun in. . . . I remember her so well, bending over the pit on cold January mornings after a hard freeze. "I just want to see how my flowers is doing," she'd say.[10]

Not only was the ritual of tending to the flower pit meaningful to Walker's mother in and of itself, but it also continues to have meant much even years later for her daughter. The idea of a flower pit, of Walker's mother continuing to garden even in winter, speaks to a theory of Black feminisms that persists in subterraneous form when the conditions are harsh, staying alive until spring. This flower pit feminism subverts expectations of what cannot be kept alive. Despite the bitter conditions, Walker's mother kept not only her flowers but also herself and her family alive throughout the Georgia winter. While Walker's later essay collection title *In Search of Our Mothers' Gardens* speaks to an elegant practice, *In Search of Our Mothers' Flower Pits* would tell a different story. Walker describes the practice as not only subversive but also an important precursor to her mother's spring garden. The cycle of the flower pit abutting the house and the garden to come altogether sustain Walker's mother and their family's lives. As the flower pit requires constant tending in a season of heightened precarity, her mother's desire "to see how my flowers is doing" is a form of Black feminist care that her daughter later transcribes as a methodology of Black feminist criticism, beginning with its rearticulation in this journal entry.[11]

While Walker memorializes the many flowers her mother grew, she also notes the "countless jars of peaches, blackberries, peas, corn, and beans" her mother canned, such that "edible jewels surrounded us."[12] In Evelyn C. White's biography of Walker, White also notes that due to Walker's mother's home gardening, her family "was able to keep hunger at bay owing to the bounty of fruits and vegetables," which Walker's mother also canned herself to stretch their food stores amid the lack of equal access to fresh food.[13] As White further notes, one of Walker's mother's anecdotes on this subject would become the basis of Walker's 1973 short story "The Revenge of Hannah Kemhuff," which narrates protagonist Hannah's struggles to keep her family afloat during the Great Depression amid a complete lack of external support. It is significant that Walker clarifies in her story that for Hannah, a home garden was not enough to mitigate a complete lack of a social safety net: "We was so hungry, and the children were getting so weak, that after I had crapped off the last leaves from the collard stalks I couldn't wait for new leaves to grow back. I dug up the collards, roots and all. After we ate that there was nothing else."[14] Subsequently, Hannah soon experiences serious hardships directly stemming from a white woman aid worker's discriminatory treatment toward her. Walker writes that later in Hannah's life, a self-sustaining space of freedom and artistry comes in the form of Hannah's telling her story to a local healer woman and her apprentice and participating in their revenge (read: healing) rituals, which eventually bloom into poetic justice—not only for Hannah but retroactively and fictively enacted for her Walker's mother, too, in writing this story. This becomes the "garden" that Hannah could not sustain on her own. Indeed, this speaks to how we as critics recognize a possible garden in our own lives or in the lives of others whom we research, especially where we have failed to find one. In the case of someone like Hannah or Phillis, there is often no trace of a garden, only fragments of a story passed down by memory—a mere outline for a garden in the making.

Such garden outlines come in many shapes and sizes, and for Black feminist critics, our own might take the shape of a classroom, a library, a collection of papers, or even something as seemingly inanimate as a single book. For example, Barbara Christian described, at the beginning of her 1985 collection, *Black Feminist Criticism*, how she had tended to the literary works of those like Alice Walker even while she was at home, "sprawling at the low table [she worked] at, surrounded by books and plants."[15] Indeed, Walker's literary critical output would rival that of Christian's, who also was a key advocate for the reading, writing, and teaching of Black women's literature from the 1960s to the 1990s, before her untimely passing due to lung cancer at the age of fifty-six in 2000. When asked by her daughter why she was working so intently one afternoon at home, Christian recounted, "I know the words that come to my mind—'If I don't save my own life, who will?'—are triggered by the Walker essay I'd been reading." For Christian, what she called "Black feminist process" was not just lifesaving, it was "fun."[16] Indeed, reading and writing about Walker and others was to be "involved in work her soul must have."[17] By the time of her passing in 2000, Christian had published several essays on Walker, along with a guide to Walker's novel *The Color Purple*, and had edited a case-book on Walker's 1973 short story "Everyday Use," in addition to her critical output on other Black women writers.[18] Christian's career-spanning work demonstrates that she and Walker were engaged in a similar critical project of searching for their (fore)mothers' gardens.

Not only an exchange of labor for material goods, an "everyday use" Black feminist critical methodology implores one to think carefully about the affective, intimate, and personal implications of one's criticism, as well as the lives of critics, in the world. I am thinking especially of Christian's argument that her criticism was an extension of "the women [she] grew up around."[19] "Everyday Use" was first published in 1973 within Walker's short story collection *In Love and Trouble: Stories of Black Women*, and one of its early critical readers was Barbara Smith.[20] In her review of the collection, Smith emphasizes Walker's short fiction as valuable if only because published stories rooted in Black women's lives were then so few and far between. Smith also admires the stories' "truthfulness. For every one of Walker's fictional women I knew or had heard of a real woman whose fate was all too similar" and knew "the cruel toll that racial hostility exerts upon black women particularly and upon black people generally."[21] A short few years later, Smith's groundbreaking 1977 essay "Toward a Black Feminist Criticism" defended Walker's *In Love and Trouble* against a white male reviewer's misreading that "there is nothing feminist about these stories." Instead, Smith proclaims that Walker's writing is part of a larger tradition that demands a particular kind of critic, a Black feminist who could "think and write out of her own identity."[22] Indeed, Christian (and several other Black feminist critics) went above and beyond to meet the teaching and service needs of their students in the absence of a greater institutional support network. Similarly, in *Community as Rebellion* (2022), Lorgia García Peña calls for a collective

> recognition for the totality of our labor: the hours spent supporting the students of color the university ignores; the months of service on committees; the emotional and mental labor required of us to exist as The One; the love and care that we put into our teaching, advising, and mentoring; and the significance of our public-facing work. That "invisible" labor needs to become visible, evaluated, rewarded, valued, and compensated as much as our research. It needs to count toward tenure and promotion.[23]

García Peña goes on to emphasize the importance of other faculty taking on this needed labor, too. Given that we know that Christian (and several other Black feminist critics) went above and beyond to meet the teaching and service needs of their students, we are faced with the difficulty of reconciling this, again, with her premature death of cancer at the age of fifty-six.

As Arlene R. Keizer, one of Christian's former doctoral advisees at UC Berkeley and now a professor at Pratt Institute, writes, "One of the most important principles that Barbara Christian imparted through her writing and her pedagogy was the significance of naming one's personal relationship to the literature about which one writes, even if one does not explicitly discuss that relationship in one's scholarly essays."[24] What could have been the outcome if many other faculty had shared Christian's burden? Would she have lived longer? Disconsolate in the wake of history, I still mourn the fact that by the time I became an undergraduate student at UC Berkeley in the late 2000s, Christian had already passed away.[25] Again, before the publication of her book on Walker's "Everyday Use" in 1994, Christian had already published several essays on Walker.[26] In one such essay first published in 1980, Christian describes supporting her UC Berkeley students who were having complex responses to Walker's work:

> I am coordinating a seminar on the works of Alice Walker. We have read and discussed *Once*, Walker's first volume of poetry, *The Third Life of Grange Copeland*, her powerful first novel. The tension in the class has steadily risen. Now we are approaching *In Love and Trouble*. There is a moment of silence as class starts. Then one of the black women, as if bursting from an inexplicable anger says: "Why is there so much pain in these books, especially in this book?" I know this student; her life has much pain in it. She is going to school against all odds, in opposition to everything and everyone, it would seem. She is conscious of being black; she is struggling, trying to figure out why her relationships as a woman are so confused, often painful. . . . "I don't want to see this, know this." There is more anger, then silence. But she is riveted by the stories in this and other class sessions and insists on staying in this class. She seems, by all appearances, to be together, well-dressed, even stylish, a strong voice and body, an almost arrogant, usually composed face. But now she is angry, resistant, yet obsessed by these stories.[27]

Christian validates her student's response to Walker (however complex) by including it in such detail in her essay, demonstrating it as a fair response to recognizing one's own pain reflected in literature while having to both discuss such literature in a predominantly white university setting and being forced to process one's relationship to respectability politics in such a setting.[28] Importantly, Christian interarticulates her students' emotional response with the text of Walker's stories: "Who are the characters in these stories? What happens to them? More to the point, what do they do that should cause this young black woman, and many others like her, to be so affected?"[29] In fact, Christian's act of publishing several works on Walker over the years suggests that she is as affected by the stories as her student is, perfecting a Black feminist criticism that encompassed Walker, the characters in her writing, her students, and even members of her family: foremother love.[30]

Thus, even when critiques of Phillis's poetry come up in the early work of Christian, Walker, or others, I may retroactively apply the critical context that Christian, Walker, and others spent their whole careers amassing and attracting. Often, Black feminist critics' responses to Phillis's work sound just like that of Christian's student: "I don't want to see this, know this." Thus, my methodology requires reading Phillis not only via her poems, or her unique context, but in and through the entire context of Black feminist criticism—a methodology that requires that one have an interdisciplinary background in Black feminisms as well as in literary studies. One who reads in this way may observe Phillis's "garden" even within the harsh criticism that earlier Black feminist critics bestowed on her. Like the flower pit in which Walker's mother kept her flowers alive, overwintering under her careful watch, I too have gathered significant cuttings from Black feminist critical works, some of which deliver harsh criticism of Phillis amid their energizing arguments, in order to plant them together in a later spring and witness their growth. One way to plant the study of Phillis back into this Black feminist context is to search for her "garden," for all that she sheltered and that which shelters our (complex) love for her. Indeed, perhaps it is something that Phillis left legible for us all along. Phillis remains well known as a poet—especially as a writer of elegies. It makes sense that this is the first place that scholars often look for greater insight into her project. Yet just as Walker's mother's flower pit was an integral part of her gardening, it is important to view Phillis's elegies, too, as an integral part of a larger project. In fact, if one is lucky as a scholar, one may come to find that their beloved writer has—and not just in more iterations of what she was able to publish in her lifetime— elegized herself. Perhaps unknowingly, within her own published or, even more extraordinarily, unpublished writing, she mourned herself and, sometime before she passed away, penned the very words that would sing the song of her own mourning long after her death.

This chapter goes on to ask what it means for Walker, author of the otherwise beautiful 1974 essay on Black feminist everyday expressive labor "In Search of Our Mothers' Gardens," to disavow Phillis and her poetry in her pursuit of late twentieth-century Black feminist critical acclaim. Both Sherley Anne Williams and Wanda Coleman also join the ranks of critics who went so far as to publish (or publicly say) disparaging remarks about Phillis despite their knowledge of her foremother status. Williams briefly mentions Phillis in her 1972 scholarly monograph, writing that Phillis's "concern as a poet was not to present the uniqueness of slave experiences in colonial New England, but to reflect the orthodox European views of Christianity and, when she touched upon it at all, African savagery."[31] Walker and Coleman's similar negative remarks about Phillis will be discussed in more detail across in this chapter, but it is key that they also come to the fore when each is asked to take on the role of the literary critic. Therefore, this chapter asks why literary criticism is the mode by which Phillis faces the most ire from her future colleagues, and what it would mean to apply the methods of Black feminist criticism as they have been previously conceived toward a generous and generative reading of Phillis rather than one that mires in critical dead ends and missed opportunities for connection. Overall, this chapter understands that a full consideration of Phillis's context enacts foremother love, a relation that does not just extend itself to Phillis but draws care around the contemporary Black feminist critics who are enacting versions of her project later, even those who may not have understood Phillis's "garden" as their own.

Alice Walker's Mother Love

In her essay "In Search of Our Mothers' Gardens," Alice Walker declared, quoting Virginia Woolf: "The key words, as they relate to Phillis, are 'contrary instincts.' For when we read the poetry of Phillis Wheatley . . . evidence of 'contrary instincts' is everywhere. Her loyalties were completely divided, as was, without question, her mind." Across her essay, Walker heartbreakingly calls Phillis out of her role as a poet, critiquing her poems as the staid productions of a young, enslaved girl loyal to her enslavers and plagued with ill health, only to go on to lament the stereotypical ways Black women have been mischaracterized across history. It is a strikingly harsh treatment in contrast to Walker's careful and loving analysis of everyday, unknown Black women in the same essay. Contrary to the set of assumptions that Walker disjointedly applies to Phillis, Walker pleads for increased understanding, care, and love of Black women thus:

> Black women are called, in the folklore that so aptly identifies one's status in society, "the *mule* of the world," because we have been handed the burdens that everyone else—*everyone* else—refused to carry. We have also been called "Matriarchs," "Superwomen," and "Mean and Evil Bitches." Not to mention "Castraters" and "Sapphire's Mama." When we have pleaded for understanding, our character has been distorted; when we have asked for simple caring, we have been handed empty inspirational appellations, then stuck in the farthest corner. When we have asked for love, we have been given children. In short, even our plainer gifts, our labors of fidelity and love, have been knocked down our throats. To be an artist and a black woman, even today, lowers our status in many respects, rather than raises it: and yet, artists we will be.[32]

Walker's attentiveness to the ongoing harm that stereotypes inflict—not only systemically in terms of delimiting Black women's access to institutional resources across society, but also personally, in terms of Black women's access to "simple caring" or "love"—helps us understand her divestiture of Phillis as akin to the dismantling of a stereotype. It is clear that in disidentifying with the (mis)characterization of Phillis that has been handed down by history, Walker is projecting her own insecurities about her prospects as a Black woman poet within a racist and sexist society and mourning the fact that, as quoted above, "to be an artist and a black woman, even today, lowers our status in many respects, rather than raises it." However, Walker's assertation "and yet, artists we will be" also provides a glimmer of hope that her reading of Phillis is not without possible reexamination.

While Walker uses her own words to explain the persistent stereotyping of Black women, it is notable that she alternatively employs the citation and paraphrase of Virginia Woolf's 1929 essay "A Room of One's Own" to effectively distance Phillis from Walker's account of the everyday Black feminist tradition. As Walker writes shortly before the passage quoted above, Woolf "wrote that in order for a woman to write fiction she must have two things, certainly: a room of her own (with key and lock) and enough money to support herself. What then are we to make of Phillis . . . who owned not even herself?"[33] What if, instead of Woolf's, we used Walker's own methodology to understand Phillis as a Black woman? What would it look like if we treated Phillis with "simple caring," "fidelity," and "love"? This might lead one to ask a very different set of questions, including these: What happens when we critique, not Phillis, but Phillis's involuntary enslavement and her care for her enslavers, using the words of Virginia Woolf, who we know occupied white English womanhood differently as queer and as someone with mental illness? And what would it mean to assert instead that Phillis, like Woolf, most likely did not want merely a room of her own but wanted "to be in the world"?[34] In large part due to the vexed position of Phillis within her essay, Walker's essay suffers its own set of contrary instincts, as her treatment of Phillis runs counter to her treatment of Black women and women writers generally. Indeed, this is precisely what highlights these moments of critique as places that call out for increased critical understanding and love. Rather than disavow Walker as she disavowed Phillis, I understand Walker's published essay as an incomplete picture of her own Black feminist critical project and as an invitation to continue to flesh out what it means to read Phillis with foremother love.

Today we might easily understand attempts, however impossible, to distance oneself from histories of slavery like those in which Phillis was embedded given how often the world reminds us how vulnerable contemporary Black women remain to harm on account of ongoing lived experiences of discrimination and mischaracterization. Projecting images of respectability is one way that Black women try to mitigate this harm. When Walker's essay collection *Our Mothers' Gardens* was first published in 1983, Walker appeared on the volume's cover in a writerly pose that rivaled Phillis's own frontispiece portrait.[35] Walker's pose signified her arrival to the role as foremother in her own right. Taking her lead, one reviewer of *Our Mothers' Gardens* emphasized Walker's status as a southern woman writer picking up the mantles not only of Zora Neale Hurston but also Carson McCullers, Flannery O'Connor, and Eudora Welty.[36] A review by Octavia E. Butler noted Walker's role as a Black woman writer in the tradition of Rebecca Cox Jackson, Hurston, Coretta Scott King, and Buchi Emecheta, each of whom Walker carefully studies in *Our Mothers' Gardens*.[37] Walker's alignment with these figures is part of a complex effort on her behalf to identify as a writer uniquely informed, rather than undercut, by her identity as a mother, as is evidenced in the poem that concludes the essay collection.[38] Emphasizing her own personal experience as a writer throughout the book perhaps gave Walker a respite from having to face the poor outcomes experienced by several generations of famous women writers, an unfortunate legacy to which even Walker has not ultimately been immune.[39] Without idealizing Walker or any other Black feminist critic, this chapter looks instead to reclaim her and others' agency and feminist practices. In the face of historical hardships or even moments in which their practices have gone on to deviate from our closest Black feminist critical values, I seek to forge a Black feminist criticism unique to our own purposes as they move beyond respectability today.

Walker's published works convey her desire to project a writerly identity in a context where she herself was subject to the kinds of critique, albeit on different grounds, that Phillis herself would receive from readers ill-equipped to understand her work. At least one reviewer of Walker's *Our Mothers' Gardens* found it to be a "piecemeal construction" and "not intended as a major statement of either esthetic or political thought."[40] Collecting more than fifteen years' worth of essays, some previously published and some not, *Our Mothers' Gardens* was designed to showcase Walker as a writer in process, but a *writer at work* nevertheless. Walker would continue to be a prolific writer and a lifelong critic not just of other people's lives and work, but her own. For example, her investigation of her personal experience as an integral counternarrative to the historical record is evidenced in the extant material that emphasizes the years of labor that predated the volume, including her previous intentions for another cover design entirely, one that did not overemphasize her own authorship in merely respectable terms. Before her own photograph portrait graced the first cover of *Our Mothers' Gardens*, a draft contained another version that featured an original print of a photograph of a garden, perhaps her mothers' actual garden, encircled by a frame of overlapping squares drawn by hand. This cover pays tribute to the materiality of Walker's authorship and expresses the heart of Walker's argument in her eponymous essay "Our Mothers' Gardens" by reminding us of the wider context in which writing takes place—that it is not self-sufficient apart from the other kinds of labor that make living possible. The unpublished cover demonstrates that Walker's own project is not necessarily piecemeal, in the way one reviewer described, but not just merely open to but solicitous of and dependent on further labor by critics today.

Like the meaning expressed by her unpublished cover image, Walker's analysis of Black feminist material culture—her mother's garden, and her handmade quilts and clothing—remains valuable for its easeful assumption of a tradition of Black feminist artistry that cannot be fully extinguished even in the most difficult of straits. Yet given the transhistorical relevance of her passages about her mother's artistry even today, how could Walker, author also of the heartfelt 1982 novel *The Color Purple*, not understand Phillis within the same Black feminist and womanist framework that would inspire me to craft the very argument of this book? Well, it is important to note that Walker's essay emphasizes mothers, her love for her own mother and Phillis's mother included: "Perhaps she was herself a poet—though only her daughter's name is signed to the poems that we know."[41] Mother love enabled Walker to imagine a Black feminist artistic tradition outside the strictly literary canon, so traditionally conceived. This book, however, demonstrates that foremother love—including love for early members of our tradition from whom we are distanced from any direct domestic or intimate understanding—requires a slightly different set of critical tools. What might Walker's methodology of Black feminist care tell us about Phillis that her own critique of Phillis cannot? If we reimagine Walker's disdain for Phillis using her own maternal method of criticism rooted in love, we might graft Phillis to Walker's familial account of gardens, quilts, and other practices of Black feminist material culture.

A draft of an alternative cover to Walker's *Our Mothers' Gardens*. ca. 1982, Alice Walker Papers, box 75, folder 1, Stuart A. Rose Manuscript, Archives, and Rare Book Library, Emory University.

While Walker and other Black feminist critics have deplored Phillis's erasure of her subjectivity in her poems, their critique might be understood as an act of mourning worthy of continued study. Indeed, in between the poems Phillis wrote, and the poems future critics wish she had written, lies a garden waiting to be explored.

In addition to the example of Walker, both Sherley Anne Williams and Wanda Coleman's creative and critical works help us better recognize Phillis as a practitioner of Black feminist material culture (her work in other genres in place of the garden she could not tend) and thereby of forms of mourning that are Black feminist in previously unnoted ways. If such an artistry went unpublished but was somehow preserved in manuscript form—deposited in the special collections acquisitions of a library, for instance—then it continues to exist intermediately between the unwritten and the permanently published as literary ephemera, what Shanna Greene Benjamin defines as "memorabilia, printed matter, or manuscripts with seemingly transitory significance."[42] Moments of scholarly discovery of such works in the history of Black feminist criticism are often bittersweet, especially when one's beloved poet has died far too soon. In blurring the line between bitter and sweet, ephemera may perform and voice that which Black feminist criticism (in its being required to publish stringent critique in polished academic tones) even cannot. While ephemera has sometimes played a secondary role within literary studies compared to more formally published manuscripts, its significance herein involves its very ability to circumvent the established conventions of mainstream publication and thus highlight power dynamics that might otherwise be subject to censorship or rejection. Following Shanna Greene Benjamin's call to acknowledge the importance of intimacy in criticism,[43] I note the ways elegiac ephemera often surfaces within moments of intimate disclosure in the archive, mourning what could not be publicly mourned in a more selective and private way. In this chapter, Phillis's ephemera enables us to better understand both her work and her own self.

Indeed, both Williams and Coleman help demonstrate that Phillis's elegiac writings speak to other significant acts of self-affirmation and determination centuries later. Echoing Phillis's own vexatious status, Williams and Coleman publicly struggled with essentialist conceptions of Black creative writing as well as criticism. For example, in 1986, Williams critiqued feminist theory generally, and Black feminist criticism specifically, for its increasing penchant for "separatism" and its inability to adequately include interpretations of Black masculinity within imaginations of feminist community.[44] Instead, Williams praised Walker's unique conception of Black feminism, what Walker termed "womanist," for its purported nonseparatist emphasis on the well-being of the entire community inclusive of all its identities, prescient of the ways that Black feminisms' inclusivity is still being debated today.[45] For her own part, Coleman is known for writing critical, sometimes to the point of being problematic, reviews of popular Black feminist writers' works, their fame notwithstanding.[46] In addition to their most complex critical legacies, both Williams and Coleman are just beginning to receive the attention for their work that they deserve, as both left behind a trove of archival material to help scholars better understand the full scope of their work and lives. Yet more support for this research is imperative, because their work also points to the ways they struggled to practice Black feminisms within the constraints of their institutional and personal lives. Further, such research provides a more nuanced understanding of Black feminisms' sometimes wayward critical routes.[47]

Sherley Anne Williams's Blues

By the early 1990s, Sherley Anne Williams was a published critic, author of the 1986 novel *Dessa Rose*, poet, professor, and recording artist working on several newer creative and critical projects. Not one to rest on her laurels, Williams continued to write scholarship that challenged earlier criticism, including her own.[48] For Williams, a living practice of the genres of criticism and creative practice would combine into a methodology that would elucidate otherwise-understudied figures in Black literature and culture, including singer Esther Phillips. In her 1991 essay "Returning to the Blues," Williams describes this methodology as "'in progress'; it is part testimony, musings toward what black intellectuals do as researchers and as the subject we research, and part eulogy to the late Esther Phillips, one amongst a horde of undercelebrated black geniuses."[49] Williams explains how listening to Phillips helps reconnect her to scenes from her childhood in the Central Valley of California, scenes that were so rarely represented in Black literature. What was otherwise viewed as ephemeral—Phillips's and others' blues records, and the working-class members of her community who listened to them, otherwise relegated to a seldom represented past—become a published part of contemporary life via Williams's criticism. Williams demonstrates that designations of what is categorized as canonical and what is not are political as well as aesthetic. By bridging a missing literature with her own criticism, Williams imbues crucial importance to the Black Central Valley, to the blues, to Phillips, and to her own position as a scholar formed by these subjects. Now when we listen to Phillips, we also hear Williams's voice. Yet even in Williams's criticism on Phillips, her own blues was circumspect. Rather, it is in her remaining unpublished archive that her own blues became "a raw civility that doesn't apologize for its wildness or knowledge."[50]

Williams practiced "raw civility" in the form of an intimate disclosure when she drafted a letter to Henry Louis Gates Jr. on November 5, 1991, subtly inquiring whether he knew of any potential fiction writer appointments in which she might have a lower teaching load and more time to write. As Williams writes to Gates in an extant manuscript from her papers at the University of California, San Diego (UC San Diego): "Teaching, in particular teaching literature, is eating me alive."[51] In 1991, Williams was a tenured professor in the Department of Literature at UC San Diego and had already published a book of criticism, a novel, and two books of poems.[52] While archival evidence suggests that Williams may have been on the academic job market soon after she wrote this letter, it is uncertain whether she seriously entertained any new offers of appointment. Nevertheless, within eight years of drafting this letter, Williams received a diagnosis of cancer that ended up being terminal. She passed away in San Diego on July 6, 1999, at the age of fifty-four.[53] Yet as her 1991 letter draft demonstrates, Williams was clearly communicating what she needed in order to thrive in her career going forward, in order to stay alive as a Black woman poet. In this way, Williams could be understood as fomenting— both being a troublemaker and at the same time nursing herself back to life. When women of color, especially Black women, make clear demands for their needs or visions of success, they are often critiqued as being "intimidating," as an undergraduate student, K., once lamented to me via email.[54] Today, Williams's letter functions as an elegiac intermediary—as a work caught in the transit not only between the privacy of her letter and the publicity of her papers in a university library, but also between her life and premature death—waiting to be heard or, better yet, attended to with a response that ensures what happened to Williams does not happen to today's generation of Black feminist critics.

Williams does not divulge the full details of her financial situation in this or other letters. This is likely because her papers at UC San Diego only contain her professional papers, not personal diaries or letters she wished to keep private. One may only assume that Williams did not receive the resources, financial or otherwise, she could expect as a figure of her renown at a more "generous" academic institution.[55] Again, Williams grew up in Fresno, in California's San Joaquin Valley, in a family that was working poor.[56] She disclosed in one interview that her childhood was "the most deprived, provincial kind of existence you can think of."[57] Later, as a self-described member of the middle class, it seems that any financial support Williams lived on came from her paycheck from UC San Diego and her creative writing, as she did not inherit any generational wealth, but few if any academics divulge their full financial truths publicly, making Williams's candid letter to Gates a rare and "unprofessional" window into intellectual history. In academia, calls to be professional are often a policing of academics' behavior by colleagues who come from privileged backgrounds. For the policed, professionalization is a process of becoming that comes at its own cost. These academics must often, as Stefano Harney and Fred Moten write, "disappear"—treating their work in the academy as a maroon community (a realm created by those who escaped enslavement)—neutralizing the threat of professionalization in a capitalist society that is ever expanding and no longer distinct from the workplace of the university, or at least holding professionalization at bay. They live a balancing act, "refusing," in the words of Harney and Moten, "to be either for the Universitas or for professionalization, to be critical of both, and who pays that price?"[58] In fact, one answer to the question of who has already paid this price is "a generation of Black feminist critics."

The systemic societal discrimination that Black women experience not only in academia but in our wider lives contributed to the premature deaths of a generation of Black poets, novelists, and literary critics, resulting in at least one cancer cluster acknowledged in finespun works of poetry as well as scholarship.[59] These works have critiqued the systems that contributed to their sister-colleagues' and foremothers' premature deaths while honoring their attempts for agency, empowerment, and privacy. For example, contrary to the public narrative of seamless academic success that corresponds with a transparent and easeful private life, Shanna Green Benjamin's intellectual biography on Nellie Y. McKay details the great lengths McKay went to hide from her colleagues the fact that she was a parent.[60] Benjamin notes that while McKay's published writings told one story, her extant archive, largely professional papers, did not necessarily tell the whole truth either.[61] Of course, not all Black feminist critics kept the same things private due to a variety of differences in their situations.[62] Sherley Anne Williams was also a single mother, and while there is no evidence that Williams kept details of her family structure quiet, her letter requesting assistance in securing a less teaching intensive appointment speaks perhaps to the presence of circumstances in her personal life she would not disclose in a professional letter.[63] Did McKay and Williams garden? Would such a practice be present somehow in their professional papers? Faith Smith, a former student of McKay's and now a professor, recalled being "struck by something [McKay's] obituaries quote her as saying: that in retrospect she wished she had spent more time in her garden."[64] McKay's regrets point, again, to a place where she cultivated a wider arc of her life recorded beyond academia. Similarly, in this chapter, Williams's public papers pertaining to her professorial life cannot possibly disclose as much as personal papers might. Yet in being as reticent as they are, they offer insight into how to study other foremother archives that are also limited in terms of extant personal information—requiring that one be able to read between the lines of the professional archive and spend more time looking for Black feminist critics' "gardens."

Proving that, on her own terms, she was a star who was burning brightly indeed, Williams's drafted letter to Gates becomes her own elegy in retrospect not only by expressing her unrealized desires for another teaching appointment but also by mourning the unfulfilled plans Williams had for her writing career, including a novel she never finished. Williams describes enclosing for Gates her future writing plans, including a short story that prefaces the events of her novel in progress: "I'm sending it to you because the story is where I found the novel's protagonist, Amah Dean, and discovered her voice."[65] Unpublished as of now, Williams's unfinished novel manuscript gains life in this letter via Williams's assertion of her protagonist's voice even before the novel was complete. Indeed, Williams's assertion of her protagonist's voice outside the bounds of the printed page suggests more than a discovery of Amah Dean's character or self: It points to a material address that emotionally engaged Williams. In 1991, the same year of her drafted letter to Gates, Williams would describe the effect of hearing blues singer Esther Phillips's voice in her criticism.[66] Across this essay, Williams discloses with great intimacy how listening to Esther Phillips and the blues that she grew up hearing in her community later helped her "survive" her graduate degree in literature and that it still helps her survive within the English professoriate.[67] Williams "worked hard and worried a lot ... [and] she felt bruised and battered by decades of doing battle in the master's house,"[68] so it is not surprising to observe her discovery of a new protagonist's voice depicted as a lifeline in Williams's own life within this letter. Nevertheless, Williams's novelization of Amah Dean's voice remains unfinished in her papers at UC San Diego, another elegy that mourns Williams's unfinished life and begs for future scholars to continue her project.

As aforementioned, Williams was a specialist not only in literature but also in other forms of Black expressive culture that tended toward the ephemeral, especially the blues and forms of oral folk culture and history, which she became instrumental in canonizing as scholarly areas of study. In fact, in 1989, when McKay solicited Williams's feedback on the tentative table of contents for the eventual 1996 *Norton Anthology of African American Literature*, Williams wrote, on one of her many pages of notes, regarding the table of contents McKay mailed her, "What happened to the folklore? What is going to be recorded?"[69] Williams's notes suggest that she cared deeply that genres like folklore were at risk of being forgotten. The draft of the table of contents McKay sent Williams in 1989 begins with Lucy Terry, Phillis Wheatley, David Walker, and George Moses Horton—all writers of works known predominantly via print. This table of contents was later revised, however: The published 1997 edition of the anthology begins instead with "The Vernacular Tradition," including spirituals, gospel, the blues, work songs, jazz, rap, sermons, folktales, and more, with asterisks denoting selections that were recorded on the accompanying CD.[70] While scholars such as Benjamin have recently and rightly underscored McKay's overarching work on the anthology, Williams's notes also denote that she is deserving of more scholarly attention as a critic of that time and not just as a creative writer. Williams's interest in what would be recorded in the *Norton* also had the effect of recording something of herself. Indeed, her correspondence points to a poetics in which the ephemeral performs essential elegiac work—essential, critical, and transformative mourning work.

This brief window reveals one way that Williams unknowingly elegized herself. While her notes throughout reveal that several of her suggestions for additions to the *Norton* were duly considered and accepted, Williams's notes on the very page of the letter McKay wrote her on February 20, 1989, reveal one key suggestion that was not taken into consideration. At the top of McKay's letter, Williams suggests organizing the *Norton* by category or genre, including "some of the more important critical

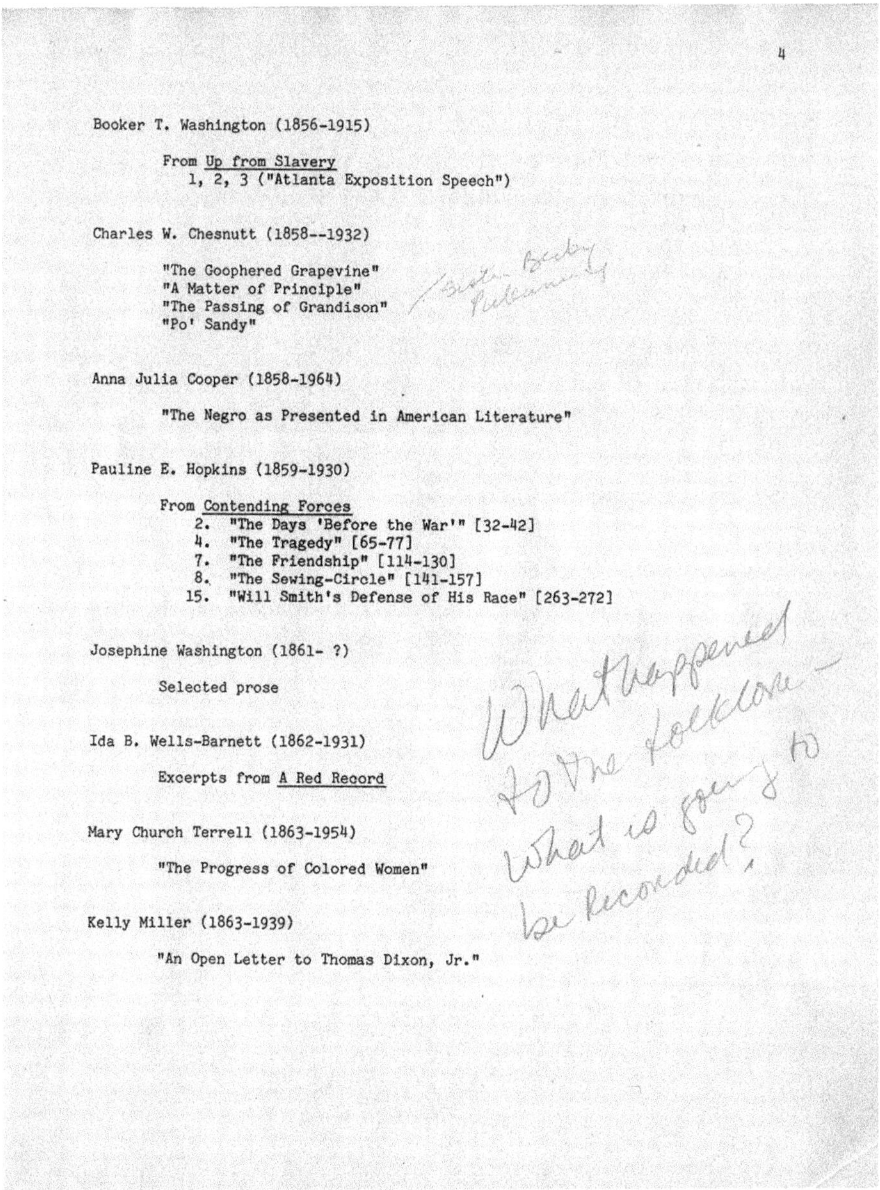

Booker T. Washington (1856-1915)

    From Up from Slavery
       1, 2, 3 ("Atlanta Exposition Speech")

Charles W. Chesnutt (1858--1932)

    "The Goophered Grapevine"
    "A Matter of Principle"
    "The Passing of Grandison"
    "Po' Sandy"

[handwritten: Sister Becky / Pulcanimy]

Anna Julia Cooper (1858-1964)

    "The Negro as Presented in American Literature"

Pauline E. Hopkins (1859-1930)

    From Contending Forces
      2. "The Days 'Before the War'" [32-42]
      4. "The Tragedy" [65-77]
      7. "The Friendship" [114-130]
      8. "The Sewing-Circle" [141-157]
     15. "Will Smith's Defense of His Race" [263-272]

Josephine Washington (1861- ?)

    Selected prose

Ida B. Wells-Barnett (1862-1931)

    Excerpts from A Red Record

Mary Church Terrell (1863-1954)

    "The Progress of Colored Women"

Kelly Miller (1863-1939)

    "An Open Letter to Thomas Dixon, Jr."

[handwritten: What happened to the folklore — What is going to be Recorded?]

Williams's marginalia on the *Norton Anthology of African American Literature* draft table of contents. ca. 1989, Sherley Anne Williams Papers, box 3, folder 1, Special Collections & Archives, University of California, San Diego.

pieces" and "autobiography."[71] In fact, at the bottom of the letter, Williams lists the names of the scholars Hortense Spillers, Helen Houston, Rita B. Dandridge, Ann Allen Shockley, Trudier Harris, and Thadious Davis, pointing us to their critical work. Unfortunately, hewing closely to a definition of literature as creative writing not inclusive of criticism, the *Norton* did not go on to include excerpts of what Williams calls "some of the more important critical pieces," making them, in this regard, even more ephemeral than the early vernacular tradition for whose inclusion Williams does successfully lobby. While the *Norton* does include a couple pages of explanation of the critical tradition before the section on literature since 1970, even acknowledging that in 1971 "Darwin Turner lamented the fact that while black poets and novelists were beginning to be recognized, the African American critic remained largely unseen," *Norton* concludes this section on a cautionary note:

> Ironically, while black scholars have been largely responsible for the increased attention given African American literature in the academy and in popular culture, their small numbers may soon decrease. During the 1980s and early 1990s, the number of black PhDs, which peaked in the mid 1970s, declined. Whether the literary critical discourses to which African Americans have been central will continue to develop is of concern. Though African American literatures have survived, even flourished, in the worst of times, the African American critic's presence in the academy may well determine whether and how these literatures will be studied in the twenty-first century United States.[72]

Not just a matter of whether this literature will be studied, at stake is whether or not it will disappear completely. As Christian wrote in 1987, "Writing disappears unless there is a response to it."[73] On the verge of disappearing in the understudied collection of her papers, Williams, too, maintained the importance of criticism, penning what would retroactively become an elegy for herself as one of the remaining few critics of this literature, a disappearing profession that if lost completely would in turn make her work as a creative writer obsolete.

Indeed, I argue that the possible disappearance of a generation of critics who would study Black literature in the twenty-first century forebodes not just the loss of creative writing but also the loss of other modes of expression that come alive with intergenerational critical study. For example, taken at face value, Williams's memorial essay "Remembering Prof. Sterling A. Brown, 1901–1989," presents a brief but laudatory portrait of Williams's professor and his wife, whom Williams calls Miss Daisy, and the memory of the occasions they hosted at their home. Williams treads carefully over the idiosyncrasies of her being a graduate student at Howard University in the late 1960s, recalling how much she and others wanted more "acknowledgment beyond the *careful criticism* of written work he gave any student who asked."[74] Significantly, the essay ends with Williams demonstrating that she is, already during her graduate studies, coming into her own as a critic of the blues, even beyond the purview of Brown. While Brown brazenly admits that he does not listen to contemporary blues, Williams stands up for the contemporary and, in a sense, herself as a representative of it as a soon-to-be critic, poet, and singer in her own right.[75] In an extant draft of a letter Williams wrote to Alice Walker dated April 5, 1989, Williams provided a bit more insight into her memorial essay for Brown, including that "a memorial wasn't the place to resolve or even display the knots in the ties that bind; so in the Sterling piece I was trying to be brief, but deep."[76] Readers of Williams's UC San Diego archive do not necessarily gain more insight into exactly "the knots in the ties that bind," but the indication that Williams is withholding the full story provides a note to future critics to be mindful of tradition's dynamic, albeit fragile, multigenerational life—with a renewed sense of the forces that make it difficult for its full story to be told.

Williams closed her 1991 draft letter to Gates like she often closed her letters to colleagues, "Stay well and working," highlighting her investment in her work not as labor for the university alone but as part of a larger project of fulfillment for herself and for the voices she kept alive in her writing.[77] While lamentations about having to teach are often interpreted as a conflict between "teaching versus the individualisation of research," Williams's desire for more time to write about the outside world seems like it is more about being unordered, about conducting a form of research that is "the negligence of professionalization" in resistance of the neoliberal university.[78] Again, in a draft of a letter to Alice Walker, Williams recounted, "Margaret Walker Alexander was here a few weeks ago; I went to the talk and the dinner afterwards. I would like to live long enough to be that outrageous."[79] Williams did not end up living nearly as long as Margaret Walker (1915–98) did, but I smile to think that she still hopefully got the chance to be as "outrageous" as she hoped she could be at an older age, recalling Alice Walker's definition of "womanish" as "outrageous, audacious, courageous or *willful* behavior."[80] At the same time, I want to respond with solemnity to the experiences of precarity that result in the need to request financial support or a professorial appointment with a manageable teaching load and smaller class sizes. Williams's words thus become an elegy for her life and honestly express a vulnerability within Black feminisms that cannot be glossed over, that call for future work to remedy. Williams's strategy of using her correspondence to facilitate her ability to pursue her true "work" was not the first, but it provides a useful contemporary frame in which to better understand the understudied and unheard voices of other Black feminist writers who found themselves in similar straits.

Phillis's Elegy for Herself

Phillis wrote many elegies for prominent white members of her Boston community, several of which were later collected and published in her 1773 *Poems*.[81] However, when I say *written for prominent white members of her Boston community*, I want to emphasize that these poems were really written for herself. Indeed, the elegies Phillis wrote were enculturated in the Puritan funeral elegy tradition, a genre whose legacy partly lies in "preserving the ephemera of memorial culture," which comes to include Phillis's own ephemera surrounding the conditions in which she crafted these poems.[82] Naturally, many other readers have desired to read Phillis's elegies less as occasional gifts for white mourners and more as expressions of early Black diasporic mourning. Beyond her poems' occasional contexts in a predominantly white community, readers continually search therein for evidence of Phillis's memorialization of her kinfolk.[83] But in the absence of archival evidence, how might scholars prove that Phillis was in fact mourning her African and Black diasporic kinfolk in her poems? Another less speculative interpretive route maintains that Phillis herself and by extension her kin are never as far away from her elegies as some of her critics may think. For those who think Phillis is a world of criticism away, on the contrary, her elegiac work maintains ties to the ephemeral in ways that are reminiscent of Walker's and Williams's work, and therein offers a striking portrait of Phillis as not only mourning for her kinfolk but also mourning for herself. In fact, Phillis's elegiac project runs parallel to those of several more contemporary Black writers whose instincts have also at times been characterized as contrary but whose implications for Black feminist criticism nevertheless glimmer forth when we find traces of themselves in and around their work.

Somewhere in the space surrounding her poems, Phillis spoke of her own life, her hardships, her successes, "her own people, her own history, her own vision."[84] Because we lack any autobiography that describes her personal life, these are the kinds of details we may never read for certain in our lifetimes. But what we do know is that, similarly to Williams, Phillis often spoke in her extant letters about her work. Instead of clear translations of her own inner life, Phillis's letters were understood not as private letters—as we are largely able to assume we may write today (barring social media and increasing tech surveillance and tracking)—but as public documents that could be read by any of the members of the network to which she had to entrust to convey her mail. Nevertheless, readers may hear Phillis's voice most clearly within these letters in the instructions she gave to the members of her network for how her poems could best gain success in the marketplace. Phillis wrote several extant letters regarding the 1773 publication of her *Poems*. Altogether, these letters express Phillis's concerns about gaining enough early subscribers to finance her book's publication, finding enough buyers of her book, ensuring that she would not lose sales due to the sale of unauthorized copies, and even attempting to recoup any unsold copies so that she might find buyers elsewhere.[85] Like Williams's draft letter to Gates in 1991, these letters retroactively elegize Phillis, who died in 1784, in part, we assume, as a consequence of dire financial straits.[86] Today these letters not only function as elegies for Phillis's life; they also continue to convey instructions for how she would have wanted us to carry forward, as a method of criticism, continued responses to her poems.

Again, while several critics have often understood the collection of elegiac poems that predominate across Phillis's 1773 *Poems* as representations of her social embeddedness in her Boston community, the inclusion of one elegy manuscript in one of Phillis's letters especially crystallizes the way in which these poems were part and parcel of the financial negotiations she carefully carried out to facilitate the conditions of her freedom even after her formal manumission. For example, Phillis's July 15, 1778, letter to Mary Wooster is particularly straightforward in its gift of an elegy written by Phillis upon the death of Wooster's husband, in exchange for unfinished financial transactions, as Phillis writes to Mary directly after she pens her elegy for her husband:

you will do me a great favour by returning to me by the first opp^y those books that remain unsold and remitting the money for those that are sold—I can easily dispose of them here for 12/Lm.° each—I am greatly obliged to you for the care you show me, and your condescention in taking so much pains for my Interest—I am extremely Sorry not to have been honour'd with a personal acquaintance with you—if the foregoing lines meet with your acceptance and approbation I shall think them highly honour'd. I hope you will pardon the length of my letter, when the reason is apparent— fondness of the Subject &—the highest respect for the deceased.[87]

In 1778, Phillis had for several years been manumitted from the Wheatley family and was now married to John Peters, but living, scholars presume, in wartime Middleton, Massachusetts, amid increasing financial difficulties.[88] Mary Wooster, whom Phillis had never met in person, was wife to one of Phillis's previous correspondents, the late Colonel David Wooster, as well as sister to one of the subjects of Phillis's previous elegies.[89] Mary had recently become a widow upon her husband David's death on May 2, 1777.[90] While much literary criticism would probably focus largely on the discovery of the elegiac poem Phillis includes in her letter, I am also interested in the content of Phillis's letter itself as a retrospective elegy for herself, mourning too the circumstances that led to the financial straits that occasion the writing of such a letter.

Joanna Brooks has described how Phillis "achieved her early reputation in large part by transacting in feelings of grief and loss among white women," emphasizing that almost one-third of Phillis's 1773 *Poems* are elegies or occasional poems "written about or for white women."[91] Brooks notes that a later version of such poems includes Phillis's "On the Death of General Wooster," in its address to the widowed Mary Wooster, and specifies its transactional nature, given that its accompanying letter includes "specific business instructions . . . concerning the New Haven sales of her book." Brooks also mentions that in "New Haven, Connecticut, Wheatley found a powerful advocate in Mary Clap Wooster," but Brooks does not include any evidence of how Mary Wooster advocated on Phillis's behalf. Mary's reply, if she indeed replied to Phillis, is not extant, as most of Phillis's papers have been lost. Mary may have been a possible "powerful advocate," but the fact that Phillis continued to struggle financially, unable to publish her second volume of poems, suggests that Mary was one of the white women who "ultimately failed her."[92] In fact, Phillis's letter to

Mary did not just contain "business instructions"; her requests of Mary were communicated in a highly affective and apologetic manner. Thus, I would qualify any assertion of white women's advocacy on Phillis's behalf by underscoring that while Phillis's poems were necessarily written largely for white members of her community, her audience is only one side of the equation. Phillis's participation on her own behalf is the other key element.[93] Phillis's poem "General Wooster" would have been published in her second volume of poems had it garnered enough subscribers, or otherwise reached publisher approval, to make it into print. The elegy's original context in her "business" letter lives on as a marker of the kinds of labor Phillis and her poetry could have gone on to do if they had been given sufficient resources.

In never being published in Phillis's lifetime, the poem "General Wooster" also remains extant only as a form of elegiac ephemera. Although Phillis's letter to Mary Wooster depicts her rhetorical savvy in requesting financial support, this is not to say that the poem itself does not also have to take on a great deal of emotional labor. Again, written while Phillis was a freedwoman, in the aftermath of the American Revolutionary War (1775–83), Phillis's letter and elegy on the death of David Wooster were not a known part of Phillis's collected works until the late twentieth century, when they were discovered by scholar Mukhtar Ali Isani. Since Isani published his findings in 1980, the authors of any scholarship published prior to that year, including Walker's original 1974 essay "Our Mothers' Gardens," would not have known about the poem. "General Wooster" succeeds in demonstrating the transformation in Phillis's orientation to poetic authority in the wake of her new life as a freedwoman. Isani describes it as "an elegy composed to comfort the general's wife but also an expression of gratitude for the interest of the Woosters in Wheatley's fortunes and in the welfare of African slaves in general. . . . While the poem is not a distinguished elegy, it contributes measurably to our understanding of the author."[94] In other words, the poem in some ways fails as a "distinguished" elegy for Wooster (it is barely an elegy in Phillis's previous sense of the genre) and thus fails as a totally successful transaction in white feminine grief. Instead, "General Wooster" may be read in hindsight as an elegy for Phillis herself. David Wooster is merely a vessel in the poem—as death has rendered him silent, mirroring Phillis's elegies on George Whitefield and Joseph Sewall—and becomes intricately embedded in what Phillis describes in her letter to Mary as the national "Cause of Freedom."[95] Wooster becomes merely a mouthpiece for the voice of a nation at war against Britain and, for Phillis, transatlantic slavery.

Following the model of her first book, for Phillis's subsequent elegies to meet success within the market of her white women readers, they required, first, "the elegist's customary prerogative of chastening other mourners for their lapses or excesses,"[96] and second, for Phillis to "mobilize images that are deeply evocative of her own experience of enslavement, such as familial separations, bereaved parents, and ocean transits."[97] This includes lines in the 1773 elegies like those in "On the Death of a Young Lady," wherein Phillis addresses the mourning parents according to these conventions, closing the poem thus:

> Why then, fond parents, why these fruitless groans?
> Restrain your tears, and cease your plaintive moans.
> Freed from a world of sin, and snares, and pain,
> Why would you wish your daughter back again?
> No—bow resign'd. Let hope your grief control,
> And check the rising tumult of the soul.
> Calm in the prosperous, and adverse day,
> Adore the God who gives and takes away;
> Eye him in all, his holy name revere,
> Upright your actions, and your hearts sincere
> Till having sail'd through life's tempestuous sea,
> And from its rocks, and boist'rous billows free,
> Yourselves, safe landed on the blissful shore,
> Shall join your happy babe to part no more.[98]

Versions of this command to be silent appear in at least nine other elegies in her 1773 *Poems*.[99] Further than a reading of Phillis's enslavement as a professionally validating experience for her white readers, I argue that understanding the interconnection of Phillis's practice of emotional withholding and her own experience of enslavement has the potential to alter our understandings of her elegies and her other seemingly assimilationist poems, including those like the infamous "On Being Brought from Africa to America," where a seeming embrace of Christian mercy is a welcomed alternative to African origins (one purported reading of the poem). In "On the Death of a Young Lady," even white parents are called to wholeheartedly embrace without protest "the God who gives and takes away." In other words, scholars have studied Phillis's frequent calls for the bereaved to be silent, or focused on mobilizations of slavery's imaginary, sometimes discoursing on both successively,[100] but none have fully detailed the ways in which these two elegiac requirements may be closely interrelated in Phillis's formation as a Black woman poet who was kept enslaved by the Wheatleys and by those in her surrounding community.

If those select readers who are addressed by Phillis's elegies are commanded to suppress their tears within a context where the setting of the elegy is transatlantic slavery, what does it mean for Phillis to absorb such readers into a discursive experience of her own enslavement? Further, what does it mean that this pool of largely white women readers neither protested this treatment nor merely accepted it, but instead embraced it? Taken together, if Phillis's elegies were known to recapitulate her own mourning as an enslaved woman in the guise of white women's mourning, then her simultaneous calls for such mourners to cease their grieving not only relieves white women from the project of mourning their kin but also theoretically frees them from the project of mourning Phillis's kin as well (perhaps intentionally blocking them from participating in this project). To cry for their own lost loved ones in the context of her elegies would mean they would have to cry for Phillis's as well. That these women ostensibly accepted without protest Phillis's invocations for dry eyes speaks volumes. Thus, it only follows that supporting the publication of Phillis's 1773 *Poems* and supporting Phillis herself in her life as a freedwoman following her exit from her volume's very stipulations for her enslavement would become mutually exclusive. To mourn otherwise is to ignore the historical conditions that produced Phillis's *Poems* and the limited possibilities of a white-sanctioned life outside it. Nevertheless, Phillis did not stop writing with the publication of her *Poems*, therefore putting pressure on the limited rubric for success which she was previously allowed.

Following her manumission from the Wheatley family, Phillis very much seems to have wished to continue performing her profession as a poet, and in part due to financial considerations. However, her new investment in writing poems that did not bear the rubrics of transatlantic slavery and the subsequent silencing of its mourners may have contributed to her publisher's inability to secure enough support to publish a second volume of poems. Phillis's enactment of a refusal to conform to the style of poems she wrote while she was enslaved demonstrates an arc of critical development akin to many of the later Black feminist critics studied in this book. This also forces readers today to reevaluate the interpretation that Phillis was in large part "failed by" and abandoned by her white women network. While certainly true, it was also the case that Phillis refused to operate within the conditions by which they would offer support, a distinction that reinscribes her agency within the narrative that white people's failings led to her demise notwithstanding. Taking Joanna Brooks's argument and research one step further, I argue retroactively that choosing the less successful path in terms of her new poetry, even if it led her to go unpublished, was the right choice insofar as it better aligned with her values. Unfortunately, we lack access to more ephemera that details the creation of both the 1773 *Poems* and her proposed second volume in order to offer a full comparison. While we cannot close-read any of Phillis's poems as though we know the full context that led to their creation, we can read the failure of her second volume to garner white people's support as a sign that perhaps those poems were not intent on subordinating to their whims. This shadow text is ultimately "more powerful" left open to the full possibilities of what it could say than perhaps any book Phillis could have written under the auspices of white publication even after her manumission.[101]

Indeed, without its accompanying letter, one might not even know that "General Wooster" was written on the occasion of Wooster's death at all, as there are few other indications that this is an elegy in the vein of Phillis's 1773 *Poems*. Gone are the invocations to cease one's tears and their correspondent images of slavery. There is also little given to the point of view of a white woman's relationship to her deceased husband. In the first lines of the poem, Phillis privileges Wooster, not his wife, but even so subjects him to the syntactical mercy of "his Country's cause." The poem begins,

> From this the muse rich consolation draws
> He nobly perish'd in his Country's cause
> His Country's Cause that ever fir'd his mind
> Where martial flames, and Christian virtues join'd.[102]

Already Wooster is mainly the sum of his Christian and soldier parts. Phillis embeds him in a poem about the nation at war, a nation that might be suddenly more sympathetic to her subject position. Yet only twenty out of the poem's forty lines dedicate themselves to Wooster as a hero slain in battle. Midway through, lines 13–32 of the poem are set apart by dialogue markers:[103]

["]Permit, great power while yet my fleeting breath
And Spirits wander to the verge of Death—
Permit me yet to paint fair freedom's charms
For her the Continent shines bright in arms
By thy high will, celestial prize she came—
For her we combat on the feild of fame
Without her presence vice maintains full sway
And social love and virtue wing their way
O still propitious be thy guardian care
And lead <u>Columbia</u> thro' the toils of war.
With thine own hand conduct them and defend
And bring the dreadful contest to an end—
For ever grateful let them live to thee
And keep them ever Virtuous, brave, and free—
But how, presumptuous shall we hope to find
Divine acceptance with th' Almighty mind—
While yet (O deed ungenerous!) they disgrace
And hold in bondage Afric's blameless race[?]
Let Virtue reign—And thou accord our prayers
Be victory our's, and generous freedom theirs.["][104]

Indeed, these lines depict Wooster as subject to an even larger battle, one in which "fair freedom" is the true reason behind the "dreadful contest," revealing this to be an elegy undermining the logic of chattel slavery, only half of which speaks about Wooster with any specificity. Rather than approaching this subject via her own position, Phillis employs Wooster as the substrate on which to base her poetic authority, a beginning of a possible life outside white women's authority in which she could use her previous subjects to speak to the nation at large.

The elegy to Mary Wooster would have needed to satisfy a threshold of elegiac obedience in order to justify the return of Phillis's unsold books and secure the widow's support as a future subscriber to her poems.[105] Able to embed her argument about the end of chattel slavery quietly and close the poem by bringing the reader back to Mary and David Wooster, Phillis tested the boundaries of the genre in combining, rather than foreclosing or divorcing, white women's grief and her own. In 1778, when Phillis wrote to Mary Wooster, her 1773 *Poems* had been already published for nearly five years. Lacking a path to publication for her second book, she likely needed to recuperate what possible sales she could in no uncertain terms. The extant manuscript of the letter and poem to Mary Wooster demonstrate how willingly, albeit apologetically, Phillis's letter transitions into poem and back from poem to letter, blurring the lines between her poetic and personal projects. However, just a few years earlier, newly published and something of a celebrity, Phillis just as politely asked for others' help in selling the "300 more copies" of her book that had recently arrived via ships from London.[106] Indeed, Phillis's "raw civility" to Mary echoes the letter Phillis sent just years earlier to Colonel David Worcester (Wooster) on October 18, 1773:

> I expect my Books which are publishd in London in [the vessel commanded by] Capt. Hall, who will be here I believe in 8 or 10 days. I beg the favour that you would honour the enclos'd Proposals, & use your interest with Gentlemen & Ladies of your acquaintance to subscribe also, for the more subscribers there are, the more it will be for my advantage as I am to have half the Sale of the Books. This I am the more Solicitous for, as I am now upon my own footing and whatever I get by this is entirely mine, & it is the Chief I have to depend upon. I must also request you would desire the Printers in New Haven, not to reprint that Book, as it will be a great hurt to me, preventing any further Benefit that I might receive from the Sale of my Copies from England. The price is 2/6[d] [two shillings, six pence] Bound or 2 [shillings]/Sterling Sewed.—If any should be so ungenerous as to reprint them the Genuine Copy may be known, for it is sign'd in my own handwriting.[107]

Phillis's authenticity is also here etched into her meticulous dedication to ensure that her *Poems* is sold for her benefit. This too is her "own handwriting." The necessary sale of the *Poems* justified her writing letters to solicit subscriptions and facilitate her readership, but the letters also function as works of criticism articulating a poetics of care for Black writers and not just their writing.

Phillis's letters, which would find their echo in future letters by Williams and other Black feminist critics, reveal much about Phillis's conception of her role as a poet, and read much like that of the letters of a critic who was also a poet. Privy to "half the Sale of the Books," which would be "entirely" hers, and a key source of income, it is clear that Phillis was writing in large part for economic security. In other words, her poems did not express Phillis to be "radiant . . . involved in work her soul must have. Ordering the universe in the image of her personal conception of Beauty," as Alice Walker so hopes they would.[108] Instead, Phillis's 1773 *Poems* prefigure the work of criticism Walker herself enacts in her own later critique of Phillis. In other words, rather than personal expression for expression's sake, Phillis's letters demonstrate that she was writing instead to radically critique and thereby change the power dynamics of her world, something much in line with Walker's own definition of Black feminism. As aforementioned, in Walker's infamous definition of *womanist*— her term for a "black feminist or feminist of color," which she wrote for the frontispiece of *Our Mothers' Gardens*—she details how she derived her term from the Black vernacular word *womanish*: "the black folk expression of mothers to female children" that "referr[ed] to outrageous, audacious, courageous or *willful* behavior. Wanting to know more and in greater depth than is considered 'good' for one."[109] Following this, a womanist is anyone who engages in the practice of criticism, who reads and writes because, as Barbara Christian asks, "If I don't save my own life, who will?"[110] Reading Phillis's elegies only as poems has delimited scholars' interpretations of her work within the absorptive, whitewashed politics of English or early American literary criticism. By contrast, this chapter understands Phillis's elegies as critical pieces that together comprise a critique of the system in which she is only permitted to participate as a beacon of death and loss.

Just as the blues used to be critiqued as a "morose" genre, as mere remnants of "slavery times,"[111] Phillis's poems have been lambasted by a generation of twentieth-century Black critics, whereas the discipline of early American literary criticism has in turn adopted Phillis as their own— often, however, to similar unsatisfactory ends. As Sherley Anne Williams writes of this critical phenomenon, "How could one work for a black revolution in which so many casualties were black?" Contrary to the critics who denigrated the blues, even her own early undergraduate scholarship, Williams recalls her eventual recognition of "the formalist and aesthetic traditions of the blues," especially that of singer Esther Phillips (despite the fact that "people liked to moralize over her and pass judgment on her character") as a kind of homecoming.[112] Conjuring her memories of hearing the blues across her childhood in the San Joaquin Valley, listening to Phillips also reminds Williams of the various ways Black people have been erased from California, despite their generations-long presence in the state. Equipped with a criticism that recognizes who people are in their historical moments while attuned to the ways they bend history to their image via their aesthetic contributions, Williams writes, "I could intellectualize [Phillips] because she had been able to intellectualize, through the medium of song, her own life. And in this, I saw some reflection of what I'd had to do in order to survive Literature."[113] After her 1773 *Poems* was published in London, Phillis wrote at least two (known) proposals for a second volume of letters and poems that was never published and whose manuscript remains underground, if not lost.[114] Rather than view this as a dead end, I view it as an invitation to do better by contemporary Black critics and poets living and recently past.

Wanda Coleman Remembers Georgiana Coleman

By the autumn of 1999, the first generation of Black feminist criticism (so formally named) was about to enter its final decade. Sadly, Williams's recent passing due to cancer over the summer was a premonition of more Black feminists' deaths to come (Barbara Christian's in 2000, June Jordan's in 2002, and, as mentioned earlier in this chapter, many others). By the close of the millennium, Wanda Coleman had published more than ten books—including her most recent 1998 volume of poems *Bathwater Wine*, which would go on to receive the Lenore Marshall Poetry Prize of $10,000 in autumn of 1999—despite great odds.[115] Like Williams, Coleman grew up in California, but in South Central Los Angeles, in a family that was also working poor. Her father had migrated to Los Angeles in 1931 after witnessing white residents in Little Rock, Arkansas, lynch a young Black man "from a church steeple."[116] Coleman's future writing would detail the class and racial inequities that influenced her poetic speakers' actions and their counterparts, the real lived experiences that impacted the subjects of her poems. As though she knew that contemporary Black women's lives were often too short to worry overly about respectability in the face of oppression, poet and multihyphenate Wanda Coleman refused to operate on any terms not her own. While the Black feminists engaged across this book often sidestepped the limited professional berths they were afforded, none did so perhaps as raucously as Coleman. It is possible to present a biographical account of Coleman that focuses only on her published poems and thereby validates a slightly tidier narrative of her life and work. But what, she might ask, would be the fun in that? The remaining pages of this chapter explore what Coleman's unconventional navigation of her public persona means for the Black feminist critical impulse to love her.

In November 2001, in the wake of the September 11 attacks, Coleman gave an hour-long talk at the Poets House in New York City and voiced a subtle argument that contextualized how Phillis's lack of self-expression in her poems nevertheless spoke to her. In "Imagining Phillis Wheatley: A Cross-Century Dialogue," Coleman begins by describing the terms that allow her to dialogue with Phillis, despite her centuries-long distance. Their reunion is at its outset facilitated by their professions as Black women poets. Coleman speaks frankly about how she began "researching" Phillis at the University of North Carolina at Chapel Hill only after being asked to speak at the Poets House, even though she also claims she had read Phillis as a child—a confession that I believe is as deliberate as the pretext of Phillis's being commissioned by white women to write her own poems. Coleman tells her audience, "I'm known for my performances but . . . I'm going to be in the mode of Professor C. tonight, a little bit" (she notes that Professor C. is what her students call her).[117] Indeed, Coleman's talk blurs the line between performance and the embodiment of professorial identity to try to communicate to her audience that academic study is an imperative prerequisite for the apprehension of Phillis's poems, especially if one has not had access to them since childhood, that is, since one's childhood as a young Black poet. Coleman's performance carefully walks the line between an apology for Phillis and a critique, and her language acknowledges that to study Phillis is to court both. What is most striking is Coleman's cutting honesty when she discloses to the audience that "if I had had my choice, I would not be discussing Phillis Wheatley, nor would I discuss her ever."[118] Coleman also voices critiques of Phillis that Black feminists have made before: "This meter and rhyme scheme, if influenced by Pope, nevertheless embodies some of Western literature's worst characteristics," "there is little to no personal pain in her poems," and "[she] seems not so much a poet as a personality for whom poetry is a social device."[119] Nevertheless, as Coleman's talk unfolds, and in the shadow cast by 9/11, she recounts how researching Phillis offers her the solace of the library's historical distance and confirms eerie similarities between their lives.[120]

Coleman's academic practices of citation are employed to walk an unknowing audience through the foundations of African American history with "Phillis," as Coleman often calls her, as her guide. Coleman's presentation collages Phillis's poems and story, the rhetoric of slavery that inscribed Phillis's time, historical accounts of Jim Crow racism, and Coleman's own experiences of modern anti-Blackness in the United States. For instance, Coleman's discussion of Phillis's "On Being Brought from Africa to America" is hesitant and inconclusive, or rather, purposefully positioned as a series of questions designed to prompt her readers to further independent study.[121] The questions Phillis poses as a poet—that limn the space between who she was and what she wrote—are so persuasive that they prompt Coleman not only to research her life but to read Phillis's poems in conversation with her own. Coleman ends her reading of this poem by echoing June Jordan's 1985 analysis of Phillis's "On Being Brought," another moment of a possible critical-poetic relationship that never came to be. That Coleman chooses to call herself Phillis's "literary descendant," even though her research about Phillis did not officially commence until 2001, emphasizes both the mutability of these lines of lineage and the amount of research and work they require to sustain.[122] Coleman also includes the fact that "Phillis had three children, Wanda Coleman had three children," and the losses, the tragic deaths of their children (one of Coleman's and all of Phillis's), is a trauma they also shared.[123] In all, Coleman extends extreme empathy around the circumstances surrounding Phillis's life and demise, and her criticism reflects exactly what she practices in her poems.

In a circuit of understanding flowing from a practice of poetry to criticism to one's lived experience, on the circumstances surrounding Phillis's death, Coleman acknowledges, "It is difficult for me to admit that I might share a like fate, even though I live in the future that Phillis has paid for."[124] Indeed, Coleman's lecture calls attention to the importance of Coleman's vulnerability. For instance, Coleman concludes with a reading of Phillis's "On Virtue," which she recites at times emphatically, at times breathily:

> O Thou bright jewel in my aim I strive
> To comprehend thee. Thine own words declare
> Wisdom is higher than a fool can reach.
> I cease to wonder, and no more attempt
> Thine height t'explore, or fathom thy profound.
> But, O my soul, sink not into despair,
> *Virtue* is near thee, and with gentle hand
> Would now embrace thee, hovers o'er thine head.
> Fain would the heav'n-born soul with her converse,
> Then seek, then court her for her promis'd bliss.

Auspicious queen, thine heav'nly pinions spread,
And lead celestial *Chastity* along;
Lo! now her sacred retinue descends,
Arrayed in glory from the orbs above.
Attend me, *Virtue*, thro' my youthful years!
O leave me not to the false joys of time!
But guide my steps to endless life and bliss.
Greatness, or *Goodness*, say what I shall call thee,
To give an higher appellation still,
Teach me a better strain, a nobler lay,
O Thou, enthron'd with Cherubs in the realms of day![125]

She repeats the final "in the realms of day," softly, twice, and the audience applauds, while Coleman can be heard laughing joyously: "I think this is a first [*laughter*]. Thank you! I've never delivered . . . well, I haven't delivered a paper like this in years," after which the audio cuts out. Coleman's lecture prompts her readers to their own further independent study to understand how the circumstances of their own lives might inspire additional research on Phillis and continued reading of her in conversation with their own lives—one of the most important tenets of Black feminist criticism, as previously discussed. Coleman does not give an in-depth close reading or gloss of "On Virtue," but her selection of that poem alone is worth noting, as it is not a popular poem in extant criticism on Phillis. Brief accounts of the poem elsewhere have classified it as one of Phillis's detours from "ordinary subject matter" toward "appropriate poetic figures in pleasing form."[126] However, I have the sense that Coleman would have even more than this to say about the poem, as her own work engaged the concept of "virtue" in very interesting ways.

Coleman was aware of her current historical moment, wherein there was still a tendency to practice code-switching in the presence of white audiences in order to remain financially solvent. For example, Coleman's own talk on Phillis in 2001 was even delivered in a much different register than that of her dual poetry reading *Twin Sister*, recorded in 1985 with Exene Cervenka, co–lead singer of the Los Angeles punk rock band X, where Coleman read poems that used "profane" language to highlight social experiences and issues, some her own personal experiences, not commonly addressed in mainstream contemporary poetry.[127] Coleman often highlighted her experiences of marginalization as not just Black and a woman, but also as a Black woman poet from Los Angeles, including in unpublished letters where she often went out of her way to try to control how she was represented in criticism. Coleman was keenly aware of the potential fallout of being pigeonholed as a Los Angeles regional writer.[128] In many instances, Coleman often stretches the practice of Williams's "raw civility that doesn't apologize for its wildness or knowledge" to its furthest reach, definitely reaching the outrageousness that Williams noted Margaret Walker evidenced at the end of her career, although even Coleman's letters are often extremely formal and fairly brief. Still, Coleman "was mean."[129] Today, respectability politics still manages and surveils Black women's behavior in white-predominant spaces, from academia to the world of poetry, even as fewer Black people have opportunities to work respectable jobs as tenure-stream or tenured professors, the result of a "thirty-year interdisciplinary shortage of African American faculty members."[130] With evidence of Black feminist critics continuing to suffer ill health in the neoliberal university, increasingly subject to the side effects of adjunctification, as was evidenced as recently as Thea K. Hunter's untimely death in 2018,[131] Coleman exemplifies the ways that these dynamics do not always translate into more "refined" behavior, and sometimes produce its opposite. Coleman did not die young, but she passed away in 2013 at the age of sixty-seven after a long illness and is only just beginning to receive the critical attention she so wanted.[132]

I have gravitated to Coleman as a critic not only because of her interesting way of reading Phillis but because so much of her work challenges respectability and certain socioeconomic and middle-class visions of Black feminist criticism. Often, though, I found her work, published and unpublished, to be problematic, leading to further questions of how to include her as part of the tradition engaged across this book. Luckily, the analytic of foremother love is a loose one, and one that gravitates toward the figures who resist easy categorization and understanding. The figures who know that if the work is too easy to like, too easy to digest, then it is no longer doing the work it set out to do in understanding why specific Black people's lives have unfolded in the ways they did. As to the question of how we read Black feminist critics who were problematic, one possible answer is to critically engage Coleman the way that she herself engages Phillis, whom she also found did not cohere with her idea of what a poet should be. Just as Coleman read Phillis's poems up against her own life and work, I, too, have read Coleman's work with an eye to the poems that have helped me think through what it means for Black poets to write as both creators and critics.[133] Whereas Coleman faced obstacles (sometimes seemingly of her own creation) when she tried to translate her life and work for academic audiences, she also often transcended editorial squabbles and departmental politics in her poetry. This is not to say that poetry is inherently a more apolitical genre; for Coleman, it provided a safe space to do the work of Black feminist criticism in a way that was both receptive to her voice and welcomed by audiences willing to listen. The rest of this chapter will engage with a small piece of Coleman's poetry as a prelude to an ongoing engagement, demonstrating her abilities to switch registers and, when addressing a beloved poetic figure, practice foremother love with aplomb.

All of this is context I bring to bear on Coleman's series of six epistolary poems written to her older sister, a sequence Coleman began in her 1998 book of poems, *Bathwater Wine*, and later extended in her 2001 book, *Mercurochrome*, which was published around the same time that Coleman was researching Phillis. The sequence sheds even more light on how to understand Coleman's poetics in the context of a Black feminist criticism that follows Phillis's legacy. Two poems, "Letter to My Older Sister" and "Letter to My Older Sister (2)," were published in *Bathwater Wine*, while the third through sixth poems in the "Letter to My Older Sister" series Coleman published later in *Mercurochrome*. Within each book, Coleman intersperses each "Letter" in between other poems such that the poems that separate them are also part of their context and fill the silence of what would otherwise be their nonexistent response. In fact, if readers extract the "Letter" poems from the rest of their books and splice them together as a series, much of their context is lost, as the poems that frame each "Letter" develop a conversation too. Yet Coleman clearly establishes these poems as an independent sequence by uniting their titles and numbering them. Reading the poems as they are situated across Coleman's books and as a separate sequence speaks to Coleman's attempt to confirm her sense of kinship with an older sister who she never had the chance to meet—whose life did affect the context of Coleman's life despite being at once separated from it. This relation is established in the epigraph that precedes the first "Letter": "*she died before christening and, therefore / had no name, but i will gladly lend her one of mine.*"[134] In the body of the poem, Coleman is only able to address her sister, "she," in the second-person "you" by letting her borrow something of "mine." Overall, Coleman's "Letter" series helps us understand how fictive kinship for an ancestor one never got the chance to meet might animate an ethical Black feminist poetics in the present.[135]

Coleman's first "Letter to My Older Sister" appears in the second section of *Bathwater Wine*, titled "Disclosures," which memorializes the history of Coleman's mother and father before they had children and their lives thereafter. Coleman is ambivalent about charting her lineage in certain terms, highlighting, too, the threats to her parents that made her future birth miraculous.[136] Thus, Coleman's first letter-poem to her sister begins with a series of questions, of which she requests careful consideration before answer at the end of the poem.[137] Of course, readers know that Georgiana does not ever answer, and that the answers matter much less than the questions themselves. Readers also stand in for Georgiana, who have the potential to respond in ways Georgiana cannot. Overall, writing to Georgiana also becomes a process of mourning Coleman's paternal grandmother, and of mourning her parents' other losses. Coleman matter-of-factly asks her sister, and the other family members she represents, if she has lived them well, demonstrating her ethical responsibility not only to those she writes poems about, but those whose lives (and losses) enabled her to write poems. Thus, Coleman and Georgiana are stitched into a cloth of kinship that collectivizes their experiences of harm. In fact, this "Letter" acknowledges Georgiana's death as an absorption into further life and as what her mother begrudges, her dying breath immortalized. The poem, however, is breathless as well. Coleman's letter is seemingly cut short as she is required somewhere else. She promises more future letters and the poem does not provide a long discourse—if Georgiana is truly a part of Coleman and if she is not forgotten, then what matters most is not what her and Coleman write but what they prompt.

Given the question of whether she has lived her sister well that Coleman asks in her first "Letter," the whole of *Bathwater Wine* takes on a new context—subsequently, what happens to Coleman in her other autobiographical poems happens also to the lives she has "absorbed." Indeed, the volume becomes less about herself than about the experiences of her entire lineage. Each poem is now a gift to her sister, a chance to relive the life her sister lost—an offering, like the bread roll left that Coleman notices in the cemetery when she visits her father's resting place in the poem just prior to her first letter-poem, "Beyond the Lake of Memories."[138] Coleman's sister may no longer embody these experiences outside Coleman's body, but having been addressed and named, she ostensibly now has the ability to share Coleman's experiences. Nevertheless, as with anyone who is conjured, it becomes difficult to know what to do when she takes on more and more flesh. Subsequent poems to Georgiana struggle with sustaining their correspondence in the same way that Coleman struggles to sustain her work as a poet.[139] Nevertheless, Coleman honors her commitment to her project of homage. In its everyday expressions of limited time and worry over the sharing of too much to an overburdened listener, Coleman's expression of her sister's familial knowledge of their mother renews the intimate reality of their correspondence. Again, the gestures to the space off the page of the poem are where Coleman's most enlivening address takes place.

Coleman's fifth "Letter to My Older Sister (5)" is the poem that most presents in the visual shape of a poem rather than prose. Its importance in the context of the entire volume is signaled by its reference to *Mercurochrome*, referencing "mercury-containing dyes developed as possible antiseptics or antibiotics" (now widely considered unsafe).[140] The poem loses track of its originary address as it suddenly falls away from Georgiana and into a memory of Coleman's mother applying lipstick in the car with elegant mastery, which strikes Coleman into a realization that her childhood is gone, and only memories remain, like her mother's lipstick, just a shade away from Mercurochrome.[141] This everyday memory of Coleman's mother comes to stand for the Mercurochrome that gives Coleman's 2001 collection of poems its title. Writing to her sister is painful but facilitates a healing memory of her mother's attention to making beauty, which Coleman carefully reads as a form of self-study, just as Mercurochrome's effects eventually render their attendant wound ephemeral. This explains the "Letter" sequence overall and its importation of a kind of healing undertaken over several everyday acts, until one hardly notices there is a scar anymore. While the sequence takes up but a small percentage of Coleman's vast collection of poems, my hope is that they help demonstrate how closely her work falls in the tradition of Black feminist poetics and deepens our ability to hold her within an account of Black feminist criticism that also tries to understand why she was so "mean" in other settings. Coleman's final "Letter to My Older Sister (6)" ends with an apology she asks Georgiana to pass on to her father.[142] Coleman's decision to delegate her address to Georgiana also falls to the task of her readers. Her project of elegy is less about a supernatural heavenly realm and more intimately tied to everyday practices of maintenance and care, and the requisite response to ameliorate violence, a practice of healing that Coleman cannot undertake alone.

Unlike Phillis, Coleman was able to leave behind a tremendous archive of poems (her "garden") that she wrote to combat economic and social inequities faced by marginalized people in Los Angeles and beyond. Thanks to Coleman's labor, Phillis is not an isolated foremother at the beginning of the tradition. Coleman chooses to consider herself Phillis's fictive descendant—even though her research on Phillis did not "officially" commence until 2001, it is clear that Coleman has spent her entire life and career preparing to be a critic of Phillis's work—emphasizing both the mutability of these lines of lineage and yet the amount of labor they require to sustain. By 2012, Coleman had counted her output at "over eleven hundred" poems.[143] Coleman's papers are now housed at the University of California, Los Angeles, in a collection of over 182 boxes (75.2 linear feet). Indeed, Coleman describes her writing habits in the language of a curator: "I collect and assemble all of my work, even the pieces. I have one notebook that consists of lines of poetry waiting to become part of something larger."[144] Coleman's daily attentiveness to her craft is evidenced in the many books and poems she was able to publish, and all the ephemera she left unpublished but carefully organized despite not gaining much critical acclaim in her lifetime (that is, according to some accounts). Just as Phillis's writing was not the final word, but a call awaiting response and an idea anticipating expression, the project of sustaining kinship across space and time remains purposefully unfinished in Coleman's work as well. Today, Coleman's readers, to whom she speaks through her poems to Georgiana and others, are asked to intercede in the matters in which Coleman can no longer speak. In 2012, Coleman wrote, "I have many unfinished works: plays, novels, articles and short stories galore, as well as notes on a memoir."[145] Resuming Coleman's and other Black feminists' unfinished work is a practice of singing their names.

we're ready

The archives engaged across this book continue to raise questions that remain unanswered in our present moment. I especially wonder what those who have since departed—Barbara Christian, Nellie Y. McKay, Sherley Anne Williams, Wanda Coleman, Robert Hayden, Audre Lorde, Phillis, and several others—would say to the scholars of Black feminist criticism today.[1] The various demands they made in order to ensure the survival of their work helps me to know what they might plausibly say: *In our final moments, we wished for more time to spend in our gardens, more time to finish our in-progress novels and poems, and for better times generally.* Thus, I encourage you, dear reader, to contemplate on what the fore(m)others of this book would say to you. As for me, I have learned that the vicissitudes of academia require ongoing vigilance to ensure equity is continuously valued across the realms of curriculum, hiring, retention, and promotion. Every day, Black feminist critics work to make the university a more just system, yet we are often faced with having to just let go and let it churn on its own for a while. In the wake of so many of my foremothers' deaths, Black feminist criticism is the method by which I organize while nevertheless prioritizing my own healing and rest—such that I may redress these deaths in ways that nourish my own spirit. Ultimately, I have learned that my spirit, and my academic work, is often sustained more by the evidence of Black feminist life and history I recognize taking place off campus (especially insofar as/if a campus lacks a Black studies/ethnic studies/gender and sexuality studies academic department or the intention to create one).

As recounted across this book, when Barbara Christian, June Jordan, Alice Walker, and others made disparaging remarks about Phillis (often relatively early in their careers), they were writing in a context in which Black studies was, overall, under threat. For them, Phillis's 1773 *Poems* consisted of work she wrote while enslaved, and her words were not consistent with the confidence, self-possession, and verve of a Black woman professor of the late twentieth century. I am a later version of them, still wondering why, at the time of this writing, Black women still experience discriminatory treatment after the PhD and even multiple tenure-track or tenured appointments (racism is rooted in structures that shape individual behavior, to put it succinctly). I understand both what Christian, Jordan, and Walker may have been experiencing when they were writing *and* what Phillis may have been experiencing when she was writing. Looking back through these former critics' output from today's standpoint, their theorizations when read across the 1970s to the 2000s have retroactively provided an analytic that makes Phillis legible within Black feminisms specifically and Black studies generally. I for one could not have embarked on such a project unless I had matriculated into a doctoral program at a public university that had hired, or was near another public sister university that had hired, a committee's worth of scholars whose work traversed Black studies, Black feminisms, white feminisms, and literary criticism. The mentorship of these scholars taught me that who trained them, whom they trained with, and whom they trained was as much an integral part of the work of the tradition as was publication. If I was ever to truly understand Phillis, I needed to understand the Black feminist critical tradition first. I needed to understand why so many scholars struggled to connect with her and why for others reading Phillis was like reading in a mother tongue. In turn, I have been able to develop a relationship with Phillis that remains as open as any relationship I would have with another critic: a singular part of a much larger community that I hope survives and continues onward.

Remembering June Jordan

Getting here has required a different kind of affective relation to institutions, a kind of affection we might practice by following the example of Phillis. One might look to her 1773 poem "To the University of Cambridge, in New-England" for a framework to this aim:

> While an intrinsic ardor prompts to write,
> The muses promise to assist my pen;
> 'Twas not long since I left my native shore
> The land of errors, and *Egyptian* gloom:
> Father of mercy, 'twas thy gracious hand
> Brought me in safety from those dark abodes.[2]

To begin, note the strange grammar of the first sentence: "While an intrinsic ardor prompts to write." Who is the subject of the verb *prompts*? And notice how Phillis qualifies each declarative statement with an example of how she is "assist[ed]"—both in writing and in being brought from Africa. Or are these lines pure metaphor and not meant to index Africa per se but Phillis's religiosity? Either way, it would seem that she is evidencing Darlene Clark Hine's 1989 concept of the "culture of dissemblance," wherein Black women have performed "the appearance of openness and disclosure but actually shielded the truth of their inner lives and selves from their oppressors," so as not to attract negative attention to the point of (sexualized) violence.[3] Yet the whole stanza also has an air of confidence. You *know* what you're doing, in other words, if you're starting a poem with a list of acknowledgments. In this way, Phillis exemplifies Alice Walker's 1983 term *womanism*, from the word *womanish*, "referring to outrageous, audacious, courageous or *willful* behavior. . . . In charge. *Serious*."[4] There's a confidence and expression of her own empowerment even though it is qualified.

In 1985, when June Jordan was first writing "The Difficult Miracle of Black Poetry in America or Something like a Sonnet for Phillis Wheatley" as an invited address at the University of Massachusetts Amherst, she seemingly rewrote the first two lines of Phillis's "To the University" so that they read, "While an intrinsic ardor bids me write / the muse doth promise to assist my pen." Jordan wrote in her address, "[Phillis] says that her poetry results from 'an intrinsic ardor,' not to dismiss the extraordinary kindness of the Wheatleys. . . . It was she who created herself a poet, notwithstanding and in despite of everything around her."[5] Jordan's citation is not a rewriting of the lines, however; rather, it is a reversion to an earlier 1767 variant of the poem Phillis wrote when she was fourteen (that variant was known to readers then and was published by the time Jordan was writing in 1985).[6] Jordan continues, "Following her 'intrinsic ardor,' and attuned to the core of her own person, this girl, the first Black poet in America, had dared to redefine herself. . . . She was making herself at home." Jordan condemns several of the 1773 poems published in Phillis's London book as "especially awful, virtually absurd," and not "accurate to the secret wishings of her lost and secret heart,"[7] but connects Phillis's "To the University" to her own thoughts about poetry. As Jordan wrote in 1977, "'What,' I sometimes wonder, 'am I trying to do, exactly?' I think that I am trying to keep myself free, that I am trying to become responsive and responsible to every aspect of my human being. I think that

I am trying to learn whatever I can that will make freedom of choice an intelligent, increasing possibility."[8] However, for Jordan, working to "keep [herself] free" required more than the poetic equivalent of "thoughts and prayers."

In 1967, when Jordan was offered a job teaching at City College of New York, it was only because a friend decided he wanted to write full time, so she took up his class and "spent the night [before] crash-rummaging among [her] books in order to choose a course curriculum reading list."[9] By 1985 things were much different for Jordan, who had become director of the Poetry Center at the State University of New York at Stony Brook. By the mid-1980s, Jordan had given a couple dozen of addresses, if not more, based on what is recorded in her papers alone, to say nothing of her many published poems, and several books of different genres, but her success was never far from her own efforts to ensure such. When I looked at Jordan's drafts of her address on Phillis, I found a letter Jordan had written stipulating the exact conditions under which she would write the address. Far from an "intrinsic ardor," Jordan demystifies any preconceptions that she would write her address on Phillis with only *a muse's assistance*. She writes on January 21, 1985, that before accepting the invitation, her original fee of "one thousand dollars" would be only for a "straightforward poetry reading," but for "the composition of an entirely new address related to the subject of" Phillis would require a fee of double that, "plus expenses of travel and lodging."[10] We find, in this moment, a valuation of the labor of criticism as twice that of poetry, but also insight into the beginning of a historical moment where universities like City College did not opt for the radical transformation of continued Open Admission despite ongoing resistance by student and faculty organizing; a moment wherein a Black woman professor's financial particulars, her honoraria—compounded by the inhumane economics of the Reagan years—needed to be meticulously negotiated far in advance, and rightly so.

Jordan's words have helped me understand what Phillis was doing when she addressed the white male students of Harvard College in 1767 and in 1773, 130 years before Alberta Virginia Scott received the first bachelor's degree awarded to a Black woman student by Radcliffe College in 1898—and then died not four years thereafter.[11] Between 1767 and 1773, one revision of Phillis's poem is a slight, though perhaps telling, shift in the agency of those Harvard students of her day. In 1767, Phillis writes,

To you, Bright youths! he points the heights of Heav'n.
To you, the knowledge of the depths profound.
Above, contemplate the ethereal Space
And glorious Systems of revolving worlds.[12]

In 1773, by contrast, these lines read,

Students, to you 'tis giv'n to scan the heights
Above, to traverse the ethereal space,
And mark the systems of revolving worlds.[13]

In 1767, an unnamed "Parent of mercy . . . points [to them] the height of Heav'n" and "knowledge of the depths profound." In 1773, who is doing the "giving" is more circumspect, and gone is any bestowal of "knowledge," but the students' inheritance as "sons of science" is limited to their "scan[ning] the heights," "travers[ing] the ethereal space," and "mark[ing] the systems of revolving worlds." She is putting the Harvard students in their place as not necessarily the sole beneficiaries of a liberal arts education but, rather, a more limited technical education. Further, something that connects both versions of the poem is Phillis's maintenance of religion as outside the university, a distinct body, so to speak, even though Harvard was originally conceived in 1636 to train clergymen. In other words, Phillis would have to structure the university differently to justify her exclusion from it—first, from knowledge, and then merely from science. These kinds of recalibrations predict the maneuvers future critics would make in their attempts to navigate the university in and beyond Black studies.

Further, down toward the end of the 1773 version of the poem, Phillis addresses the Harvard students with urgency:

Suppress the deadly serpent in its egg.
Ye blooming plants of human race divine,
An *Ethiop* tells you 'tis your greatest foe.[14]

Thus, one must appreciate the license Phillis takes to describe the students as members of a "human race divine" and herself as neither a member of the "human race divine" nor a servant nor someone who was enslaved but, rather, "an *Ethiop*." Phillis does not negate white men's standing at the top of the American racial-social hierarchy, but neither does she locate herself at the bottom of such a schema; instead she stands outside it. Her warning stems from her subject position, carefully articulated around what cannot be acknowledged—slavery—as she defines and delimits the students' academic purview and entreats them to be aware of their "privileges while they stay." If we read this also as a caution voiced to us today, whereas Black feminisms might provide a roadmap for curtailing the entrenched exclusion in science, technology, engineering, and mathematics (STEM) that has outpaced social investment in critical care, we must understand that, ultimately, it is up to each of us to choose how to use or to protest the limited conditions of our educational system. Just as Phillis sounded her caution as early as 1767, recent scholars of Black and feminist science and technology studies have corroborated Phillis's caution to the early-career scientists of today as STEM has continued to veer toward artificial intelligence and other forms of posthuman technologies.[15]

Phillis's revision of her "To the University" poem (versus Jordan's selection of the older version as her own personal favorite) and Jordan's stipulations of her own value as a public speaker and her commitment to providing a critical context, and thus value, for her own poetry have much in common. Similarly, Joshua Myers asks in his book *Of Black Study* (2023) "whether or not the university truly had the capacity to do this work for and with us. Could it be a space that moved against its tradition of affirming the rationality of plunder and pain?"[16] His question echoes Jordan's 1969 essay "Black Studies: Bringing Back the Person," in which Jordan asks, "Is the university prepared to teach us something new?"

> *Black studies.* The engineer, the chemist, the teacher, the lawyer, the architect, if he is Black, he cannot honorably engage career except as Black engineer, Black architect. *Of course, he must master the competence, the perspectives of physics, chemistry, economics, and so forth.* But he cannot honorably, or realistically, forsake the origins of his possible person. Or she cannot. Nor can he escape the tyranny of ignorance except as he displaces ignorance with study: study of the impersonal, the amorality of the sciences *anchored by Black Studies.*[17]

I would add: Could the university be what it was to Phillis at fourteen (a place where she could grammatically proclaim intrinsic ardor) before she revised her poem for publication at age twenty? Probably not, for as Myers writes of our own moment, "as the university became more and more 'neoliberal,' individual academics more entrepreneurial, and human life and possibility more vulnerable, the 'legitimization and institutionalization' of Black Studies in the 1980s made sustaining the originary radical communal impulse all the more difficult."[18] In fact, just as Phillis revised her poem, Jordan revised her own ideas throughout her lifetime of what the university can do. Not only do her words enable me to celebrate her life and mourn her death due to cancer in 2002 while she was a professor at UC Berkeley, just a few years before I matriculated there; they also enable me to better understand the weight she and other Black feminist critics were carrying as ongoing purveyors of Black studies. Indeed, they were doing so within the context of a university structure that could proclaim, upon Barbara Christian's promotion to full professor in 1986, that one of her reviewers warned against "the danger of responding to the numerous requests that her expertise stimulates. Some of her later work seems to be variations on a theme."[19]

Remembering Barbara Christian

What I hope this book imparts is a better understanding of how Black feminist critics, including myself, have attempted to ameliorate the fact that their places of work did not often come with ready-made feminist communities dedicated to their collective survival. The kind of communities envisioned by Black feminist criticism are as diverse as their founding critics, yet they each share a glimmer of marronage, a whisper of a safe haven that keeps us returning to the bookshelf, the blank page, and the seminar table at the beginning of each term in perpetual search of a possible blueprint. Black feminist criticism has never been set in didactic stone within the university. Nevertheless, it survives, even as an ephemeral practice, and may help one survive one's journey through traditional academic settings, akin to the first letter Nellie Y. McKay wrote to Barbara Christian on October 1, 1982 ("I have wanted to write to you for some time"), to praise the publication of Christian's 1980 book, *Black Women Novelists*, commencing their acquaintance and eventual colleague-friendship:

> My reasons for writing to you are not complicated. I think that it is important for black women scholars across the country to develop links between themselves. We need each other for intergroup and outside of the group support. We need to know who each other is, where each is, and what

each is doing. We need to share information between us all—all kinds of information, but most certainly that which involves our professional lives. In short, we need to build a strong network that links us to each other.[20]

Given that we have now come to understand that McKay was disappointed in the opportunities for Black feminist community at the University of Wisconsin, it is wonderful to discover evidence that she began strategizing to build a national community to supersede the conditions of Black women's home institutions, that she was "not convinced that the 'scholar in isolation' is the best way of getting work done." While the fact remains that so many of this generation died prematurely in ways that signal the likely lack of general institutional support the university could have afforded them, we should not let their efforts to mitigate this reality die in vain.

I visited UC Berkeley, my alma mater, for the first time in roughly a decade to research an archive for *Foremother Love*, which had by now grown alongside me throughout several phases in my postdoctoral and tenure-track career as well as throughout the global COVID-19 pandemic. As I walked to campus preparing to read the archive of papers belonging to the late Barbara Christian, I realized that I still mourned her as if she had been my own professor. Again, Christian had passed away of cancer in 2000, nine years before I matriculated at the university, but I was fortunate to later have the chance to study under her former advisee, Arlene R. Keizer, who was a professor at UC Irvine when I was accepted into their English doctoral program. In a 2021 panel on Christian's legacy, Keizer lovingly recalled "some of the things [she] learned from her that aren't written down anywhere," including the fact that Barbara, "a serious gardener, . . . thought of her doctoral students as flowers and nicknamed us according to the bloom she thought we resembled."[21] Thus, I felt a mixture of closure and shyness while I was heading to UC Berkeley's campus to read Christian's papers, as if I was going to meet her for office hours, and, in a way, I was. Defaulting to my quiet shyness, I felt inadequate to the task of accounting for the emotional, intellectual, and spiritual significance of Christian's life and work. I do not think this feeling, a varietal of imposter syndrome, will ever truly go away, but I quickly had other words I could place alongside that feeling, like Christian's own wondering about whether any students would care enough to study Black women, and her mantra that what she does and writes she does and writes for herself only.[22] Christian's words embodied a tradition that was, to me, grounding.

I never got to be her student at UC Berkeley, but through her work I was able to learn from her students and from the writings that she gifted to herself and to the world.

Christian's archived papers were beautiful to me in a way I recalled beauty throughout the papers of other Black feminist professors that I had visited before the pandemic. However, I had never done archival research as a tenure-track professor before. I loved the way I could just sit and read and be fully present in the archive, slowly turning over page by page within folders upon folders of the ephemera detailing Christian's academic career. I felt the beauty of what it meant to be a Black feminist critic now, as though I was encountering the remnants of a long-lost library in a world where books had been destroyed. Given the subject matter of my own book, the obvious thing to look for was any mention of Phillis in Christian's archive, but I had long recognized having finished the bulk of the writing for my project that my interest in these papers was not so much if Phillis herself exactly was ever in Christian's thoughts, but a larger theoretical investment in how Christian's life and work had prepared me to read Phillis in ways that may not have been possible otherwise. At the same time, I could not but help reflect on all the ways it was also hard for me to be a reader of Christian's papers in the same way I read other Black feminist critics' papers, even if I had access to more resources for research now than ever before. First, because one of my doctoral committee members had been Christian's advisee, I felt like Christian was akin to a grand-adviser to me, and I wanted to tread especially lightly when perusing and writing about an archive that felt more personal to me than the others I had encountered from a more "objective," scholarly standpoint. Second, being back at UC Berkeley and back in the official, university archive for the first time since 2019, I was forced to reflect on all the ways I had changed as a person and as a scholar since the pandemic started, and how deeply the world had changed.

However, many of my anxieties melted away and transformed into purpose as I began to carefully peruse Christian's papers in the reading room of the Bancroft Library. I became quickly immersed in Christian's world and understood the awe that so many of her students proclaimed for her in their evaluations of her teaching.[23] She went so confidently about her work that any trepidation I had felt was replaced by the need to simply do her archive justice. Her papers comprised not only a record of her own research materials but also her correspondence and countless other kinds of ephemeral evidence of the ways she built community at UC Berkeley and beyond. Extant in Christian's papers are also unpublished essays and letters, including one on the importance of the humanities and another on her personal journey at UC Berkeley, how she transitioned from the English Department to the African American Studies Department, and letters and memos detailing information about one of the books she wanted to write, "Contemporary African American Women Writers as Theorizers," building on her essay "The Race for Theory."[24] Also of interest to today's scholars is the entire box dedicated to Christian's extensive work as an editor of the 1996 *Norton Anthology of African American Literature*.[25] While today the anthology is largely known as being coedited by Henry Louis Gates Jr. and Nellie Y. McKay, I was intrigued to learn that Gates wrote to Christian regarding the anthology and it was she who recommended collaboration with McKay as well as several other scholars.[26] Finally, I learned from reading her syllabi that Christian's office had been in 347B Dwinelle Hall, thus I had the chance while I was on campus to make a pilgrimage and visit her one time for "office hours."

I am also happy to report that Christian's papers yielded a surprise appearance by Phillis. For example, even though I was not exclusively searching for her, I did find evidence of Phillis in one of Christian's publication drafts. Within the folder dedicated to her correspondence with her editors at the Feminist Press who invited her to draft the 1980 *Teaching Guide to Accompany Black Foremothers*, Christian included several drafts of her guide, including a handwritten outline that included two teaching suggestions related to Phillis. One such prompt read, "Mary Church Terrell named her daughter after Phyllis Wheatley. Write a short essay on who Phyllis Wheatley was, and Terrell's reason for naming her child, Phillis," and another read, "Have students write a short biography on the life of a well-known black woman.—e.g. The early years of Phyllis Wheatley."[27] Unfortunately, Christian's editors at the Feminist Press recommended that she "limit the number of these teaching suggestions," since "many students will not have the library resources for this type of research"—and as a result, Phillis was entirely erased from her published teaching guide.[28] An editorial decision such as this has ramifications for the future growth of libraries and public support for and understanding of their importance, as well as for the repositioning of professors in the contemporary neoliberal university as the select members of a society to have access to such resources. Such a decision contrasts with Christian's teaching style at UC Berkeley, as is evidenced by her extant syllabi, assignment prompts, and teaching evaluations. Christian was a celebrated lecturer, but it was also clear that she expected her students to be involved in their own learning and research.

In terms of other histories of missed opportunities for Black feminist connection, I also learned that the Bancroft Library had flagged one of Christian's folders as a "Wow" item, including a letter that Alice Walker wrote to Christian on September 14, 1981, in which Walker asked Christian to read the latest draft of her newest novel, *The Color Purple*, before it was to be published.[29] The letter demonstrates how much figures like Walker participated readily in both creative writing and criticism, and how much she treasured Christian's feedback specifically. However, a subsequent letter from Walker on October 21, 1981, reveals that Christian never responded to Walker's original request to read her novel ("I get the feeling from your long silence that sending *The Color Purple* to you was indeed the imposition I feared").[30] Paradoxically, the second letter also ends up being a fitting example of Black feminist criticism and the many imperfect manifestations of foremother love as Walker defers to Christian's busy schedule rather than the other way around. Even though Christian would go on to publish extensive scholarship on *The Color Purple*, this correspondence subverts our expectations for a tidy expression of solidarity among Black feminists in lieu of more realistic accounts of the various textural vacillations of engagement and absence across the tradition's history.[31] While this is only one small window into this story, reflective of my research up until today—and I'm sure the other side of Christian's correspondence in Walker's papers may hold more clues as to what exactly happened—I appreciate what this unfinished exchange says about the history of Black feminist criticism and the ongoing need to read intricately around its rather "Wow" moments.

Returning to the archive to remember Christian was both beautiful and challenging. It had been years since I had sat intently in special collections trying to be receptive to what the archive might be trying to say, the ways it often corrects or skews the public record, sometimes in ways I do not realize until months or years later. Despite the pandemic and other crises of the past few years, what I largely felt among Christian's papers was gratitude and validation. So much of what I encountered in her papers confirmed something I had long wondered or sometimes supplied a piece of a puzzle that had been long missing. More than anything, I felt strongly that the Black feminist critical tradition was still alive and well and that

Christian and others had not worked in vain. Even though I did not have a chance to be Christian's student, I recognized the ways in which she shaped the University of California campuses I attended—including by supporting affirmative action despite the 1996 University of California ban, contributing to the institutionalization of Black studies, and training doctoral students who would end up being my professors—thereby making the public university more habitable for me than it would have been otherwise. As I reflected on my own position nearing the completion of *Foremother Love*, I agreed with Christian's expression on February 21, 1994, as she reflected on all the labor she had completed so far on the *Norton Anthology of African American Literature*: "I'll be glad when this project is over and I do feel I've done more than my share."[32] Indeed, I was grateful that it was Christian's foundational work that made my research on Phillis possible, and grateful to realize that my book on Phillis could be written in close collaboration with her spirit. I like to imagine that Phillis, Jordan, Christian, and I are part of a large tapestry of (Black) feminist critics speaking truth to the university and other institutions forged from slavery, with an entire row of untied threads at the end eagerly awaiting the warp and weft of whoever is next. We're ready.[33]

I am grateful to all who came before and to all who supported me on my journey to *Foremother Love*.

For their considerable and kindhearted mentorship at multiple key junctures along my career path and the parallel writing of this book, I thank Virginia Jackson, Arlene Keizer, and Fred Moten.

For helping me sow the book's beginnings, I thank the members of various academic departments at UC Berkeley and UC Irvine; the University of Michigan–Ann Arbor; and UC Riverside. I am grateful to Laura O'Connor, Julia Lupton, Tiffany Willoughby-Herard, Martin Harries, David Lloyd, Yopie Prins, Gillian White, Sandra Gunning, Michael Awkward, Aida Levy-Hussen, A. Van Jordan, Xiomara Santamarina, Adela Pinch, Angela Dillard, Madhumita Lahiri, Aliyah Khan, Scotti Parish, Andrea Zemgulys, David Porter, Geoffrey G. O'Brien, Donna V. Jones, and Jessica Fisher. I thank the undergraduate students in my Fall 2020 course at Michigan, Black Women Heroines: A Legacy Continues, who formed a collective and asked questions that I hope have grown into answers in these pages. Lastly, I thank all department and campus staff.

For their support of the humanities at Caltech, I would like to thank Black@Caltech, the Caltech Center for Inclusion and Diversity, and members of administrative, facilities, and other campus staff.

I am grateful for the fellowship year I received at the Stanford Humanities Center and thank Roland Greene, Kelda Jamison, and the 2024–25 fellows, especially La Marr Jurelle Bruce, as well as all center staff.

I thank Duke University Press, especially Senior Editor Elizabeth Ault and Assistant Editor Benjamin Kossak, and Black Feminism on the Edge series editors Jennifer C. Nash and Samantha Pinto, for their invaluable input and support of this book throughout the entire process and for making space for ongoing Black feminist scholarship. I also thank the two anonymous readers and the production team.

I appreciate the librarians and staff who lent their archival expertise to this project, especially their support with interlibrary loan and document delivery. In addition to the universities mentioned above, I thank staff at the Charles E. Young Research Library at UCLA; the John Hay Library at Brown University; the Margaret Walker Alexander National Research Center at Jackson State University; the Massachusetts Historical Society; Special Collections and Archives at UC San Diego; Spelman Archives at Spelman College; and the Stuart A. Rose Manuscript, Archives, and Rare Book Library at Emory University.

I thank, for their financial support, the Stanford Humanities Center; the Division of the Humanities and Social Sciences at Caltech; the Department of English Language and Literature and the LSA Collegiate Fellows program at the University of Michigan–Ann Arbor; the Department of English at UC Riverside; the John Hope Franklin Dissertation Fellowship from the American Philosophical Society; the WW Dissertation Fellowship in Women's Studies from the Institute for Citizens and Scholars; the Graduate Dean's Dissertation Fellowship at UC Irvine; and the University of California, including the UC Consortium for Black Studies.

An earlier version of part of chapter 2 appeared in *African American Review* 53, no. 4 (Winter 2020): 299–313.

My gratitude goes out to my family, friends, and othermothers for their care and friendship over the years, especially Natividad ("Nativa") Martinez, Gertrude Clue, Nofoao Leau-Wilson, Esther Gonzalez, Andrea Mills, Patricia New, Juanita Lewis, Karla Greenlee, Gwenda Pollard, Elizabeth Ayala, Cynthia Estrada, Pamela J. Bjorkman, Ruth Medina, Ariadna Mesa, and Anna-Mary Lopez.

My thanks go to longtime and newer colleague-friends navigating their early academic careers alongside mine: Jeania Ree Moore, Winnie Wong, Camille Cannon, Jennifer Geraci, Suzanne Manizza Roszak, Morgan Slade, SJ Zhang, Kaneesha Parsard, Sophia Azeb, Tina Post, Melissa Phruksachart, SaraEllen Strongman, Andrea Bolivar, Angela X. Ocampo, Ania Aizman, Niloofar Sarlati, and Samantha Adams.

I have been able to become the Black feminist critic I am today because of my younger sister, Kara Murphy, and her ongoing creative spirit, and because of my father, Timothy Murphy, and his longtime work in the garden.

Andrew Hill read and supported this book, which became a lived counterpart to our sunny coastal/inland Southern/Northern California

The author, her younger sister, and their mother in her office in the Norman W. Church Laboratory for Chemical Biology at Caltech, July 6, 1999. Author's personal collection.

days, and made it possible, through various forms of care, for me to joyfully do this work.

This book also could not have been written without my mother, Marta Gonzalez Murphy, and her efforts as a (fore)mother and colleague-friend to me, family members, friends, and more. This book begins and ends with you, Mama.

Preface

1 Bambara, *The Black Woman*, 1, 6, 7.
2 I use Phillis's first name to invoke a different kind of familiarity than that of her enslavers, the Wheatley family, as I explain in more detail in my introduction in the section titled "From Foremother to Black Feminist Critic."
3 Bambara in Tate, *Black Women Writers at Work*, 32, 34, 33. (Tate completed *Black Women Writers at Work* in 1983 and published it in 1985; see publisher's note at beginning of 2023 edition, vi.) While Bambara was writing *The Salt Eaters*, she was working a great deal—and, of course, doing the labor required to simply maintain academic employment, such as her lengthy negotiations for a visiting position at Spelman College to teach their first course on Black women writers, as Holmes noted across "Making Dreams Work."
4 Tate, *Black Women Writers at Work*, 13.
5 See Phillis, *Poems on Various Subjects*, iv.
6 Mason, *Poems of Phillis Wheatley* (1989 ed.), 45n2. Mason also writes that Phillis "had been publishing poems for some years and had tried to publish a book of her poems in Boston in 1772 (see her 1772 Proposals)." This is a bit different from what Mason wrote over two decades earlier below the same preface in Mason, *Poems of Phillis Wheatley* (1966 ed.): "It is probably true that she did not originally write with publication in mind, and her friends probably did suggest publication to her and even attempt it without her permission" (n.p.; n. 2, a couple of pages before p. 1). The preface precedes John Wheatley's authenticating letter to the publisher in the second and third 1773 editions of *Poems* published in London, as noted in Robinson, *Phillis Wheatley*, 83.
7 See Phillis, *Poems on Various Subjects*, iv.
8 B. Smith, "Toward a Black Feminist Criticism," 20.
9 Griffin, "Conflict and Chorus," 118, and *In Search of a Beautiful Freedom*, 245 (Griffin's 2023 collection of new and selected essays). While there was a concentrated theorization of Black womanhood across Bambara's 1970 *The Black Woman*, it was a theorization that was not yet calling itself "Black feminist." That term would be used with more frequency in 1973 to refer to

organizations such as the National Black Feminist Organization (1973–75), the National Alliance of Black Feminists (1976–80), and the Combahee River Collective (1975–80) (see Springer, *Living for the Revolution*, 1). Barbara Smith was a founding member of the Combahee River Collective and published the essay "Toward a Black Feminist Criticism" in 1977.

10   B. Smith, "Toward a Black Feminist Criticism," 20. Smith here cites Alice Walker's 1974 essay "In Search of Our Mothers' Gardens," collected in the 1983 volume of the same name, as a key example of this historical arc underlying Black women's creativity.

11   Lorde, "Age, Race, Class, and Sex," in *Sister Outsider*, 116.

12   David Waldstreicher writes that "there are no fewer than four possible concrete scenarios for how Phillis Wheatley became free by the autumn of 1773, three of which are supported by her few words on the subject" (*Odyssey*, 215). Each was dependent on the London publication of her book, if not due to public opinion than due to sales. "Now she held a copyright, a property. That changed something, if not everything" (*Odyssey*, 220).

13   Griffin, "Conflict and Chorus," 126, and *In Search of a Beautiful Freedom*, 255.

14   Holmes, "Lessons in Boldness, 101," 154. Beyond academia, Bambara often participated in other cultural institutions that she believed in and that were receptive to her organizing for Black people, people of color, and other marginalized groups.

15   "Baby-Baby-Baby" is the twelfth track on TLC's *Ooooooohhh . . . On the TLC Tip* (LaFace, 1992, CD).

16   While there are many scholarly definitions of this term, what a colleague-friend once described to me as "an ethos of white patriarchy," I will provide one brief anecdotal example here: In the wake of 9/11, a national movement away from multiculturalism toward exclusion is perhaps embodied in the fact that I lost my sixth-grade run for school president to a young man whose surname was Bush and who ran under the slogan "Two Bushes Are Better than One."

17   R&B singer Tinashe is one of the few fellow Black women students who attended my public middle and high schools in La Crescenta (out of over two thousand students) at the same time as my sister and me. Tinashe's music video to "Bouncin,'" from the album *333* (Tinashe Music, 2021), especially the joyful choreography on the mini trampolines, reads to me as a healing reclamation.

18   Black feminist criticism was memorialized in two 2007 retrospectives: Farah Jasmine Griffin's "That the Mothers May Soar" and Arlene R. Keizer's "Black Feminist Criticism."

19   I later learned that James was born in Los Angeles proper, which deepened my sense of imagined kinship with her. The combination of vast numbers of books and ever-playing music, mostly from the radio, led my father to dub my room "the Jazz Library."

20   James and Ritz, *Rage to Survive*. First published in 1995, Etta James's autobiography certainly reads today as a work of Black feminist criticism.

21   Randall, *The Black Poets*, 38. There is no mention of Phillis's biography in this anthology, and I would later learn that the single poem of hers anthologized is quite abridged. Dudley Randall (1914–2000), who named his first daughter Phyllis, was also a poet and an instrumental editor of Black poetry via his Detroit publishing house, Broadside Press, founded in 1965 (see Boyd, *Wrestling with the Muse*, 51, 2).

22   James and Ritz, *Rage to Survive*, 264. Even today, when I listen to Etta James's "cover" of Etta Jones's 1960 "Don't Go to Strangers," its opening notes transport me. And as the song closes, I *believe* James when she belts out the final lines of the song in a way that Jones's version reminds me, rather, of a much younger version of myself.

23   This is in the vein of Erika de Casier's song "Story of My Life" from *Essentials* (Independent Jeep Records, 2019), her debut album.

Introduction

1   I did at some point purchase a reader for the Spring 2010 course, which I've fondly perused over the years.

2   June Jordan, "African American Studies 158A Tuesday Class," February 13, 2001, Jordan Collection, UC Berkeley, https://archive.org/details/cabeuaas _000213, 16:30–31.

3   Muller and the Blueprint Collective, *June Jordan's Poetry for the People*, 13.

4   In the winter of 2015, I took a graduate seminar titled Contemporary Experimental Poetry with Fred Moten at the University of California, Riverside, where he asked us this question.

5   The next section of this chapter provides more information on my decision to use this name. Recent biographies of Phillis by historians and literary scholars include the 2023 editions of Vincent Carretta's *Biography* and David Waldstreicher's *Odyssey*. Throughout this book I cite alternatively from both for moments of literary-historical consonance. Carretta cautions that while Waldstreicher's biography is "worthy of its subject," it also includes several examples of apocrypha, "slipping seamlessly from supposition to assertion"; see Carretta's review of Waldstreicher, *The Odyssey of Phillis Wheatley*, 158, 156.

6   Bynum, "Phillis Wheatley on Friendship," 42, and *Reading Pleasures*, 50.

7   To which would be added the sudden trauma then slow burn of the COVID pandemic (2019–) and other harrowing events since 2017—part of a long cascade of crises characteristic of life for millennial and zillennial scholars.

8   June Jordan, "The Difficult Miracle," in *Some of Us*, 175, 178.

9   Boyd, *Discarded Legacy*, 26. Boyd's description of her approach to reading
     Frances E. W. Harper's work as "a voice-over," a creative and critical mode of
     intertextual or intersonic conversation, is a praxis I hope to extend herein.

10   As described in my preface above, Black feminist criticism arises in special
     relation to "a consistent feminist analysis" about "Black women writers and
     Black lesbian writers" (B. Smith, "Toward a Black Feminist Criticism," 20). It
     is part of, though not to be confused with, Patricia Hill Collins's pivotal term
     Black feminist thought, which often encapsulates Black feminist criticism to
     describe a wider "critical social theory" about "heterogeneous Black feminist
     intellectual traditions" (*Black Feminist Thought*, 20). Note this is a revision of
     what Collins wrote in her first 1990 edition, in that there was "*a* distinctive
     Black feminist intellectual tradition." See Collins, *Black Feminist Thought:
     Knowledge, Consciousness, and the Politics of Empowerment* (Boston: Unwin
     Hyman, 1990), 16. Ultimately, my understanding of Black feminist criticism
     is akin to Marina Magloire's description of "Black feminism [as] a kind of
     poetry that must constantly conjure a relationality said to be innate but
     which actually requires active pursuit" (*We Pursue Our Magic*, 4).

11   June Jordan, *Some of Us*, 179.

12   McKay, "Naming the Problem," 367–68.

13   Griffin names Hazel Carby, Barbara Christian, Beverly Guy-Sheftall, bell
     hooks, Nellie Y. McKay, Valerie Smith, Hortense Spillers, Eleanor Tray-
     lor, Gloria Wade-Gayles, Cheryl Wall, Sherley Anne Williams, and more
     throughout the essay as "a few of the architects of black feminist criticism,"
     noting that Guy-Sheftall, Traylor, and Wade-Gayles, worked in "histor-
     ically black institutions," and the others at "elite white institutions in
     unprecedented (though still small) numbers" ("That the Mothers May
     Soar," 491, and *In Search of a Beautiful Freedom*, 268). Keizer also engages in
     retrospection of several of these critics, adding Carole Boyce Davies, Fran-
     ces Smith Foster, Mae Gwendolyn Henderson, Audre Lorde, Mary Helen
     Washington, and others, in "Black Feminist Criticism," 158.

14   Keizer, "Black Feminist Criticism," 155.

15   While I am careful about historical facts, I balance what cannot be known
     with plausible speculation about historical gaps using a Black feminist critical
     context. Also, while my archival work draws on academic archives of critics
     and writers who often worked at universities, I am aware of the intertwined
     histories of colonialism and chattel slavery and ongoing exclusive dynamics
     of these spaces, too, as detailed in Hartman, *Lose Your Mother*, and "Venus in
     Two Acts." My book also traverses my very uneven institutional experiences as
     a researcher from graduate student through tenure-track assistant professor.

16   Chapter 1, "Obour Outsider," details Phillis's relationship with Obour, a
     Black woman who was enslaved by the Tanner family in Newport, Rhode
     Island, and who safeguarded and later bequeathed at least seven letters
     from her and Phillis's correspondence.

17   This includes poems like Robert Hayden's "A Letter from Phillis Wheatley, 1773," in *Collected Poems*; Nikki Giovanni's "Linkage," in *The Collected Poetry of Nikki Giovanni*, 313–15; Evie Shockley's "wheatley and hemmings have drinks in the halls of the ancestors," in *a half-red sea*, 25–26; drea brown's *dear girl: a reckoning*; Allison Clarke's *Phillis*; Honorée Fanonne Jeffers's *The Age of Phillis*, a work of poetry and poetics; the poems collected in Danielle Legros Georges and Artress Bethany White's *Wheatley at 250*; and more. See also those cited in Waldstreicher, *Odyssey*, 454–55.

18   For the use of the word *progenitor* see Gates, "In Her Own Write," x. Rowan Ricardo Phillips describes Phillis as an "epigraph" and "an *ab ovo* figure" in *When Blackness Rhymes with Blackness*, 13, 17.

19   This term, coined by Evelyn Brooks Higginbotham, has remained alive in the critical conversation since *Righteous Discontent*. See Jenkins, *Private Lives, Proper Relations*; Morris, *Close Kin and Distant Relatives*; Cooper, *Beyond Respectability*; and C. L. Smith, *Race and Respectability in an Early Black Atlantic*.

20   Christian, "The Race for Theory," 62.

21   Grounding texts for this intention across this book include those by the Combahee River Collective, "Statement"; B. Smith, *Home Girls*; Lorde, *Sister Outsider*; Crenshaw, "Mapping the Margins"; Collins, *Black Feminist Thought*; Quashie, *Black Women, Identity, and Cultural Theory*; Muñoz, *Cruising Utopia*; Mock, *Redefining Realness*; Ellis, *Territories of the Soul*; Ahmed, *Living a Feminist Life*; Taylor, *How We Get Free*; Nash, *Black Feminism Reimagined*; and more.

22   I cite and take inspiration from Janet Mock's definition of *mahu*, or *mahuwahine*, the Indigenous word reclaimed by Hawaiian trans women, in *Redefining Realness*, 102–3.

23   See especially O'Neale, "A Slave's Subtle War," and "Challenge to Wheatley's Critics"; Foster, *Written by Herself* (see also Foster's 2008 introduction to *Love and Marriage*); and Bassard, *Spiritual Interrogations*.

24   Hull, *Color, Sex, and Poetry*; Shockley, *Renegade Poetics*.

25   Howe, *My Emily Dickinson*; Lootens, *Lost Saints*; Prins, *Victorian Sappho*; Jackson, *Dickinson's Misery*; and G. White, *Lyric Shame*.

26   Gumbs, *Spill, M Archive*, and *Dub*; Williamson, *Scandalize My Name*; Nash, *Black Feminism Reimagined*; Sullivan, *The Poetics of Difference*; Tinsley, *The Color Pynk*; and Thorsson, *The Sisterhood*. Joshua Myers's *Of Black Study* has chapters especially relevant to Black feminisms on June Jordan, Sylvia Wynter, and Toni Cade Bambara. After my book entered production, I was also happy to read Gumbs, *Survival Is a Promise*; Nash, *How We Write Now*; and Savonick, *Open Admissions*.

27   For a recent (2022) special issue of *Early American Literature* on Phillis, see Bynum, Fielder, and Smith, "Special Issue Introduction." Other recent scholarship includes Ford, "The Difficult Miracle"; Pinto, *Infamous Bodies*;

Jackson, *Before Modernism*; Bynum, *Reading Pleasures*; and C. L. Smith, *Race and Respectability in an Early Black Atlantic.*

28 McKay and Benjamin, "Breaking the Whole Thing Open," 1680.

29 Christian, "The Race for Theory," 61.

30 Toward the close of my 2018 dissertation, I thought it best to honor Phillis's later married surname, Peters, but have since thought it more radical to try to imagine a name for her beyond the cisheteropatriarchal institutions of slavery and marriage. Others' recent positions include Honorée Fanonne Jeffers's decision to use the surname Wheatley Peters in alignment with her positive imagination of Phillis's marriage and of the way Phillis signed her name after her marriage to John Peters, in *The Age of Phillis*, 179. Similarly, Zachary McLeod Hutchins justifies the surname Wheatley Peters based on the fact that Phillis "chose to marry" and the fact that scholars regularly use white women writers' married names ("'Add New Glory to Her Name,'" 666). Also, Jennifer Y. Chuong uses the surname Wheatley, critiquing others' attempts to navigate her naming, including "the feminist alternative of referring to women artists by their first names [as] equally problematic" ("Engraving's 'Immoveable Veil,'" 84n2). Finally, Cassander L. Smith takes a measured stance that both Phillis's enslavers and her husband's surnames "stand in for what we cannot know about the conditions of Wheatley's birth and early childhood" (*Race and Respectability in an Early Black Atlantic*, 188–89n1).

31 June Jordan imagines a new full name: "Phillis Miracle Wheatley" ("Miracle" being Jordan's own appellative addition), in "The Difficult Miracle," in *Some of Us*, 176.

32 Alexander, *Pedagogies of Crossing*, 294, 293, 294.

33 Philip, *Zong!*, front cover.

34 Far from any judgment on John Peters (à la the 1834 memoirist Margaretta Matilda Odell's account), I am just less interested in the institution of marriage within the scope of this project.

35 R. R. Phillips, *When Blackness Rhymes with Blackness*, 13.

36 Waldstreicher writes that of the "ninety-six people" who left Africa on *The Phillis*, "between seventy and eighty survived" (*Odyssey*, 19).

37 Jones, "Poetics," 149 (strikethrough in original).

38 It has long been common among the members of my maternal family to refer to ourselves within family settings via shortened versions of our names.

39 Moody et al., "In Memoriam," 7.

40 Cavitch, *American Elegy*, 192.

41 "Phillis, n.," OED *Online*, Oxford University Press, https://www.oed.com /dictionary/phillis_n?tab=factsheet#30766709, accessed March 26, 2023.

42 Odell, *Memoir and Poems*. Information about Odell and her life is detailed by Glatt, "'To Perpetuate Her Name.'"

43   Frazier, "Some Afro-American Women of Mark," esp. 102–5; Hopkins, "Famous Women of the Negro Race"; and Mossell, *The Work of the Afro-American Woman*, 55–56, 68–69.

44   Johnson, "Preface," in *The Book of American Negro Poetry*, xxiv; and S. A. Brown, *Outline for the Study of the Poetry of American Negroes*, 1.

45   Henry Louis Gates Jr.'s *The Trials of Phillis Wheatley* provides a comprehensive history of criticism on Phillis, and by Black masculinist critics specifically on 74–81.

46   For a synopsis of scholars working in Wheatley (Peters) studies, see Sesay, "Remembering Phillis Wheatley." Carretta's revised 2023 version of his 2011 biography uses the name Wheatley Peters in its title.

47   Prins, "'What Is Historical Poetics?,'" 14.

48   While my research has demonstrated that uses of the word *foremother* to describe Phillis increased after the 1990s, I argue that the concept has been operative in criticism on her long before this.

49   For example, in her introduction to the 1990 edited collection *Wild Women in the Whirlwind*, Joanne M. Braxton includes Phillis in her multipart definition of a foremother: a "female ancestor" or a figure "at the foreground of cultural experience" (Braxton and McLaughlin, *Wild Women in the Whirlwind*, xxv). Herein, Phillis is grouped with other early literary figures, distinct from those who practiced "forms of material culture including quilting and furniture making . . . [such as] our mothers and grandmothers . . . 'ordinary women of courage.'"

50   Bynum, Fielder, and Smith, "Special Issue Introduction," 664; and Gates, "In Her Own Write," x.

51   Combahee River Collective, "Combahee River Collective Statement," 16.

52   Christian, *Teaching Guide*, 1.

53   Bynum, Fielder, and Smith, "Special Issue Introduction," 663, abstract. They continue, "There aren't enough poems, extant materials, or quite simply not enough interest in her" (664).

54   Pinto, *Infamous Bodies*, 33.

55   Bynum, Fielder, and Smith, "Special Issue Introduction," 664.

56   All my references to Phillis's writings are from the 2024 *Writings of Phillis Wheatley Peters* edited by Vincent Carretta, unless otherwise noted.

57   I also admire Kerry James Marshall's 2007 acrylic on PVC panel painting, *Scipio Moorhead, Portrait of Himself, 1776*, which portrays Scipio amid the process of painting (gazing directly at viewers), while a sketch of Phillis is poised in the background, seeming to gaze almost directly at viewers: Marshall places viewers in the position of Phillis as she is being painted.

58   This line is from Christian's speech on Black women poets, "Majority Report," December 4, 1982, *Pacifica Radio Archives*, https://archive.org /details/pacifica_radio_archives-AZ0642.12, 2:07–11. This speech was later published as the essay "Afro-American Women Poets" in *Black Feminist*

Criticism, 120. I typically refer to Christian's full name without reference to her middle initial, which she often omitted in her own later publications. Across this book, I largely refer to her by her last name, in alignment with today's convention of subsequently referencing scholars by surname. I also do my best to align with the ways other twentieth- and twenty-first-century scholars most regularly published their names.

59 Christian paraphrases Walker's 1974 essay "In Search of Our Mothers' Gardens," which was later published in a collection of the same name in 1983 (see A. Walker, *Our Mothers' Gardens*, 237). Walker defined *womanism* at the very beginning of this volume (xi–xii). Emphasis original to *Gardens*.

60 In 1978, Christian became the first Black woman to earn tenure at UC Berkeley, see Bowles, Fabi, and Keizer's introduction to *New Black Feminist Criticism*, esp. x.

61 One of Phillis's few appearances in this triple biography is in the brief albeit fascinating detail that Terrell named one of her daughters after Phillis, spelled as Phyllis, in Sterling, *Black Foremothers*, 133.

62 And named as Phyllis, in Christian, "Afro-American Women Poets," in *Black Feminist Criticism*, 120.

63 See Gilmore, *Golden Gulag*, 28.

64 Lorde, *The Cancer Journals*, 14. Across this book, Lorde demonstrates that she considered her cancer to be a direct result of a "carcinogenic" food chain and environment as well as a symptom of the body's broader attempt to survive marginalization like racism and sexism in the United States, in *The Cancer Journals*, 9. Sadly, Phillis's death in her early thirties in 1784 was in line with "the average life expectancy" of all Black people in the United States around that time, as noted in Carretta, *Biography*, 197.

65 Priest, "Salvation Is the Issue"; Gumbs, "We Can Learn," 21; Hong, *Death Beyond Disavowal*, 126; Thorsson, *The Sisterhood*, 200–202.

66 DuCille, "Feminism, Black and Blue," 151, 152.

67 Carretta, *Biography*, 196, 197.

68 DuCille, "Tribute to Barbara T. Christian," xvi.

69 Christian, "Your Silence Will Not Protect You," 1.

70 Murphy, "Praisesong," 299. In terms of "everlasting . . . life," the idealism of this statement is meant to counter the lived reality in which few Black feminists specifically and Black people generally are afforded this kind of mythic status.

71 DuCille, "Tribute to Barbara T. Christian," xvii, xviii.

72 Christian, "Your Silence Will Not Protect You," 1. Alexis De Veaux writes that Lorde described herself as a "black, lesbian, feminist, mother, poet warrior" despite stigma at that time against lesbianism (whereas June Jordan's bisexuality was more accepted) and against possessing other identities in addition to Blackness, in *Warrior Poet*, 179.

73 Christian, "Introduction," in *Black Feminist Criticism*, x, xi.

74   Christian, "The Race for Theory," 58, 59.

75   Lorde, "Uses of the Erotic," in *Sister Outsider*, 57.

76   Smith defines "home girls" as "the girls from the neighborhood and from
      the block, the girls we grew up with" (B. Smith, introduction to *Home Girls*,
      xxiv). Quashie defines the "girlfriend" as "the other Black woman who is a
      subject's girl," e.g., "an othermother, play sister, god sister, cousin, or sister-
      friend . . . who makes it possible for a Black female subject to bring more of
      herself into consideration" (*Black Women, Identity, and Cultural Theory*, 17,
      18). Dove poeticizes "mother love" across her eponymous book of poems
      and in one particular poem, "Mother Love," which combines a dark form of
      love and mourning via the Greek myth of Demeter and Metanira (*Mother
      Love*, 17). Hartman articulates the concept of losing one's mother as a
      metaphor for transatlantic slavery: "To lose your mother was to be denied
      your kin, country, and identity" (*Lose Your Mother*, 85).

77   Christian, "The Race for Theory," 56. Arlene R. Keizer writes that Chris-
      tian's essay resulted in "polarizing controversy" and that Christian herself
      was "pilloried" (*Black Subjects*, 14).

78   Christian, "The Race for Theory," 52.

79   Christian, "The Race for Theory," 53. Christian also emphasizes that it is
      important to "share our process" with others as this is ultimately "a collec-
      tive endeavor."

80   Crenshaw, "Demarginalizing the Intersection," 140.

81   For similar information on formulations of like concepts that have been
      theorized at least since the nineteenth century, see Collins, *Black Feminist
      Thought*, 21; Taylor, *How We Get Free*, 4–5; Nash, *Black Feminism Re-
      imagined*, 6–11, 40–42; and Sullivan, *The Poetics of Difference*, 5–8.

82   Crenshaw, "Demarginalizing the Intersection," 149; and Nash, *Black Femi-
      nism Reimagined*, 9.

83   Gates, "In Her Own Write," xi.

1: Obour Outsider

1   I still have not located this essay. I hope someone reading this will be able to
     locate it—and I look forward to future scholarship on it.

2   My memory tells me that it was not a colorism issue that was at play, but
     more of a general indifference to Black sisterhood generally. It could also
     have been a sign of falling numbers of Black students at the university due
     to the 1996 ban on affirmative action in California after the passing of
     Proposition 209. UC Berkeley has recently come under fire "for having the
     worst campus climate for Black students in the University of California
     system," and a total Black enrollment that hovers around 3 percent of the
     student population, as Teresa Watanabe writes in "UC Berkeley Has a Poor

Reputation Among Black Students," *Los Angeles Times*, July 20, 2020. Since the passage of Prop. 209, effectively banning affirmative action in public university admissions, most prospective Black students from the United States have chosen to attend other universities due to feeling "unwelcome" at UC Berkeley, as J. Douglass Allen-Taylor notes in "Why Black Students Are Avoiding UC Berkeley," *East Bay Express*, November 6, 2013.

3   Citation of all such scholarship would be too vast to include in one note. Some of the most formative examples for this book include Barbara Christian's 1994 essay "Diminishing Returns: Can Black Feminism(s) Survive the Academy?," wherein she discusses her research on her "sister/colleagues"— "how the black woman professor is often called upon to serve as mentor, mother, and counselor in addition to educator to African American students who experience the academy as a hostile and alien place and that she is often expected to serve on committees to make certain the minority and woman perspective are represented" (Bowles, Fabi, and Keizer, *New Black Feminist Criticism*, 212). Nellie McKay writes of the extracurricular "networks" Black professors must develop to meet "the need for mentors and supportive colleagues" at the postdoctoral and early-career stage, noting how "everyone was sad when some colleagues failed to achieve tenure in their institutions," suggesting a systematic lack of home-institution support, in "Naming the Problem" (361, 362). More recently, Sara Ahmed relays the importance of understanding that feminist professors, especially feminist professors of color, do "diversity work, whether or not we think of ourselves as doing this work," in *Living a Feminist Life* (91); and Lorgia García Peña also notes the several kinds of service labor expected of women of color professors that is subsequently not rewarded at the tenure or renewal stage (*Community as Rebellion*, 29).

4   Hartman, *Lose Your Mother*, 15. Notably, Hartman was awarded "early tenure" at UC Berkeley "on the strength of her draft of 'Scenes of Subjection'" and later recalled the "freedom" that came from such a decision (from the place of "low expectations" of the department chair telling her "there was no need to finish the book"), which allowed her to finish her book, as Alexis Okeowo notes in "How Saidiya Hartman Retells the History of Black Life."

5   Hartman, *Lose Your Mother*, 16, 17. This practice of theorizing not just the archive but the shape it takes in relation to oneself is articulated across Hartman's *Lose Your Mother* and via her later concept of "critical fabulation," wherein if "'fabula' denotes the basic elements of story," then to engage fabulation critically means to call attention to the conditions of its creation, elements, and sense of historical coherence and order ("Venus in Two Acts," 11).

6   Christian and Jordan have stood out in my mind as two of several possible models. Christian's professorial life, and turn from the British literature that was the focus of her graduate program's training toward African American

literature as her specialization, stemmed largely from her experiences with students in the City College of New York SEEK (Search for Education, Elevation, and Knowledge) program: "At SEEK, I was fast discovering African-American writing (in response to which my students suddenly exhibited the writing capacity they were not supposed to have)" (Bowles, Fabi, and Keizer, *New Black Feminist Criticism*, 120). Similarly, June Jordan often taught her students to love their own vernacular speech, to recognize it as worthy of academic attention, and thus to love themselves, across "Nobody Mean More to Me Than You and the Future Life of Willie Jordan," in *Some of Us*.

7 Carretta writes that Obour "was probably born around 1750" and passed away on June 21, 1835, according to record books in the First Congregational Church, Newport, Rhode Island, in *Biography*, 45. See also 217–18n46. Bynum writes that Obour's name was likely spelled "Orbour," with an additional *r*, as is evidenced in a later extant writing by her, in *Reading Pleasures*, 124–25. I use "Obour," for now, for consistencies sake with how Phillis referred to her.

8 Likely shortly before Obour passed away in 1835. See "November Meeting," 268 note †. All references to the historical record surrounding Obour's bequest refer to pages 267–79 of the November 1863 Massachusetts Historical Society (MHS) meeting proceedings. While Phillis is discussed in the main text and seven of her letters to Obour are reprinted therein, discussion of Obour mainly occurs in footnotes. As discussed later in this chapter, an eighth Phillis-Obour letter was discovered in 2005, which Edes Beecher gave to Amasa Walker a couple of years prior to 1863, "about 1860" (Moonan, "Slave Poet's 1776 Letter"). This February 14, 1776, letter from Phillis is included in Carretta's 2024 edition of her writings (p. 131) and is held in a private manuscript collection. After consulting several libraries, I still have not found an original copy of Edes Beecher's letter at the time of this writing.

9 Both Obour and Phillis were what has been termed "saltwater" enslaved women. They were born on the African continent, miraculously survived their captivity, their passage to colonial North America, subsequent sale, and continued enslavement into their adult years. One must keep in mind that this status was coterminous with, as Stephanie E. Smallwood notes, "an unforgiving journey into the Atlantic market that never drew to full closure" (*Saltwater Slavery*, 8). Albert J. Raboteau also noted that for most saltwater enslaved people, "the internal slave trade made social cohesion an impossibility" (*Slave Religion*, 54).

10 Phillis's letters were the main source when I originally drafted this chapter around 2018, but, as I discuss later in this chapter, Bynum's 2023 chapter "Coda; or, Reading Pleasures: Looking for Arbour/Obour/Orbour" details Bynum's discovery of additional archival evidence of Obour's life (*Reading Pleasures*, 123–33).

11   Carretta writes that "Obour initiated their correspondence in late 1771 or early 1772" (*Biography*, 45). This is plausible given that Obour would have likely kept an originative letter from Phillis and passed it on (if her inheritors maintained her full collection). Phillis's first extant letter in response to Obour reads like it was her first: She addresses her as Arbour.

12   Bynum writes that Phillis's "position as 'first' is irrelevant when her writing is placed within the many communities that she wrote for, communities that included enslaved, Christian, Methodist, English, or free African populations" ("Phillis Wheatley's Pleasures"). And that she is "part of many, interconnected stories" (*Reading Pleasures*, 15).

13   As aforementioned, all my references to Phillis's writings are from the 2024 *Writings of Phillis Wheatley Peters* edited by Vincent Carretta, unless otherwise noted. Excerpts from five letters from Phillis to Obour: on May 19, 1772, 32; October 30, 1773, 111; March 21, 1774, 121; May 29, 1778, 135; and May 10, 1779, 137.

14   Carretta, *Biography*, 45. Carretta notes that we do not know if Obour and Phillis "ever met" and "there is no evidence" in clear support of the "possibility" they arrived on the same ship.

15   Phillis to Obour, May 19, 1772, 32.

16   See Carretta, *Biography*, 197. Noting that Phillis's husband John Peters advertised for the return of Phillis's manuscript from whoever borrowed it so it could be published, Carretta writes that this figure was "Elizabeth Walcutt's daughter." In Carretta's 2011 edition of *Biography* he writes that the manuscript was not recovered but that Peters "surely would have published it had he acquired it" (190). In 2023, Carretta writes, "Peters later recovered the manuscript" (197), but he could not gather enough subscribers for publication and the manuscript was not in his "effects recorded after his death in 1801" (198). Margaretta Matilda Odell notes in 1834, "Previous to Phillis's departure for Wilmington, she entrusted her papers to a daughter of the lady who received her on her return from that place. After her death, these papers were demanded by Peters, as the property of his deceased wife, and were, of course, yielded to his importunity. Some years after, he went to the South, and we have not been able to ascertain what eventually became of the manuscripts" (*Memoir*, 29).

17   Bassard, *Spiritual Interrogations*, 25. Bassard also relies on the language of intimacy and friendship ("Obour Tanner, her confidante") to describe the letters, even though they are often "'favd by' someone, and 'in care of,' which marks the problematics of ownership for black women slaves, a qualification that framed even their most intimate attempts to communicate with each other." Bassard also writes, "the sense of surveillance that collapses the distinction between public and private confers on this correspondence the possibility of an audience larger than the letters' original addressee."

18 Bassard, *Spiritual Interrogations*, 25.

19 Bynum, "Phillis Wheatley on Friendship," 43; and *Reading Pleasures*, 25, 43.

20 Phillis to Obour, May 10, 1779, 137.

21 At the time this letter was written, the "hindrances" included, as Carretta writes, arranging for the publication of her "second volume" of poems (*Biography*, 183).

22 Phillis to Obour, May 10, 1779, 137.

23 Carretta specifies that "Obour was baptized and admitted in the First Congregational Church in Newport on 10 July 1768" (*Biography*, 45).

24 Phillis to Obour, May 19, 1772, 32.

25 Phillis to Obour, October 30, 1773, 112; Phillis to Obour, March 21, 1774, 121; and May 6, 1774, 123.

26 Bynum, "Phillis Wheatley on Friendship," 44; see also *Reading Pleasures*, 45. Waldstreicher also reads this as sincerity, as "with Obour she emphasizes Christ much more than she does even in her poems about religion" (*Odyssey*, 113).

27 Bassard, *Spiritual Interrogations*, 23. Bassard notes that Obour's articulation (and Phillis's rearticulation) of "the saving change" is a synonym for Christian conversion as well as "the promise of a radical change in subjectivity"; "if one could move from 'sinner to saint,' she/he could also move 'from slave to free,' 'from bondage to freedom.'" As Bassard also writes earlier, Black women participated in religion "for the purpose of both self-empowerment and communal political engagement" (4).

28 Phillis's October 18, 1773, letter to Colonel David Worcester (Wooster) solicits his help finding subscribers and says she would receive "half the Sale" proceeds from her 1773 *Poems*: "This I am the more Solicitous for, as I am now upon my own footing and whatever I get by this is entirely mine, & it is the Chief I have to depend upon" (110).

29 Brooks, "Our Phillis, Ourselves," 15, 8.

30 Carretta writes that "Phillis was baptized in 1771," in Boston's "Old South church" (*Biography*, 44). It seems plausible, therefore, that the "saving change" she expresses hope to Obour in her May 19, 1772, letter to one day experience could be something beyond Christian conversion (32).

31 Phillis wanted to achieve economic independence via her writing alone, but in 1778 she married free Black man John Peters, out of likely a "desire for some degree of social and economic security," as noted in Carretta, *Biography*, 177. Phillis's manumission in 1773 coincided with the increasing instability of the War of Independence in 1775 with Boston at its epicenter. Carretta writes that "Phillis and John Peters were victims of the severe depression throughout the former colonies that followed the end of the Revolutionary War" (193). Just before these pages, Carretta offers new details on Phillis and John's life, which was not present in his 2011 edition of the biography. See also Dayton, "Lost Years Recovered." While Phillis's

plans did not coalesce, I read her own intentions as a blueprint for what could have been possible.

32   See Griffin, "Albert Raboteau: An Appreciation," in *In Search of a Beautiful Freedom*.

33   Raboteau, *Slave Religion*, 48.

34   Raboteau, *Slave Religion*, 43. While Raboteau does not note this, my own research confirms that Adeline's narrative derives from the oral history transcripts from former enslaved people conducted by the Federal Writers' Project between 1936 and 1938 and this quotation in Adeline and Peel, *Federal Writers' Project*, 12. Adeline's narrative ends with a note on her current life at age eighty-nine, ostensibly written by her amanuensis: "Aunt Adeline talks 'white folks language,' as they say, and seldom associates with the colored people of the town" (Adeline and Peel, *Federal Writers' Project*, 16). I wonder if Raboteau indeed cherry-picked here or if it is possible that the source of the transcript, as he consulted it around 1978, was itself abridged or incomplete.

35   Quoted in Raboteau, *Slave Religion*, 44 (close to the original "On Being Brought").

36   Quoted in Raboteau, *Slave Religion*, 43 (ellipsis in original).

37   Phillis to Obour, May 19, 1772, 32.

38   Phillis, "On Being Brought," 56, line 1.

39   S. A. Williams, "Returning to the Blues," 819.

40   Again, see Adeline and Peel, *Federal Writers' Project*.

41   Raboteau, *Slave Religion*, 47, 48. In other words, Raboteau relies on very explicit traces of Black diasporic religious influence and privileges religions such as "*candomblé, vaudou, santeria,* and *shango,*" even though these religions, too, took from multiracial and multiethnic sources (47). Raboteau risks exoticizing these examples of Black diasporic religion as opposed to "black religion in the United States," not accounting for the difference in circumstances and histories that led to their more easy recognizability as African-influenced (47).

42   Griffin, "Albert Raboteau: An Appreciation," in *In Search of a Beautiful Freedom*, 100.

43   Truth, *Narrative*, 12, 41.

44   Similarly, it is not a coincidence that, early in her career, Truth believed her prayers were responsible for the death of her son's enslaver, in Truth, *Narrative*, 39. Truth's close involvement in writing her *Narrative*, which she dictated to a white woman named Olive Gilbert who served as Truth's amanuensis, has since been corroborated by Nell Irvin Painter's research. See Painter's 1998 edition of Truth's *Narrative*, xvi–xx, and her 1996 biography *Sojourner Truth*, especially 103–12.

45   Bynum, "Phillis Wheatley on Friendship," 44. Bynum writes here that "with every greeting [to Obour], Wheatley accesses and writes of a 'pleasure

deep down,'" citing not Phillis but the scene in Toni Morrison's 1987 novel *Beloved* in which Denver recalls Grandma Baby's ("Baby Suggs") advice: "I should always listen to my body and love it" (Morrison, *Beloved*, 247). In this passage, Morrison not only validates Baby Suggs's sexuality despite her enslavement, but she passes this down as knowledge for her granddaughter Denver. See also Bynum, *Reading Pleasures*, 43–44.

46 Bynum, "Phillis Wheatley on Friendship," 42, 43; see also 44. Lorde's writings, including her essay "Uses of the Erotic," were decidedly not situated in a Euro-Christian context. Obour and Phillis would seem to be more legible within works like D. S. Williams's *Sisters in the Wilderness*. As Williams writes, "Womanist theology attempts to help black women see, affirm, and have confidence in the importance of their experience and faith for determining the character of the Christian religion in the African-American community" (xiv). However, that Williams is only able to discuss "sexual pleasure" in relation to rape by white men enslavers (166) explains Bynum's turn instead to Lorde to theorize what is impossible to say about enslaved women's sexuality (in and beyond sex) in a strictly Christian context.

47 Bynum, "Phillis Wheatley on Friendship," 44, and *Reading Pleasures*, 44.

48 Lorde, *Sister Outsider*, 53.

49 Lorde, *Sister Outsider*, 54. Sharon Patricia Holland writes that Lorde's essay originated in a paper Lorde gave "at the Fourth Berkshire Conference on the History of Women at Mount Holyoke" in 1978, where she tasked herself with validating the importance of women's sexuality in response to growing conflations of expressions of women's sexuality with pornography. Beyond this terrain, Holland also writes that "the erotic is under constant revision and reimagining" (Holland, "The Erotic," 84, 85).

50 Lorde, *Sister Outsider*, 54, 55, 58.

51 Strongman, "'Creating Justice Between Us,'" 42; Lorde, *Sister Outsider*, 57, 56. Strongman derives the quoted portion of her essay title from Adrienne Rich's November 10, 1979, letter to Lorde, which ends, "but I love you, and I care more than you believe about creating justice between us" ("'Creating Justice Between Us,'" 54).

52 Strongman, "'Creating Justice Between Us,'" 48.

53 Lorde, *Sister Outsider*, 57.

54 Lorde, *Sister Outsider*, 54, 56. Embedded in Lorde's definition of the erotic is her articulation of what would become a career-long engagement with "difference," which Lorde defines in her 1978 essay "Scratching the Surface: Some Notes on Barriers to Women and Loving" as "a dynamic human force, one which is enriching rather than threatening to the defined self, when there are shared goals" (*Sister Outsider*, 45).

55 Sullivan, *The Poetics of Difference*, 2.

56 Strongman writes that Lorde, serving as poetry editor from 1976 to 1979 at *Chrysalis*, experienced microaggressions from the other staff that became

the subject of Lorde's "infamous letter to the white feminist theologian Mary Daly" which led to her falling out with Rich, who was Daly's friend, in "'Creating Justice Between Us'" (51).

57 A series of letters between Rich and Lorde are discussed in Strongman, "'Creating Justice Between Us'" (52–55). My own research has led me to an LP recording of Lorde and Rich reading their poetry alongside Joan Larkin and Honor Moore, titled *A Sign / I Was Not Alone* (Out & Out Books, 1977, vinyl), the extant photographs displaying their joy during this shared experience.

58 Lorde, "An Interview," in *Sister Outsider*, 103. Lorde notes that the "interview, held on August 30, 1979 in Montague, Massachusetts, was edited from three hours of tapes we made together" (81, bottom of page).

59 Lorde, *Sister Outsider*, 103.

60 Lorde, *Sister Outsider*, 102, 103. Lorde participated in the Combahee River Collective and their retreats following their break from the National Black Feminist Organization on the grounds that it wanted to be "a broad, maybe electorally focused, not necessarily by any means radical or left, formation" (Taylor, *How We Get Free*, 53; see also 25). Black feminist organizers of the 1970s and '80s would continue to experience rifts and question their ties to each other. Such would chart paths to—not a more homogeneous "Black feminism" but—an increasing theorization of plural "Black feminisms" that do not fear difference. Lorde's difference, among others' coalitional theorizations, offered a way of acknowledging the possibilities difference produces at the outset, rather than as a retroactive corrective, and the importance of pre-informing Black feminist theorizing with this intention.

61 See Glave, "To Hell with the Goddess." Glave cites Alexis De Veaux's biography of Lorde, *Warrior Poet*, as a work that did not shy away from telling these moments.

62 Subsequent pages in this folder list possible course books published in and before 1973, and there is a listing of the course offerings of the Department of Afro-American Studies at Brooklyn College, where Lorde was teaching at the time. Lorde Papers, box 82, folder titled "Readings for Proposed Course—The Black Experience in Poetry. No Date."

63 Lorde to Christian, September 5, 1986, Christian Papers, box 1, folder 32.

64 De Veaux, *Warrior Poet*, 151.

65 Brooks, "Our Phillis, Ourselves," 15.

66 Phillis's letter to Obour, on May 19, 1772, 32, uses "favour." Phillis switches to the term *Epistle* on July 19, 1772 (p. 36), and again on October 30, 1773 (p. 111).

67 Phillis to Obour, October 30, 1773, 112.

68 Carretta, *Biography*, 85. See also Waldstreicher, *Odyssey*, 139.

69 Phillis to Obour, October 30, 1773, 111.

70 "November Meeting," 268.

71 "November Meeting," 268, 269.

72 Bynum, "Phillis Wheatley on Friendship," 47. Bynum uses this term. *Bestie* is a colloquial contemporary term for "best friend." According to the online *Oxford English Dictionary*, the term is original to Britain, with an earliest use in 1991 cited to a description in *The Observer* of the late Princess Diana's friendships "from the days BC (Before Charles)," accessed October 28, 2022.

73 Phillis to Obour, March 21, 1774, 120.

74 Phillis to Obour, March 21, 1774, 120; and P. Gabrielle Foreman et al., "Writing about Slavery/Teaching About Slavery: This Might Help," www.naacpculpeper.org/resources/writing-about-slavery-this-might-help/, accessed September 28, 2021.

75 Carretta, *Biography*, 146.

76 Phillis to Obour, March 21, 1774, 120–21. Phillis writes at the close of this letter, "I shall send the 5 Books you wrote for, the first convenient Opportunity. if you want more, they Shall be ready for you."

77 Jackson, *Dickinson's Misery*, 1. Virginia Jackson served as my faculty mentor and dissertation committee chair, championing this very project in its early stages at UC Irvine, in the mid- to late 2010s.

78 Jackson, *Dickinson's Misery*, 8. Jackson writes that these reading practices develop in relation to a specific idea of poetry, "the idea of the lyric," which "was itself produced by a critical culture that imagined itself on the definitive margins of culture." Across the book, Jackson charts Dickinson's legacy largely in terms of a historical twentieth-century form of Anglo-American literary criticism called New Criticism, instead defining feminist criticism on Dickinson as centered on "the problem of metaphorical gender in the lines" (4). I would argue, rather, that feminist criticism is more than just about gender; it is about feminist critics and the work they do in all the ways that may be possible.

79 Following this opening passage, Jackson's argument pivots and thereby progresses across her book that this "exercise in supposing" provides "some indication of what now, more than a century after the scene in which you have just been asked to place yourself, can and cannot be imagined about reading Emily Dickinson" (*Dickinson's Misery*, 1). While this is necessary work, I would also like to linger in the practice of supposition that Jackson stages as the open-hearted invitation to her book on the history of Dickinson criticism, and poetics broadly. While the history of Dickinson's criticism depends on the fact of her corporeal death, as this staging of feminist critical recovery demonstrates, that same loss nevertheless begets an enlivened paper trail. Obour and Phillis's criticism, however, lacks the basis of a substantive paper archive on which to restage critical imagination, making access to even supposition even more desired.

80 Jackson does note that "Dickinson's sister did burn many of her extant papers though there is nothing in the will directing her to do so" (*Dickinson's Misery*, 241n1).

81 Stowe, *Saints, Sinners and Beechers*, 140.

82 "November Meeting," 267–68 note †.

83 "November Meeting," 268–69 note † (ellipsis in original).

84 "November Meeting," 267, 268, 269 note †. Also, Carretta notes that "Rev. Samuel Hopkins (1721–1803) married Obour Tanner to Barra (also spelled Barry) Collins in the First Congregational Church in Newport on 4 November 1790" (*Biography*, 45).

85 Stetson, "Studying Slavery," 82–84. Stetson's 1982 essay recounts the difficulty of teaching not from the enslaver's point of view but from the experiences of enslaved women, and the difficulty of finding historical texts that may express an unmitigated enslaved women's voice (61). Stetson concludes that Black women's narratives of enslavement transpose various genres, a strategy that enables them to speak on various levels. The blurring of genre distinctions also renders the impossibility of reading either "the authentic voice of the Black slave woman" or "the adopted masks of white women" as transparent and uncomplicated texts (69).

86 Andrews, *To Tell a Free Story*, xi. Andrews also wrote that a general description of an "amanuensis-editor" of autobiographies by enslaved or formerly enslaved people is someone who transcribes and publishes "the experiential facts recounted orally by a black person . . . with editorial prefaces, footnotes, and appended commentary" (20; see also 19).

87 In 2010, Carretta announced the discovery of Phillis's first poem and its transcription in two print versions, which he found in the archives of none other than the MHS. Both versions of the poem were hand-transcribed in the 1773 diary of a white man, Jeremy Belknap, who would establish the MHS in 1791 (Carretta, "Phillis Wheatley's First Effort," 796). Belknap's transcription of one version in prose and the other in verse, "as if he could not decide whether it was prose or poetry," marks Phillis's earliest known writing as well as the commencement of a critical debate as to how to understand her work within preexisting literary genres (795). There is no extant manuscript version in Phillis's own handwriting, and readers are left not fully knowing the circumstances that resulted in this transcription.

88 While Stetson does not include Phillis's poems as an example of a Black woman's narrative of enslavement, she does cite an 1864 book titled *Letters of Phillis Wheatley, the Negro Slave Poet of Boston*, the earliest published collection of the Obour-Phillis correspondence, leading us to better understand the ways this text had to speak in multiple voices, some not their authors' own ("Studying Slavery," 84).

89 Santamarina, *Belabored Professions*, 39, 40. Santamarina's naming of this conflict through the example of Sojourner Truth and her amanuensis's writing—"the complicated maneuverings that structured Truth and Gilbert's collaboration" (43)—refuses to downplay the unequal power dynamics embedded in these texts' collaborative inceptions and at the same time

points to the epistemological value of their originating authors' agency in and around their transcribers and the resulting texts themselves.

90 Stetson, "Studying Slavery," 71.

91 Coincidentally, the Edes Beecher bequest also led to the letters' future discovery by a Black feminist critic like me, but I do not subscribe to forms of logic that contend that violent literary histories alone have made my work possible.

92 Ellis et al., "Special Meeting," 130. Deane would go on to publish one hundred pamphlet copies of Phillis's side of the Obour-Phillis correspondence as the *Letters of Phillis Wheatley, the Negro-Slave Poet of Boston.*

93 Ellis et al., "Special Meeting," 137, 140.

94 "November Meeting," 268.

95 See Carretta, *Biography*, 197–98.

96 "November Meeting," 268 note †.

97 Boyd, *Discarded Legacy*, 26, 26–27.

98 Christian, "The Race for Theory," 61. Christian writes, "For me literature is a way of knowing that I am not hallucinating, that whatever I feel/know *is*. It is an affirmation that sensuality is intelligence, that sensual language is language that makes sense. My response, then, is directly to those who write what I read and to those who read what I read." Christian argues across this essay that the relationship she has with herself as a critic is synonymous with the relationship between herself as critic and the writers she studies.

99 For example, Hartman gestures beyond single authorship to theorize a Black feminist collective response to Black girls' experiences in the early twentieth century, what gains figuration as "italicized phrases and lines . . . utterances from the chorus" (*Wayward Lives*, xvi).

100 "November Meeting," 268 note †.

101 Loretta Ross, "Don't Call People Out—Call Them In," TED video, 5:51–57, filmed in August 2021 in Monterey, CA, https://www.ted.com/talks/loretta _j_ross_don_t_call_people_out_call_them_in. An outright call-out is, by contrast, a prelude "to a fight, not a conversation, because you're publicly humiliating them" (03:56–4:02).

102 This also harks back to Audre Lorde and Adrienne Rich's attempts to build solidarity with each other across difference and the genuine attempt, as Rich says, to try "to translate from your experience to mine" (Lorde, "An Interview," in *Sister Outsider*, 104).

103 Moonan, "Slave Poet's 1776 Letter." The *New York Times* is also the first historical record I have found to identify the Mrs. William Beecher of the MHS proceedings as *Katherine Edes* Beecher.

104 Moonan, "Slave Poet's 1776 Letter." I had not read the letter when this chapter was originally drafted around 2018. The letter is printed in Carretta's 2024 edition of Phillis's *Writings*, 131.

105 See Felicia R. Lee, "Letter by 18th-Century Slave Fetches Record Price," *New York Times*, November 24, 2005.

106 Hartman, "Venus in Two Acts," 8.

107 "November Meeting," 268 note †.

108 Slauter, "Looking for Scipio Moorhead," provides a full account of Scipio's life and significance.

109 Odell, *Memoir*, 18. Paradoxically, because Susanna Wheatley could not "see," or simply refused to see, past her version of Phillis, she could not possibly visualize Phillis as a fugitive, now technically free on London soil. With the 1772 *Somerset v. Stewart* ruling, "an enslaver could not legally force an enslaved person in England back to the colonies" (Carretta, *Biography*, 124; see also 123). For more on James Somerset, the Black man behind this victory, see Waldstreicher, "The Movement," in *Odyssey*, 151–64.

110 "November Meeting," 268 note †.

111 "November Meeting," 268 note †.

112 A. Walker, *Our Mothers' Gardens*, 231–32, 233.

113 "November Meeting," 268, 269 note †.

114 Muñoz, *Cruising Utopia*, 1.

115 In Lyman Beecher Stowe's 1934 family biography *Saints, Sinners and Beechers*, Edes Beecher makes a brief appearance via her marriage in 1830 to William Henry Beecher (1802–89), one of the older brothers to Harriet Beecher Stowe, who is hailed in the text as "The Unlucky" (138; see also 140). According to Lyman Beecher Stowe, William Beecher tried his way at preaching at various churches. William Beecher's only printed pamphlet, *The Duty of the Church to Her Ministry*, "indicted the system which condemned the rank and file of evangelical clergymen to overwork, underpay and constant changes of parish, induced by backbiting and petty persecution" (143). Nothing is said in *Saints, Sinners and Beechers* about William Beecher's (or his wife's) purported work in abolitionism.

116 Stowe, *Saints, Sinners and Beechers*, 140.

117 Bynum, *Reading Pleasures*, 125. Bynum writes that the letter evidencing Obour's participation in this society is in William H. Robinson's 1976 edition of *The Proceedings of the Free African Union Society and the African Benevolent Society, Newport, Rhode Island, 1780–1824* (*Reading Pleasures*, 153n1).

118 Williams wrote in 1980, "I was a 'man' in *Give Birth to Brightness*"—and while that helped her "come into [her] own voice," Williams felt she was akin to "the women I speak of in my stories, my poems" (S. A. Williams, "From Meditations," 770).

119 S. A. Williams, "Author Note," in *Dessa Rose*, 5. In the author's note prefacing *Dessa Rose*, Williams writes that her research into the life of a pregnant enslaved Black woman who led a revolt of enslaved people in 1829 (and was executed after the birth of her child) led her to discover

the existence of a white woman in 1830 who harbored fugitives from slavery. Williams wrote *Dessa Rose* to provide the occasion for their fictional meeting, despite their having missed each other in historical time and space: "How sad, I thought then, that these two women never met" (5). Williams also pays homage to the twentieth-century scholarship that connected these women by association: "Angela Davis' seminal essay, 'Reflections on the Black Woman's Role in the Community of Slaves' (*The Black Scholar*, December 1971)" and "Herbert Aptheker's *American Negro Slave Revolts* (New York, 1947)" (5).

120 See Lisa Lowe, "Sherley Anne Williams: In Memoriam," October 1999, lit-erature.ucsd.edu/people/faculty/memoriam/swilliams.html.

121 S. A. Williams, "From Meditations," 769 (parenthetical in original). Williams's biographical statement was originally published in Mary Helen Washington's 1980 anthology, *Midnight Birds*, and was reprinted posthu-mously in 1999 in an issue of *Callaloo*.

122 S. A. Williams, "From Meditations," 770.

123 Henderson, "In Memory," 763.

124 "When confronted by such an unexpected situation as this, what does one say?" (Ellison, "Portrait of Inman Page," 113).

125 Ellison, "Portrait of Inman Page," 119. For example, Ellison recalls, "I remember [Page] in a context of ceremonies, in most of which he acted as the celebrant—but never in my wildest fantasies would I have anticipated my being called upon to play a role in a ceremony dedicated to his memory" (113). Ellison's candid remarks echo others' experiences of criticism, wherein one's active remembrance leads one to experience atemporality: "My sense of time has begun leaping back and forth over the years in a way which assaults the logic of clock and calendar, and I am haunted by a sense of the uncanny" (114).

126 Henderson, "In Memory," 765.

127 DuCille, "Feminism, Black and Blue," 151. DuCille emphasizes that Wil-liams "felt bruised and battered by decades of doing battle in the master's house . . . the marginalization, the isolation, the exhaustion . . . I have to wonder at the toll it takes."

128 Christian, *Black Feminist Criticism*, ix. Christian continues, "Interruptions would be normal and she would likely be reinterpreting the book she is reading without even being aware of it, reinventing herself in the midst of patriarchal discourse, as to who she is supposed to be."

129 Christian, *Black Feminist Criticism*, ix. Williams also wrote that she understood her writing as part of her role as a single mother, as a way of helping her only son come to know her: "Women must leave a record for their men; otherwise how will they know us?" (S. A. Williams, "From Medi-tations," 770).

130 Henderson, "In Memory," 766.

131　Christian, "The Race for Theory," 58.

132　Henderson, "In Memory," 763, 766 (emphasis in original).

133　Henderson, "In Memory," 766.

134　Lorde, "Uses of the Erotic," in *Sister Outsider*, 53.

135　Lorde, *Sister Outsider*, 53.

136　Taylor, *How We Get Free*, 25. I cite these examples of how the Combahee River Collective modeled Black feminist criticism in and around the traditional setting of academia.

137　Henderson, "In Memory," 764.

138　Henderson, "In Memory," 766. Henderson and E. Patrick Johnson would coedit *Black Queer Studies: A Critical Anthology*, one of the earlier critical works to gather work that was both Black studies and queer studies.

139　Washington, *Black-Eyed Susans / Midnight Birds*, 3, 278. Washington's *Black-Eyed Susans / Midnight Birds* is Washington's 1990 combined edition of two of her anthologies, the 1975 *Black-Eyed Susans* and the 1980 *Midnight Birds*. This information is unique to the 1990 edition and alludes to the sparse criticism following the publication of Williams's 1986 novel, *Dessa Rose*.

140　Henderson, "In Memory," 766.

2: Their Eyes Were Watching Phillis

An earlier version of part of chapter 2 appeared as "Praisesong for Margaret Walker's *Jubilee* and the Phillis Wheatley Poetry Festival," *African American Review* 53, no. 4 (Winter 2020): 299–313, https://doi.org/10.1353/afa.2020.0042.

1　McKay, "Naming the Problem," 368. McKay herein deploys Phillis to posit a definition of Black criticism that is inclusive to scholars of all identities while maintaining the importance of having an equitable number of Black-identified scholars. A similar conclusion was drawn by McKay's colleague Barbara Christian in her 1989 essay "But What Do We Think" as well as her 1994 essay "Diminishing Returns," collected in *New Black Feminist Criticism*. In 2013, P. Gabrielle Foreman also "attempts to answer earlier calls by academic foremothers for affirmative accountability and responsibility" ("A Riff, a Call," 308). McKay's former student Kimberly Blockett would respond to Foreman in 2014, articulating the importance of "cultural ethics" ("Do You Have Any Skin in the Game?," 64). Similar expressions on the state of the tradition appear in Ann duCille's 1994 essay "The Occult of True Black Womanhood," and in Frances Smith Foster's 2007 essay "The Personal Is Political."

2　See R. M. Benjamin, "Tenured Black Professors," 79.

3　McKay, "Naming the Problem," 368.

4   See Rutledge et al., "The Nellie Tree," and Moody et al., "In Memoriam," the latter of which begins with a photograph of McKay standing in her office before an image of Phillis, her "muse-mentor" (n.p.).

5   Rutledge et al., "The Nellie Tree," 41, 49 (emphasis in original). Notably, McKay not only taught Black literature and Black students but encouraged the study of all literatures and mentored students of all backgrounds (see especially 42, 47, 48, 63).

6   McKay, "Black Woman Professor," 147. Despite the difficult and challenging experiences of racism and sexism that McKay describes across the essay, she emphasizes Black women professors' overarching fight to "stay." For example, McKay's abstract closes, "This paper looks at the experiences of one black woman in a prestigious Midwestern university and documents the nature of her experiences as a double minority. She voices the opinion that black women intend to struggle on to their rightful places in the academy. They can't go back, and they aim to stay" (143).

7   McKay and Benjamin, "Breaking the Whole Thing Open," 1678–79. For more biographical information on McKay's doctoral experience at Harvard, including her two-year absence from her program to teach at Simmons College and subsequent reenrollment, see S. G. Benjamin, *Half in Shadow*, 47–53, 59–60. Benjamin writes that Harvard in the late 1960s was "an elitist space that perpetually placed white men and their interests atop the educational hierarchy" (48). Ultimately, McKay earned her doctorate there not because she aligned with the institution but because it was a necessary hurdle in order to "pursue the life she wanted" (60).

8   McKay and Benjamin, "Breaking the Whole Thing Open," 1679, 1680; see also S. G. Benjamin, *Half in Shadow*, 56–57. Benjamin writes that these informal meetings in which McKay took part, in conjunction with each woman's formal teaching assignments, "moved Black women's literature a step closer to becoming a field unto itself" (57). The women in this Boston community included Thadious M. Davis, Gayle Pemberton, Andrea B. Rushing, Barbara Smith, Hortense J. Spillers, and others, as detailed in McKay and Benjamin, "Breaking the Whole Thing Open," 1679; Washington, foreword to *Their Eyes*, ix; and S. G. Benjamin, *Half in Shadow*, 56.

9   McKay and Benjamin, "Breaking the Whole Thing Open," 1680.

10   The novel had been out of print since its original publication date in 1937. Fawcett Publications reissued it in 1965, and University of Illinois Press reissued it again in 1978, according to Newson, *Zora Neale Hurston*, xxxv.

11   Wright, "Between Laughter and Tears," 25.

12   McKay and Benjamin, "Breaking the Whole Thing Open," 1681.

13   In some ways, this underground recirculation of Hurston's *Their Eyes* was a form of poetic justice as Hurston's final experiences with her publisher J. B. Lippincott included the rejection of her last two novels on Black life, which led her to write her 1948 final novel, *Seraph on the Suwanee*, about

southern white characters with publisher Charles Scribner & Sons, see Carby, foreword to *Seraph*, vii. However, Black feminist critics of the time would not disavow even this novel or other complex parts of Hurston's oeuvre. Hazel V. Carby overall describes the novel as "a very modern text, a text that speaks as eloquently to the contradictions and conflict of trying to live our lives as gendered beings in the 1990s as it did in 1948" (xvi).

14   DuCille, "Feminism, Black and Blue," 152–53. Here duCille recounts her experiences of teaching out-of-print Black women's writing at Hamilton College in the 1970s.

15   DuCille, "Feminism, Black and Blue," 153. DuCille also cites the overarching representation of Hurston on Amazon.com.

16   Originally published in 1975 in *Ms.* magazine, Walker would later retitle this essay "Looking for Zora" in her 1983 essay collection *Our Mothers' Gardens*.

17   A. Walker, "Zora Neale Hurston," in *Our Mothers' Gardens*, 84 (emphasis added). Subtitled "A Cautionary Tale and a Partisan View," this essay was originally the foreword to Robert E. Hemenway's *Zora Neale Hurston: A Literary Biography* before later appearing in Walker's *Our Mothers' Gardens*.

18   DuCille, "Feminism, Black and Blue," 152.

19   DuCille, "Feminism, Black and Blue," 153.

20   Washington, foreword, *Their Eyes*, xi–xii. Washington's specification of *Their Eyes* as "a shared text" echoes Nellie McKay's description of Black feminist criticism in the 1970s as a "sharing community" (McKay and Benjamin, "Breaking the Whole Thing Open," 1680).

21   Jennifer Jordan writes of "the unsupportable notion that the novel is an appropriate fictional representation of the concerns and attitudes of modern black feminism," and that at the end of the novel Janie's "life has passed" ("Feminist Fantasies," 107, 115).

22   Hurston, *Their Eyes Were Watching God*, 191, 192–93.

23   See duCille, "Feminism, Black and Blue," 152–53.

24   DuCille, "Notes on 'Hamilton,'" March 10, 2017, duCille Papers, box 2, folder 10.

25   Phillis to David Worcester (Wooster), October 18, 1773, 110. Again, all my references to Phillis's writings are from the 2024 *Writings of Phillis Wheatley Peters* edited by Vincent Carretta, unless otherwise noted. Again, in this letter Phillis specifies her hope that New Haven printers do not reissue her book "as it will be a great hurt to me, preventing any further Benefit that I might receive from the Sale of my Copies from England." This letter also indicates that Phillis purchases, at the urging of the Earl of Dartmouth, a collection of works by Alexander Pope, and chooses herself to buy *Hudibras*, by Samuel Butler; *Don Quixote*, by Miguel de Cervantes; and *Fables*, by John Gay. It appears that Sir Brook Watson gifted her *Paradise Lost*, by John Milton.

26 A. Walker, *Our Mothers' Gardens*, 237; June Jordan, "The Difficult Miracle," in *Some of Us*, 179.

27 For how recent scholars have engaged with the complexities of reading the archive of slavery see Hartman's 2008 essay "Venus in Two Acts" and the essays written in response in the Fall 2016 special issue of the journal *History of the Present* (6, no. 2), including Hartman's own response, "The Dead Book Revisited." In 2008, Hartman wrote that "it might have been possible for me to represent the friendship that could have blossomed" between two enslaved girls amid the horrendous conditions aboard the ship the *Recovery*, concluding, "I could not change anything. . . . It was better to leave them as I had found them. Two girls, alone" ("Venus in Two Acts," 8, 9). Hartman here does not advocate relinquishing the practice of our profession, rather, the question remains how to read when the archive appears foreclosed to further interpretation. Smallwood emphasizes that scholars might "read a slave ship's ledger as a literary text that [tells] a story," rather than as a statement of fact, and thus understand criticism "as work that does not re-violate the enslaved but rather disrupts the archive's naturalization of the violence it narrates" ("The Politics of the Archive," 126, 129). Hartman later wrote, "I neglected to take into account the ways the other captives might have attended to these girls and responded to their deaths," foregrounding another possible way to read the archive ("The Dead Book Revisited," 209).

28 Keizer, *Black Subjects*, 169. Arlene R. Keizer writes that Douglass's copybook entrance into literacy sets the stage for his first autobiography, *Narrative of the Life of Frederick Douglass, an American Slave, Written by Himself*, and subsequent autobiographies. As teaching literacy to enslaved people was illegal, Douglass teaches himself using his enslaver's "old copybook" and "covertly writes between the lines of that copybook, an act which will prepare him to write [*Narrative*], a text whose reason for being was the will to freedom" (Keizer, *Black Subjects*, 169). See also Douglass, *Narrative*, 44.

29 Carretta, *Biography*, 221n41. Carretta's lengthy endnote details helpful background to the Emory copybooks as well as the likelihood that its contents are not written in Phillis's handwriting. See also Waldstreicher, *Odyssey*, 43.

30 Gumbs, "We Can Learn," 337, 338 (emphasis in original). Reading poems not authored by Phillis, we inevitably look for the poems we wanted her to write. The interpretation of Phillis's copybooks as enabling her to say what she cannot in her own poems leads Gumbs to comb the poems in the copybooks for lines like "How many nations have long since / Been slaves to a usurping prince, / Let Britain's history relate," and "When liberty is put to sale / For wine, money or ale / The sellers must be abject slaves" (338, 339). While it is inconclusive whether these are Phillis's views on chattel slavery in these lines, as someone who has read the copybooks, Gumbs's observation and subsequent transcription of these lines from their penned originals

is impressive, and so is her arrival at this conclusion from a collection of poems that seems, to this reader, truly quite random.

31 See Carretta, "Phillis Wheatley's First Effort."

32 Burkett, "Re: Phillis Wheatley Manuscript," September 8, 1997, and "Phillis Wheatley Manuscript Poems Discovered," n.d., Foster Papers, box 17, folder "Hymn to Humanity." About two years later, on October 20, 1999, Burkett forwarded the memo to Frances Smith Foster, who would later donate her own papers to Emory. I would come across Burkett's memo detailing acquiring the copybooks within Foster's papers during my visit to Emory's library in November 2018.

33 Burkett, "Phillis Wheatley Manuscript Poems Discovered," n.d., Foster Papers, box 17, folder "Hymn to Humanity." Even now, Phillis's "Hymn" variant is Emory's pride and joy, evidenced by its ongoing life as meaningful ephemera, including as a postcard reproduction of the manuscript that in 2018 visitors to the library could pick up and take home with them, giving the poem an afterlife via the US Postal Service.

34 Carretta, *Biography*, 221n41.

35 Phillis, "An Hymn to Humanity," 91, and Burkett, "Re: Phillis Wheatley Manuscript," September 8, 1997, Foster Papers, box 17, folder "Hymn to Humanity."

36 Burkett, "Re: Phillis Wheatley Manuscript," September 8, 1997, Foster Papers, box 17, folder "Hymn to Humanity." Burkett writes, "It is conceivable that Phillis Wheatley was tutored by the person (S. P. Gallowy??) who tutored these students."

37 Phillis, "An Hymn to Humanity," 92, lines 23, 25–30. This address is specified to "G——y" in the 2001 edition of Phillis's complete writings (92, line 23).

38 Phillis, "2: Hymn to Humanity," December 12, 1773, Wheatley Collection, box 1, folder 2. The double "Command" I have quoted reflects, I believe, the use of the word as a "catchword" in the manuscript version. While the poem would not be read aloud in a way that repeated the word, it would ensure the poem would be read in the correct page order if published.

39 McKittrick, *Demonic Grounds*, xxv, xxvi (emphasis in original).

40 Wynter, "Beyond Miranda's Meanings," 355, first published in *Out of the Kumbla*, edited by Carole Boyce Davies and Elaine Savory Fido. McKittrick's foremother love for Wynter is a pluralization of Wynter's subtitle to this essay, "Un/Silencing the 'Demonic Ground' of Caliban's 'Woman,'" a coapplication of Wynter's own use of the terms "the demonic" and "the grounds" that may subsequently articulate Black feminist geographies. Wynter's essay superseded its editors' request for an afterword, refusing closure by refusing to "be included here in its entirety."

41 Ellis, *Territories of the Soul*, 155. Although I apply this phrasing to Phillis, Ellis is here describing an alternative "diasporic subjectivity" beyond

"colonial history" and whatever found or newfound nationalism into which Black subjects may have arrived.

42 I will trace some of this history in this chapter but note here one example of literal rewriting: the performance of readerly "resourcefulness" that compels Henry Louis Gates Jr. to rearrange every letter in Phillis's poem "On Being Brought" in order to transform it into a direct protest poem; see Gates, *The Trials of Phillis Wheatley*, 87, 88.

43 Stepto, *From Behind the Veil*, 3 (emphasis in original).

44 Hartman, *Lose Your Mother*, 15. Again, Hartman's figure of the lost mother (or lost great-great-grandmother) is akin to the foremother, who is often not lost so much as removed from us by time and absented by a lack of criticism.

45 Phillis, "On Being Brought," 56, lines 7–8. This argument is also made at the level of punctuation. The seventh line of the poem stitches together "*Christians, Negros*" with a comma that one might read as separating coordinate adjectives of the same noun or as separating distinct clauses in a series of nouns. Lorenzo Thomas writes that "depending upon where you place the caesura," whether in the traditional center of the line, or after "Remember," determines whether the line employs direct address to a specific audience (Christians) or indirect address to an audience unknown (*Extraordinary Measures*, 3). After four commas and a line break, after physical and temporal movement, cohesion and constraint, surrendering Phillis to "th' angelic train" would require readers to exert a decisive interpretation of her conditional "May be refin'd" as a definitive. Phillis is there, or not there, in that line and in that poem, depending on how much one's interpretation sutures grammatical proximity and spiritual transformation or how greatly skepticism dictates close reading the poem in pursuit of Phillis's memory of her African origin.

46 E. Smith, "Phillis Wheatley," 403; Gates, *The Trials of Phillis Wheatley*, 71.

47 Phillis, "On Being Brought," 56, lines 1–8.

48 O'Neale, "Challenge to Wheatley's Critics," 507. O'Neale draws on historical use of the word *redeem* in relation to "eighteenth-century white indentured servants who were working to earn the funds to buy themselves out of slavery," who "were known as 'redemptioners'" (507–8). The possibility that Phillis could have understood her enslavement as more akin to indentured servitude and that redemption was an outcome that ultimately rested with the servant's own labors toward freedom is certainly enticing.

49 Included in Phillis's 1772 book proposal, her poem "Thoughts on Being Brought from Africa to America" was written in 1768; see Phillis, *The Writings*, 186.

50 Phillis, "On Being Brought," 56, lines 5–6.

51 As Jennifer Thorn writes, "[I]n the original Ovid, [the poem is] a homosocial story of female rivalry and maternal suffering" ("'All Beautiful in

Woe,'" 240). In Phillis's version, the poem remains true to its original locus of power.

52 Phillis admits the poem's own original wrestling with its male-dominant heritage and uses a classical (masculine) poetic technique to call on women goddesses to help her write it again. When Phillis begins with the lines "Apollo's wrath to man the dreadful spring / Of ills innum'rous, tuneful goddess, sing!" it is important that Apollo's characteristic violence is here mediated and shaped by a woman's language, and by the ability of a goddess to enable a Black woman poet to sing about it, 94, lines 1–2. It is this "tuneful goddess," in fact, who may be responsible for Ovid and Wilson's abilities in the first place: She "did'st first th' ideal pencil give, / And taught'st the painter in his works to live" (94, lines 2, 3–4).

53 Thorn, "'All Beautiful in Woe,'" 234, 242; see also 245.

54 Phillis, "Niobe in Distress," 94, lines 5–6.

55 Phillis, "Niobe in Distress," 95, lines 33–34; 96, line 88.

56 *Ovid's Metamorphoses in Fifteen Books* (ed. Garth), 183, 185, 188. Garth's edition included the translations of several famous writers of the time. Jennifer Thorn notes that Samuel Croxall translated the sixth book in which Niobe appears, presenting her "as inexcusably arrogant and justly punished as a bad mother, where Wheatley's Niobe errs primarily in failing to gauge accurately the power of profoundly unjust gods" ("'All Beautiful in Woe,'" 246).

57 Ovid, *Ovid's Metamorphoses in Fifteen Books* (ed. Garth), 182, 183.

58 Ovid, *Ovid's Metamorphoses in Fifteen Books* (ed. Garth), 189.

59 Phillis, "Niobe in Distress," 95, lines 53–58.

60 Phillis, "Niobe in Distress," 98, line 157; 96, line 104.

61 Slauter, "Neoclassical Culture," 117.

62 Phillis, "Proposals," in *The Writings*, 27–28.

63 Phillis's poem "America" remains in manuscript form at the Historical Society of Pennsylvania, 12–13; her poem and letter "To His Excellency General Washington" were published in *Virginia Gazette* in 1776, 129–31; and "Liberty and Peace" was published by a printing house in 1784, 141–43, and see corresponding notes.

64 Phillis, "America," 12–13, lines 6–7, 17, 19, 22.

65 Phillis, "To His Excellency General Washington," 130; 130, lines 3; 131, lines 32, 39–40.

66 Phillis, "Liberty and Peace," 141, lines 1–2.

67 A. Walker, *Our Mothers' Gardens*, 237.

68 A. Walker, *Our Mothers' Gardens*, 236. These lines are cited as they appear in Phillis, "To His Excellency General Washington," 130, lines 9–12.

69 A. Walker, *Our Mothers' Gardens*, 237 (emphasis in original).

70 Phillis, "Niobe in Distress," 99, lines 213–24. In the 2024 Carretta edition of her writings, quotation marks appear all along the left margin of these

lines. Carretta writes that "William H. Robinson . . . believes that these lines were 'probably the work of Mary Wheatley'" (195). Robinson also notes that these lines may be translated, in *Phillis Wheatley and Her Writings*, 274.

71   According to Slauter, slavish is "a word that had come specifically to signify a lack of mental originality only in the 1750s" ("Neoclassical Culture," 83).

72   Slauter, "Neoclassical Culture," 116n96.

73   C. N. Thomas, *Alexander Pope and His Eighteenth-Century Women Readers*, 63.

74   Ford, "An African Diasporic Critique," 77.

75   Phillis, "Niobe in Distress," 99, line 225.

76   Phillis, *Poems on Various Subjects* (1773), 112. The asterisk appears at the beginning of this final stanza, with the note at the bottom of page, with the poem continuing onto the next page. In the 2001 edition of Phillis's writings edited by Carretta, quotation marks are not included all along the left margin.

77   Walker in Washington's foreword to *Their Eyes*, xii (emphasis in original).

78   Ford, "An African Diasporic Critique," 77.

79   Hayden, "Arachne," in *Collected Poems*, 113.

80   One may compare the lines at the beginning of "Niobe in Distress" to *Ovid's Metamorphoses in Fifteen Books*, see Ovid (ed. Garth), 182.

81   This rendering of Arachne as stripped down to weaver appears in Ovid's *The Metamorphoses*, translated by Mary M. Innes, 138; translated by Horace Gregory, 167; translated by Frank Justus Miller, 299; and translated by William S. Anderson, 42, 170n144.

82   D. Smith, "Quarreling in the Movement," 455. See also the first two chapters of Smith's book *Robert Hayden in Verse*. Also, Hayden's own 1967 biographical note in *Kaleidoscope* reads, "Hayden is interested in Negro history and folklore and has written poems using materials from these sources. Opposed to the chauvinistic and the doctrinaire, he sees no reason why a Negro poet should be limited to 'racial utterance' or to having his writing judged by standards different from those applied to the work of other poets" (108).

83   Hayden was promoted to full professor at Fisk in 1967 but returned to teach at the University of Michigan–Ann Arbor, "with great relief" in 1968 (visiting professor) and 1969 (full professor), a complex decision that, due to department politics, then deferred his acceptance of the position of Consultant in Poetry to the Library of Congress, see Hatcher, *From the Auroral Darkness*, 40–42.

84   D. Smith, "Quarreling in the Movement," 456–57.

85   Boyd, *Wrestling with the Muse*, 128. Also quoted in D. Smith, "Quarreling in the Movement," 457.

86   D. Smith, "Quarreling in the Movement," 457; see also D. Smith, *Robert Hayden in Verse*, 27. Hayden did not attend the subsequent 1967 conference.

87   To get a sense of the magnitude of Hayden's readings of this poem, one live reading is over ten minutes long. Hayden prefaces his reading with a humble disclaimer: "Perhaps now it's time for me to read this poem. It's long and it has different voices in it and I'm not always up to it. I think, though, that I think I can get through it tonight" (beginning of reading of "Middle Passage," *Poetry Foundation*, https://www.poetryfoundation.org /poems/43076/middle-passage, accessed January 13, 2018; also posted on YouTube, https://youtu.be/z3Z4FEj7LJo). Hayden's poem was first published in 1945 in the journal *Phylon*. A revised version later appeared in his volume of poems *A Ballad of Remembrance* (1962).

88   Dargan, "Kyle Dargan (1980–)," 434.

89   The poem, originally published in Dargan's book of poems *The Listening*, is reprinted in Rowell's 2013 anthology of contemporary Black poetry, see Dargan, "Kyle Dargan (1980–)," 435.

90   Hatcher, *From the Auroral Darkness*, 90.

91   The poem and interview are in Corral, "To Robert Hayden"; see also P. T. Williams, *Robert Hayden*, 120. Corral notes the pain of Hayden's terminal illness; as heart attack (note above), as cancer (see D. Smith, *Hayden*, 192).

92   On Hayden's work at the Library of Congress, see Hatcher, *From the Auroral Darkness*, 41–42, 45–48.

93   Hayden, *Kaleidoscope*, xxi, 3.

94   Hayden, *Kaleidoscope*, 4–7. Phillis's poem to Dartmouth is similarly abridged in Dudley Randall's 1971 anthology *The Black Poets*, 38, and as early as in the preface to James Weldon Johnson's 1922 anthology, *The Book of American Negro Poetry*, xxviii.

95   Lines quoted as they appear in Hayden, *Kaleidoscope*, 4. These lines from *Kaleidoscope* are similar to other published versions of these lines, although Hayden's version uses "pursue" rather than "peruse," and "the soul" rather than "that soul." Compare to Phillis, "To the Right Honourable William, Earl of Dartmouth," 81–82, lines 20–31.

96   Hayden, *Kaleidoscope*, 2.

97   Phillis to Huntingdon, June 27, 1773, 106.

98   Hayden, *Kaleidoscope*, 2.

99   Carretta, *Biography*, 141. Carretta also confirms that Phillis "departed London for Boston on 26 July 1773" and "arrived back in Boston on 13 September." And that she had originally departed Boston for London on "8 May 1773" (99), arriving on "17 June 1773" (131).

100   Julian D. Mason Jr. writes that "the countess was in Wales" and Phillis could not visit her due to news of Susanna's illness in Boston (*Poems of Phillis Wheatley* [1989 ed.], 185n1), although Waldstreicher notes that Phillis had not yet heard of Susanna's illness (*Odyssey*, 210).

101   Hayden certainly had read some of Phillis's letters, for they appeared one year earlier, as he wrote in his biographical note for her, in a "definitive edition,

which includes the poet's letters . . . in 1966" (*Kaleidoscope*, 3). Hayden is referring to Mason's 1966 edition of *Poems of Phillis Wheatley*, which includes seven of Phillis's letters to Obour, her February 9, 1774, letter to the Reverend Samuel Hopkins, and her October 10, 1772, letter to the Earl of Dartmouth (but no letters to Huntingdon), 103–11. Phillis's letters to Huntingdon, among others, were later added to Mason's 1989 edition; see 184–212.

102   Phillis to Obour, October 30, 1773, 111.

103   Phillis to David Worcester (Wooster), October 18, 1773, 109–10.

104   Phillis to Huntingdon, June 27, 1773, 106.

105   The version of the poem from Hayden's *American Journal* appears in Hayden's *Collected Poems*, 147–48. Previous to this, Hayden published a version of this poem in 1977 in the *Massachusetts Review* with very slight changes.

106   Phillis to Obour, October 30, 1773, 111.

107   "Middle Passage" is collected in Hayden, *Collected Poems*, 48–54.

108   Morrison, *Beloved*, 248.

109   Phillis to Huntingdon, July 17, 1773, 106.

110   Carretta, *Biography*, 202. Phillis wrote that without the patronage of the countess, her poems would be subject to "Severe trials of unpitying Criticism" (Phillis to Huntingdon, June 27, 1773, 106).

111   In his two cameos in the poem, Nathaniel Wheatley's emotions are oppositely calibrated with Phillis's. Nathaniel, the Wheatley son who monitored Phillis's London visit, cries when Wheatley does not and frowns on her expression of pleasure later in the poem.

112   Hayden, *Collected Poems*, 148, line 45, lines 46–49.

113   Murphy, "Praisesong for Margaret Walker's *Jubilee*."

114   Christian, "Ritualistic Process," 83.

115   M. Walker, "Phillis Wheatley and Black Women Writers," 35. This is also corroborated by Walker's journals: in between pages in which Walker drafted a sonnet in honor of Dunbar, she sketched an outline of a festival of "20 Black women poets" to honor Phillis "on the 200th anniversary of the publication of her book" (M. Walker, Personal Journals, September 1972, journal 91, p. 75).

116   Parks, "Report on a Poetry Festival," 92 (brackets and ellipsis in original).

117   M. Walker, "How I Wrote *Jubilee*," 50. This moment is recounted for all its complex economic, familial, and gendered dynamics in Maryemma Graham's biography of Walker (*The House Where My Soul Lives*, 16–17).

118   In addition to the women listed, "Johari Amini," "Gwendolyn Brooks," and "Julia Fields" are listed on the festival's original program but could not attend and are not included in the copy of the program in the festival's published proceedings. See Rowell and Ward, "Ancestral Memories," 129, 139. I call each writer by the name she used during the festival.

119   Murphy, "Praisesong," 299.

120   Lee, "Archives," 858–59.

121 M. Walker, Personal Journals, October 22, 1972, journal 91, p. 101.

122 M. Walker, Personal Journals, August 5, 1973, journal 92, p. 241.

123 M. Walker, Personal Journals, September or October 1973, journal 93, pp. 67, 69.

124 M. Walker, Personal Journals, March 8, 1973, journal 92, p. 135.

125 M. Walker, Personal Journals, September 1, 1973, journal 93, pp. 185, 187.

126 M. Walker, Personal Journals, November 11, 1973, journal 93, p. 233.

127 Murphy, "Praisesong," 309; M. Walker, Personal Journals, November 11, 1973, journal 93, p. 234. Graham also observed Walker's notes about Fabio and writes in her biography that "Walker's moralistic views separated her from the new generation" (*The House Where My Soul Lives*, 471).

128 Harney and Moten, *The Undercommons*, 26.

129 Rowell and Ward note the poems Fabio read, including one dedicated to Walker's *Jubilee*, and praised Fabio's "dazzling" performance, noting that "with all the charisma of a voodoo priestess, she blacktrocuted the audience" ("Ancestral Memories," 138).

130 Graham, *The House Where My Soul Lives*, 452.

131 "With a few exceptions" (Graham, *The House Where My Soul Lives*, 470).

132 Murphy, "Praisesong," 308, 309.

133 Tate, *Black Women Writers at Work*, 252. See also preface, note 3. I chose not to attend the 2023 version of the festival in order to finish writing this book, among other matters. After this book entered production, I learned in October 2024 that the journal *Callaloo* would be publishing a special issue on the 2023 festival—released late fall: 42, no. 3 (Summer 2024).

134 M. Walker, Personal Journals, 1997 or 1998, journal 133, p. 137.

3: In Search of Our Foremothers' Gardens

1 Davies, *Caribbean Spaces*, 3–4.

2 Dungy, *Black Nature*, 149–50.

3 Dungy, *Soil*, 14.

4 A. Walker, *Our Mothers' Gardens*, 241. Walker's 1974 essay "In Search of Our Mothers' Gardens" was first published in *Ms.* and later collected in 1983 in Walker's essay collection of the same name. Citations throughout are to this collection. Minnie Tallulah Grant was Walker's mother's maiden name, as detailed in Evelyn C. White's biography, *Alice Walker*, xvii.

5 A. Walker, *Our Mothers' Gardens*, 241. These conditions were so harsh that White spends the first chapter of her biography delineating the histories that made Jim Crow Georgia, its roots of slavery, and its modern component, sharecropping, such a violent setting, in E. C. White, *Alice Walker*, 3–8. This setting runs counter to Walker's family's great efforts to stay well despite these circumstances, but it is important not to confuse their survival

as acquiescence to these circumstances. Walker also recalls these positive childhood memories of her mother's garden despite the trauma of an injury she sustained at the age of eight when she was blinded in her right eye when her brothers were playing with BB guns and were ignored by white members of their community while seeking emergency care, in E. C. White, *Alice Walker*, 34–35, 40, 7.

6   A. Walker, *Our Mothers' Gardens*, 241. This phrase will bear continued relevance in this chapter's charting of the practice of Black feminist critical work despite the predominance of racist, sexist, and cisheteropatriachal workplaces.

7   Walker knows that each of these women would have longed for the freedom of self-expression in the arts of their choosing—a freedom that coincided with the desire to be free from slavery and from further racialized-economic discrimination thereafter.

8   A. Walker, *Our Mothers' Gardens*, 234. But women who could not become such writers due to barriers a society placed in their path. Interestingly, Walker herself practiced each of these genres and clearly saw the multiplicity of literary expression as a crucial component of her critical project.

9   A. Walker, *Gathering Blossoms*, xiii. Edited by Valerie Boyd, the collection gathers selections of journal entries that Walker approved for publication, while the rest remain embargoed until 2040.

10   A. Walker, *Gathering Blossoms*, 19. Boyd describes Eric as a current acquaintance ("comrade") of Walker's and a white man "movement type." According to White, in the summer of 1966, Walker was recently graduated from Sarah Lawrence College (January 1966) and newly transplanted in Mississippi to work at the NAACP Legal Defense and Educational Fund (E. C. White, *Alice Walker*, 119, 130, 134).

11   A. Walker, *Gathering Blossoms*, 19. Dated August 1966, the journal entry is penned a few years before Walker would write the essay "In Search of Our Mothers' Gardens," first published in 1974 in *Ms.* magazine, whose title she would later borrow for her 1983 essay collection of the same title.

12   A. Walker, *Gathering Blossoms*, 20. Walker thus recuperates her family's denied economic value as sharecroppers via her mother's domestic artistry.

13   E. C. White, *Alice Walker*, 27. White also quotes Walker's sister Ruth, who described how their mother "gave away enough flowers to be the official florist of Georgia" (56). As flowers and food intertwine in these passages, they are inextricably linked as forms of sustenance across body and soul, and family and community.

14   A. Walker, "The Revenge of Hannah," 62.

15   Christian, "Introduction," in *Black Feminist Criticism*, ix. I imagine Christian alternating between experiencing their beauty and benefiting from the oxygen they respired, while providing them with the means for further growth and life.

16 Christian, "Introduction," in *Black Feminist Criticism*, ix, xv. Again, by the publication of *Black Feminist Criticism* in 1985, Christian had published multiple books, dozens of essays, and had since become the first Black woman tenured professor at UC Berkeley in 1978.

17 A. Walker, *Our Mothers' Gardens*, 241.

18 See Christian, *"Everyday Use."* In Alice Walker's story "Everyday Use," an intergenerational rift between a mother ("Mama") and her eldest daughter ("Dee," who prefers "Wangero") deepens due to their respective approaches to quilting, with Mama preferring the quilts as enjoyable every-day objects, and Dee as art objects to display. The story speaks particularly to Christian's distinction between scholarship that was meant for display (to showcase the critic's skill or reflect prestige) and scholarship that was meant to be put to "everyday use" beyond academia, where it had utility in the world. The space of the garden/yard is also significant at the beginning of the story. Christian's essay, "Novels for Everyday Use: The Novels of Alice Walker," appeared in Christian's 1980 book, *Black Women Novelists*. Christian published other essays on Walker in 1980, 1981, and 1984—each collected in Christian, *Black Feminist Criticism* in 1985. Christian also wrote *Alice Walker's "The Color Purple" and Other Works: A Critical Commentary*.

19 Christian, "The Race for Theory," 52.

20 Smith was organizing via the National Black Feminist Organization and, shortly thereafter, the Combahee River Collective as well as Kitchen Table: Women of Color Press, in Taylor, *How We Get Free*, 42–47. Inter-estingly, Smith's biography at the close of her 1974 review of Alice Walk-er's *In Love and Trouble* emphasizes instead her academic qualifications: "Barbara Smith is currently completing her doctorate in English at the University of Connecticut and is teaching a course on black women writers at Emerson College" ("The Souls of Black Women," 78).

21 B. Smith, "The Souls of Black Women," 43, 78.

22 B. Smith, "Toward a Black Feminist Criticism," 21, 23.

23 García Peña, *Community as Rebellion*, 29.

24 Keizer, "Introduction," in Bowles, Fabi, and Keizer, *New Black Feminist Criticism*, 2–3.

25 I was fortunate in that years later I met and was taught by Christian's former student, Keizer, in the English graduate program at UC Irvine in the mid-2010s.

26 See Christian's essay "Novels for Everyday Use" in *Black Women Novelists*, as well as several essays collected in Christian's *Black Feminist Criticism*.

27 Christian, "The Contrary Women," in *Black Feminist Criticism*, 32–33. Simi-larly, Barbara Smith writes, "Even as a black woman, I found the cumulative impact of these stories devastating. I questioned the quantity of pain in these sisters' lives and also wondered why none of the men and women were able to love each other" ("The Souls of Black Women," 43).

28   By contrast, Shanna Greene Benjamin notes how in Houston A. Baker Jr.'s
      1992 address to the Modern Language Association, Baker related how
      he had been teaching Phillis's use of "neoclassical literary conventions,"
      when one of his students, a Black woman, asked if their class could instead
      discuss "what Phillis means to the black community per se" and "talk about
      Wheatley in more direct ways," but Baker turned back to the discussion on
      conventions. Baker's feelings of shame after this encounter led him to later re-
      consider his pedagogy from a Black "womanist" lens (the student "redeemed"
      his teaching). See S. G. Benjamin, *Half in Shadow*, 125–26; Baker, "Presiden-
      tial Address," 403. What Baker describes is a pedagogy that is the result of his
      graduate training in the field of "British Victorian literature" (400).

29   Christian, "The Contrary Women," in *Black Feminist Criticism*, 33.

30   Christian foregrounds her relationship with her young daughter as one, too,
      of complex intellectual exchange. Christian introduces *Black Feminist Crit-
      icism* by recounting a conversation wherein she explains to her daughter
      why her work matters and how it is connected to the kinds of uneven power
      dynamics her daughter is already beginning to understand.

31   S. A. Williams, *Give Birth to Brightness*, 35. However, Williams would later
      revise some of the points she made in this monograph. As will also be
      discussed in this chapter, Williams also wrote disparagingly of the blues
      tradition in her early work, an interpretation she would later revise in the
      criticism she wrote after becoming a published poet who emulated the blues
      tradition, providing the possibility that she may have changed her views
      about Phillis as well.

32   A. Walker, *Our Mothers' Gardens*, 235–36, 237 (emphasis in original).

33   A. Walker, *Our Mothers' Gardens*, 235.

34   Jack Halberstam, "The Wild Beyond," in Harney and Moten, *The Undercom-
      mons*, 10. Other questions might include these two: What does it mean to as-
      sume that Phillis did not own herself interiorly, even while she was enslaved
      in the eyes of the law? Further, what of the many Black women, even today,
      who do not have their own rooms or sufficient money of their own?

35   The now ephemeral cover portrait of the 1983 edition was later replaced for
      a design in 2004 featuring that of an unknown young Black woman leaning
      over the flower petals in her cupped hands.

36   B. Brown, review of A. Walker, *In Search of Our Mothers' Gardens*, 351.

37   Butler, "Black Feminism," B2. Butler's matter-of-fact review is striking
      for its generous synopsis of Walker's volume's contents without any harsh
      criticism. It concludes with Butler's assessment of Walker's "basically
      thoughtful common-sense writing of a kind that might once have been
      called humanist before that word was pushed into disrepute."

38   A. Walker, "*One Child*," in *Our Mothers' Gardens*, 392–93.

39   In her later years, Walker has come under fire for antisemitic remarks. See
      Burton, "Alice Walker's Terrible Anti-Semitic Poem Felt Personal—to Her

and to Me." Walker's daughter, Rebecca Walker, discusses her half-Jewish
ancestry in her autobiography *Black, White, and Jewish: Autobiography of
a Shifting Self*. Marina Magloire's article "Moving Towards Life" discusses
June Jordan and Audre Lorde's "Black feminist falling-out over Zionism"
and "Palestinian resistance."

40 Vigderman, "From Rags to Rage to Art," 637. ·

41 A. Walker, *Our Mothers' Gardens*, 243. Walker emphasizes Phillis's mother,
about whom we cannot possibly know anything definitively, but Walker
speculates, "Perhaps she painted . . . perhaps she sang . . . perhaps she
wove . . . or told the most ingenious stories." It appears Walker was working
out the fact that even if she and Phillis had little in common, perhaps their
mothers had more. This turn to her mother would find its echo in Honorée
Fanonne Jeffers's poems about Phillis's mother in 2020 in *The Age of Phillis*.

42 Benjamin and McKay, "Intimacy and Ephemera," 16.

43 Benjamin and McKay, "Intimacy and Ephemera," 17. Benjamin's 2015
essay precedes her 2021 biography of McKay and details how "intimacy as
a methodology is invisible trust-building work that initiates or facilitates the recovery and reconstitution of the lives and literature of black
women." While Benjamin acknowledges that ultimately her biography
will be "unauthorized" because McKay's daughter would "not have final
approval over the content," Benjamin waited until she "had granted me
permission," and it is clear Benjamin adheres to a Black feminist critical ethos throughout the process (Benjamin and McKay, "Intimacy and
Ephemera," 18).

44 S. A. Williams, "Some Implications," 304. While Williams concurred that
feminism was better than the predominating alternative, she was concerned
that its failure to theorize Black men as part of its aims would prevent the
study of Black masculine writers who do practice Black feminisms and lead
to further division and rifts. By her own account, Williams later felt that her
early scholarship overly focused on Black masculine writers. Of her 1972
scholarly monograph, Williams wrote, "I was a 'man' in *Give Birth to Brightness*," but "I am the women I speak of in my stories, my poems" ("From
Meditations," 770).

45 S. A. Williams, "Some Implications," 304.

46 Lizzy LeRud, "Heart First into This Ruin," *Poetry Foundation*, May 11, 2020,
https://www.poetryfoundation.org/articles/153468/heart-first-into-this
-ruin. LeRud writes that Coleman's "critic's pen could prove vicious." Famous writers whom Coleman critiqued in problematic terms include Maya
Angelou and Audre Lorde.

47 A special issue dedicated to Sherley Anne Williams's work advertised a call
for papers in 2017 to appear in the journal *Callaloo* to be guest edited by
Wendy W. Walters. Unfortunately, despite Walters's best efforts, the special
issue has not progressed as of the time of this writing.

48 For example, Williams describes her "earlier disdain for the blues as the misguided arrogance of the undergraduate," and her determination "to be on guard against such parochialism in the future" (S. A. Williams, "Returning to the Blues," 819–20).

49 S. A. Williams, "Returning to the Blues," 816.

50 S. A. Williams, "Returning to the Blues," 827.

51 Williams to Gates, November 5, 1991, Williams Papers, box 1, folder 31. Williams often kept copies of drafts of her own professional correspondence.

52 Williams received tenure at UC San Diego in 1975, as noted by Lisa Lowe, "Sherley Anne Williams: In Memoriam," October 1999, literature.ucsd.edu /people/faculty/memoriam/swilliams.html. Williams was "the first black woman in a department dominated by white males" (Gable, "Understanding the Impossible").

53 "Sherley Anne Williams, 54, Novelist, Poet and Professor," *New York Times*, July 14, 1999.

54 As this student, K., wrote further, "I hear this so much from people because I care about succeeding and making a positive change in the community. I'm always 'doing too much' or I 'stand out too much'" (personal correspondence, August 5, 2022).

55 A large percentage of Williams's papers at UC San Diego relate to her teaching. Classes with high enrollments are also common in the University of California system. While I am skeptical of the system's track record when it comes to supporting Black women professors, this is not to say that other, better-endowed state or private universities have supported them more, only that one could assume they could be able to support a celebrated writer with a higher salary and a lower teaching load, so long as doing so coincided with their mission of prestige.

56 See S. A. Williams, "From Meditations," 768–70. Williams describes being raised by one of her older sisters after her parents, who were agricultural workers, passed away when Williams was young. Williams later became a professor at a prestigious public research university despite these early barriers, and she would return her family's care by caring for her older sisters later in life.

57 Williams continues, "Even in a poverty-stricken environment, we were enormously poor." Yet Williams describes her present-day situation as decidedly middle class, saying, "I kind of lucked into this middle-class occupation, and those times I might have fallen and did not want to get up, there was this middle-class system propping me up" (Gable, "Understanding the Impossible").

58 Harney and Moten, *The Undercommons*, 26, 33.

59 For example, in addition to Williams and Christian, Evie Shockley's 2011 poem "good night women (or, defying the carcinogenic pen)" also

commemorates Audre Lorde, Toni Cade Bambara, Claudia Tate, June Jordan, and Nellie Y. McKay, all of whom died of cancer between 1992 and 2006, in Shockley, *the new black*, 12. In the main body of Shockley's poem, the women are figured like stars, but their heavenly ascent is not to last forever. At its close, the poem expresses the sheer magnitude of the loss of their lives, occurring far too often. Also, Alexis Pauline Gumbs's poetic scholarship is informed by this legacy of elders dying from cancer or other diseases. She writes in her 2011 dissertation, "The material I am working with here is a maternal trace (not an inherited property) that scares me to death. And has made me obsessed with the deaths of people like Audre Lorde, June Jordan, Claudia Jones, Barbara Christian, Nellie McKay, Elizabeth Amelia Hadley, Octavia Butler, Gloria Anzaldua and more" ("We Can Learn," 21). Myisha Priest in 2008 also notes the deaths of Virginia Hamilton and Beverly Robinson, in "Salvation Is the Issue," 118; and Grace Kyungwon Hong in 2015 also notes the deaths of Endesha Ida Mae Holland, Toni Yancey, Stephanie Camp, and Marlon Riggs, a beloved gay Black man filmmaker, poet, and UC Berkeley professor who died of complications from AIDS in 1994, in *Death Beyond Disavowal*, 126, 143.

60   S. G. Benjamin, *Half in Shadow*, 2. Up until her death, McKay felt she had to keep the truth of her two children, including a daughter whom she told colleagues was her sister, among other select details about her life, private. As Benjamin writes, "McKay gave her colleagues and her students access on her own terms" (5).

61   S. G. Benjamin, *Half in Shadow*, 11–13. Benjamin roots her biography largely in McKay's professional ephemera, as access to personal ephemera required that she establish rapport with McKay's family, some of whom could not participate or passed away before their full story could be told.

62   Barbara Christian also became a single mother later in life after a divorce and, as previously detailed in this chapter, she selectively used her personal life as a frame through which to contextualize her scholarship, contrary to any stigma.

63   Williams wrote about her son publicly in her poems, especially in her 1975 *The Peacock Poems*, and made motherhood a cornerstone for interracial feminist solidarity in her 1986 novel *Dessa Rose*. Again, in 1980, Williams wrote that she wanted to care for her older sisters, Ruise and Learn, in return for their having raised her after her parents passed away ("From Meditations," 769).

64   Rutledge et al., "The Nellie Tree," 50.

65   Williams to Gates, November 5, 1991, Williams Papers, box 1, folder 31. Before she passed away, Williams was working on the novel *Licensed to Dream*, which, though unpublished, resides in her papers in proposal, outline, and draft forms. The novel was intended as the sequel to *Dessa Rose*.

Williams also wrote a novel earlier in her career which was never published about "a young single mother in Fresno working as a maid to support her child and brother," and in 1986, Williams was thinking of writing "a trilogy set in the Central Valley that examines the societal strivings of black people during the '60s" (Gable, "Understanding the Impossible").

66 Williams writes that "it hurt me to hear her voice; it frightened me," and it "seemed to me like an open wound, proclaiming that its owner had survived unspeakable things" ("Returning to the Blues," 824, 817).

67 S. A. Williams, "Returning to the Blues," 824.

68 DuCille, "Feminism, Black and Blue," 151.

69 McKay to Williams, February 20, 1989, Williams Papers, box 3, folder 1. While Williams is not listed on the *Norton*'s main prefatory page of general editors at the forefront, she is listed in the acknowledgments as an editorial editor, one of around one hundred academics the general editors consulted. McKay coedited the *Norton Anthology of African American Literature* with Henry Louis Gates Jr. In its first 1996 edition, the anthology's other editors included, in alphabetical order, "William L. Andrews; Houston A. Baker Jr.; Barbara T. Christian; Frances Smith Foster; Deborah E. McDowell; Robert G. O'Meally; Arnold Rampersad; Hortense Spillers; and Richard Yarborough" (Gates and McKay, *Norton Anthology of African American Literature*, iv).

70 Perhaps her interest in what would be recorded was also instrumental in the production of the accompanying CD of recorded oral culture that was sold with the *Norton*, as no mention of such is made in the table of contents McKay originally sent Williams in 1989, suggesting it was a later addition to the project stemming from the wider editorial advice received. The contents of the CDs that were included with the *Norton Anthology of African American Literature* changed slightly with each subsequent edition. Comparing the 1989 draft of the *Norton* table of contents to the published 1997 edition also reveals some other interesting changes, such as the fact that several works by figures whom we consider canonical today, including Olaudah Equiano, Sojourner Truth, and Nella Larsen (whom Williams points out in her notes), were originally absent but were added to the anthology by 1997. Of course, on the flip side, some figures in the 1989 table of contents were later omitted.

71 McKay to Williams, February 20, 1989, Williams Papers, box 3, folder 1.

72 Gates and McKay, *Norton Anthology of African American Literature*, 2019, 2020.

73 Christian, "The Race for Theory," 62.

74 S. A. Williams, "Remembering Prof. Sterling A. Brown," 107 (my emphasis).

75 As Williams writes at the close of her 1975 poem "Any Woman's Blues": her song is not over (*The Peacock Poems*, 25, line 24). The first 1975 edition

of *The Peacock Poems* features a different spelling of Williams's first name (Shirley), which is changed in subsequent 1975 reprints.

76   Williams to Walker, April 5, 1989, Williams Papers, box 1, folder 1.

77   Williams to Gates, November 5, 1991, Williams Papers, box 1, folder 31.

78   Harney and Moten, *The Undercommons*, 28. While there is every indication in the large body of teaching materials collected in her UC San Diego papers that Williams was a proficient, if not beloved, teacher, she was also trying to be successful, or to survive, in, as they call it, the "UC system." I also believe she would not have subscribed to the model of university teaching as a "call to order," as a violent implementation of colonial power, surveillance, and prescribed knowledge (*The Undercommons*, 125).

79   Williams to Walker, April 5, 1989, Williams Papers, box 1, folder 1.

80   A. Walker, *Our Mothers' Gardens*, xi (emphasis in original).

81   Joanna Brooks writes that Phillis wrote elegies to especially gain favor with white women in exchange for access to their network and support: "While Wheatley built her career with support from both black and white women, it was her white female agents who asserted a definitive influence over the content of her poems" ("Our Phillis, Ourselves," 10).

82   Cavitch, *American Elegy*, 33. While Phillis's elegies are often studied in relation to eighteenth-century print culture, the Puritan funeral elegy is also renowned for its having preceded and exceeded its Puritan context, in part due to its "more-than-occasional implication in matters of familial, communal, and cultural continuity" (34), a continuity that I argue comes to include Black feminisms.

83   Several scholars have speculated that Phillis perfected her use of the Puritan elegy to be able to, in part, clandestinely practice her own mourning for her African kinfolk and thus quietly prophesy a time when print would accommodate, annunciate, and center Black grief within the elegy's enterprise. See Bassard, *Spiritual Interrogations*, 8, 64; Bennett, "Phillis Wheatley's Vocation and the Paradox of the 'Afric Muse,'" 70; Brooks, "Our Phillis, Ourselves," 12; and Cavitch, *American Elegy*, 188–89.

84   June Jordan, "The Difficult Miracle," in *Some of Us*, 175.

85   Again, all my references to Phillis's writings are from the 2024 *Writings of Phillis Wheatley Peters* edited by Vincent Carretta, unless otherwise noted. Attempts to organize (or mitigate potential lost) sales include Phillis's letters to David Worcester (Wooster) on October 18, 1773, 110; to Obour on October 30, 1773, 112, and again on May 6, 1774, 123; to Samuel Hopkins on February 9, 1774, 118–19, and again on May 6, 1774, 123–24; and to Mary Wooster on July 15, 1778, 135–36.

86   Carretta, *Biography*, 196–97.

87   Phillis to Mary Wooster, July 15, 1778, 136. Carretta writes that the cost Phillis specifies is "12 [shillings]/Lm.o [lawful money] each" (*Biography*, 179).

88   Carretta, *Biography*, 193–94. See also Dayton, "Lost Years Recovered."

122 Coleman, "Imagining Phillis," 31:23–24.

123 Coleman, "Imagining Phillis," 47:03–7. Coleman says, "Her poems, like her children, died, not of neglect by Phillis but out of the circumstances of her time" (57:27–35), and "like Phillis, I too have lost a child, an adult son" (58:23–27). Coleman's son "died of AIDS-related complications in 1997" (Ryan, "The Transformative Poetics of Wanda Coleman's *American Sonnets*," 422).

124 Coleman, "Imagining Phillis," 1:00:09–19.

125 Phillis, "On Virtue," 54–55, entire poem.

126 Mason, *Poems of Phillis Wheatley* (1989 ed.), 15.

127 Cervenka and Coleman, *Twin Sisters*.

128 In various moments in the archive of Coleman and others' papers, Coleman corresponded with critics to criticize their own accounts of her work. Today, it is perhaps more well understood that classifications of who has "national fame" or not is not necessarily the fault of a poet's writing but rather their connections and privilege, but these moments communicate a great deal of friction and misunderstanding perhaps on both sides.

129 See Terrance Hayes's introduction to Coleman, *Wicked Enchantment*, xi. Hayes writes that Coleman "only softened when she understood/believed I was a fan."

130 McKay, "Naming the Problem," 363.

131 All professors, whether tenured, tenure-track, or untenured, are harmed by adjunctification, as its effects—the insidious chipping away of mentorship, resources, and support—inevitably creep up the ranks. On Thea K. Hunter, see Harris, "The Death of an Adjunct." Harris writes that "To be a perennial adjunct professor is to hear the constant tone of higher education's death knell. The story is well known—the long hours, the heavy workload, the insufficient pay—as academia relies on adjunct professors, non-tenured faculty members, who are often paid pennies on the dollar to do the same work required of their tenured colleagues." This system is unsustainable, economically and otherwise. Fortunately, Hunter's "professional and personal papers will be donated to the Schlesinger Library on the History of Women in America, at Radcliffe/Harvard" ("In Memoriam: Thea K. Hunter, April 25, 2019, https://www.oah.org/insights/archive/in-memoriam-thea-k-hunter/).

132 Ryan and Coleman, "'Come. Glory in My Wonder's Will,'" 196.

133 This is also similar to how Terrance Hayes navigates introducing Coleman in his recent edition of her poems, by focusing on "my own true introduction to her" (Coleman, *Wicked Enchantment*, xi).

134 Readers learn that "Georgiana" was to be her older sister's name before it later became Coleman's middle name—the space between Coleman's first and last name haunted and enchanted by someone who died young. Using this name to hail someone back into life would allow Coleman to speak to

other family members she had lost too. *Bathwater Wine* and *Mercurochrome* honor especially the loss of Coleman's oldest son, see P. A. Brown, "What Saves Us," 645. Coleman describes feeling "like I had wasted my life" (645), and the books are an attempt to take stock of that life.

135 The poems that precede Coleman's first "Letter to My Older Sister" detail her childhood and adolescence; the poems that precede "Letter to My Older Sister (2)" her young adulthood; "Letter to My Older Sister (3–4)," her early motherhood; "Letter to My Older Sister (5)," her lifestyle as a maturing poet; and following the death of her son comes her final "Letter to My Older Sister (6)."

136 Although the precariousness of her parents' early lives, their survival, and their ability to craft joyous lives mark Southern California as a kind of haven, the poems in the "Disclosures" section of *Bathwater Wine* remain skeptical, and several poems acknowledge Coleman's own painful childhood. In this section, Coleman also writes a series of elegies for her father.

137 Coleman, "Letter to My Older Sister," in *Bathwater Wine*, 47, lines 23–24.

138 Coleman, "Beyond the Lake of Memories," in *Bathwater Wine*, 46, line 16.

139 See especially Coleman, "Letter to My Older Sister (2)," in *Bathwater Wine*, 86, lines 11–15; "Letter to My Older Sister (3)," in *Mercurochrome*, 50, lines 23–24; "Letter to My Older Sister (4)," in *Mercurochrome*, 52, lines 12–13, and 52–53, lines 32–38.

140 Coleman, "Letter to My Older Sister (5)," in *Mercurochrome*, 70, lines 14–17; see also "mercurochrome, *n*.," OED *Online*, Oxford University Press, https://www.oed.com/dictionary/mercurochrome_n?tl=true, accessed September 5, 2022.

141 Coleman, "Letter to My Older Sister (5)," 70, lines 43, 17–22. The poem's jagged structure, long lines alternating with short lines, seem to approximate *Mercurochrome*'s vacillation between healing and pain.

142 Coleman, "Letter to My Older Sister (6)," in *Mercurochrome*, 248, lines 27–29.

143 Coleman, "Wanda Coleman: The TNB Self Interview."

144 Magistrale and Ferreira, "Sweet Mama Wanda Tells Fortunes," 494.

145 Coleman, "Wanda Coleman: The TNB Self Interview."

Conclusion

1 Continued scholarship in this vein in California alone might look to the papers of Vèvè A. Clark at the University of California, Berkeley; Shirley Kennedy at the University of California, Santa Barbara; Jewelle Gomez at the San Francisco Public Library; and many more across the United States and elsewhere.

2 Once more, my references to Phillis's writings are from the 2024 *Writings of Phillis Wheatley Peters* edited by Vincent Carretta, unless otherwise noted. Phillis, "To the University" (1773), 55, lines 1–6.

3   Hine, "Rape and the Inner Lives of Black Women in the Middle West," 912.

4   A. Walker, *Our Mothers' Gardens*, xi (emphasis in original).

5   June Jordan, *Some of Us*, 177. See also a draft of this essay in Jordan Papers (Harvard), box 59, folder 14.

6   Phillis, "To the University" (1767), 10, lines 1–2.

7   June Jordan, *Some of Us*, 178, 179, 180; and Jordan Papers (Harvard), box 59, folder 14.

8   June Jordan, *Civil Wars*, 123. Jordan says of this essay, "Thinking About My Poetry," that when her latest volume of selected poems was published by Random House, only two periodicals reviewed it, "an unexpected silence that pushed [her] to further re-examine [her] assumptions of community," since at the time she was a contributor to at least three Black or feminist periodicals, so, she "decided to pretend that somebody wanted to know how [she] came to be a poet" (122) and wrote an essay on that topic.

9   June Jordan, "Black Studies," in *Civil Wars*, 45.

10   Jordan Papers (Harvard), box 103, folder 3. Marina Magloire's article "Moving Towards Life" emphasizes that around the mid-1980s to mid-1990s Jordan's career was stymied by backlash to her support for Palestinians. See also Sriram Shamasunder, "June Jordan's Legacy of Solidarity."

11   While several of the earliest Black men graduates of Harvard, including Richard Theodore Greener, who received his bachelor's degree in 1870, and W. E. B. Du Bois, who received in PhD in 1895, went on to have illustrious careers and long lives, Alberta V. Scott (ca. 1875–1902) did not. Scott became a "teacher" in "Indianapolis" and at "Tuskegee," but "died . . . after an illness of 16 months. Death was attributed to a nervous break down, brought on partly by overwork, but largely caused, it is believed by her relatives, by the shock given her by the sudden death of her father, nearly two years ago" (*Cambridge Chronicle*, September 6, 1902).

12   Phillis, "To the University" (1767), 10, lines 8–11.

13   Phillis, "To the University" (1773), 55, lines 7–9.

14   Phillis, "To the University," 55, lines 26–28.

15   I give a synopsis of this history in my essay "Imagining Black Steminist Care."

16   Myers, *Of Black Study*, 4.

17   June Jordan, *Civil Wars*, 53, 52.

18   Myers, *Of Black Study*, 6.

19   The letter does say this was "a very subordinate position to the great praise" (E. Peters to Christian, March 10, 1986, Christian Papers, carton 2, folder 25).

20   McKay to Christian, October 1, 1982, Christian Papers, carton 1, folder 33.

21   "Barbara Christian and the Futures of Black Studies," Social Sciences at UC Berkeley, January 25, 2021, YouTube video, 10:50–53 and 11:27–36, https://youtu.be/rd5OpjD6Jxo. In her presentation, Keizer also offered words of caution about the future of the field.

22 I am also grateful to Kevin Quashie for his theorization of "quiet"—which especially helped me begin research for my doctoral dissertation—as a choice or practice we might understand as interiorly empowering, in *The Sovereignty of Quiet.*

23 Several of Christian's teaching evaluations are collected in her papers in carton 8, folder 37. Christian's high evaluations are also discussed in the letter from Margaret B. Wilkerson to Gerald A. Mendelson recommending Christian's merit increase on February 26, 1993, in Christian Papers, carton 2, folder 26.

24 Christian, n.d., carton 9, folder 29; Christian, n.d., carton 2, folder 24; and Christian to Hinton, October 10, 1994, carton 12, folder 20, all in Christian Papers. Christian envisioned this book would focus on Toni Morrison, Alice Walker, Octavia E. Butler, Audre Lorde, June Jordan, Angela Davis, and bell hooks.

25 Christian Papers, carton 10.

26 Christian to Gates, March 31, 1987, Christian Papers, carton 10, folder 1. Gates's letter to Christian on January 27, 1987, states that Mary Helen Washington was originally asked to fill the role of associate general editor; see Christian Papers, carton 10, folder 1.

27 Christian, n.d., Christian Papers, carton 11, folder 14.

28 Christian, n.d., Christian Papers, carton 11, folder 14. This correspondence unfolds over several letters. See especially the December 11, 1978, letter from the Feminist Press.

29 Walker to Christian, September 14, 1981, Christian Papers, carton 11, folder 11.

30 Walker to Christian, October 21, 1981, Christian Papers, carton 11, folder 11 (underlining in original).

31 In later years, Walker later wrote to Christian to correct several parts of Christian's book *Alice Walker's "The Color Purple" and Other Works*, which Walker was not invited to review, I believe, before publication. She asked, "I must ask you: do you have an editor?" (Walker to Christian, February 14, 1985, Christian Papers, carton 3, folder 24).

32 Christian to Burton, February 21, 1994, Christian Papers, carton 10, folder 1.

33 I close with an homage to Tracy Chapman's "I'm Ready," the final song in her album *New Beginning* (Elektra, 1995)—with its cover photograph of a sunflower upon purple.

Archives

Christian, Barbara. Papers. Bancroft Library, University of California, Berkeley.

Coleman, Wanda. Papers. UCLA Library Special Collections, Charles E. Young Research Library, University of California, Los Angeles.

duCille, Ann. Papers. John Hay Library, Brown University.

Foster, Frances Smith. Papers. Stuart A. Rose Manuscript, Archives, and Rare Book Library, Emory University.

Jordan, June. Collection. Department of African American and African Diaspora Studies, University of California, Berkeley.

Jordan, June. Papers. Schlesinger Library, Harvard Radcliffe Institute.

Lorde, Audre. Papers. Spelman College Archives.

Phillis [Wheatley]. Collection. Stuart A. Rose Manuscript, Archives, and Rare Book Library, Emory University.

Walker, Alice. Papers. Stuart A. Rose Manuscript, Archives, and Rare Book Library, Emory University.

Walker, Margaret. Personal Journals. Margaret Walker Personal Papers Digital Archives Project, Margaret Walker Alexander National Research Center, Jackson State University. https://www.jsums.edu/margaretwalkercenter/collections/digital-archives-project/.

Williams, Sherley Anne. Papers. Special Collections and Archives, University of California, San Diego.

Other Works

Adeline, Aunt, and Zillah Cross Peel. *Federal Writers' Project: Slave Narrative Project*, vol. 2: *Arkansas*, part 1: *Abbott–Byrd*, 11–16. November–December 1936. Manuscript/Mixed Material. https://www.loc.gov/item/mesn021/.

Ahmed, Sara. *Living a Feminist Life*. Durham, NC: Duke University Press, 2017.

Alexander, M. Jacqui. *Pedagogies of Crossing: Meditations on Feminism, Sexual Politics, Memory, and the Sacred*. Durham, NC: Duke University Press, 2005.

Andrews, William L. *To Tell a Free Story: The First Century of Afro-American Autobiography, 1760–1865.* Urbana: University of Illinois Press, 1986.

Baker, Houston A., Jr. "Presidential Address 1992: Local Pedagogy; or, How I Redeemed My Spring Semester." *PMLA* 108, no. 3 (1993): 400–409.

Bambara, Toni Cade, ed. *The Black Woman: An Anthology.* 1970. Reprint, New York: Washington Square Press, 2005.

Bassard, Katherine Clay. *Spiritual Interrogations: Culture, Gender, and Community in Early African American Women's Writing.* Princeton, NJ: Princeton University Press, 1999.

Benjamin, Richard M. "Tenured Black Professors in the English Department of the Nation's 25 Highest-Ranked Universities." *Journal of Blacks in Higher Education*, no. 8 (1995): 79–82.

Benjamin, Shanna Greene. *Half in Shadow: The Life and Legacy of Nellie Y. McKay.* Chapel Hill: University of North Carolina Press, 2021.

Benjamin, Shanna Greene, and Nellie Y. McKay. "Intimacy and Ephemera: In Search of Our Mothers' Letters." *MELUS* 40, no. 3 (2015): 16–27.

Bennett, Paula. "Phillis Wheatley's Vocation and the Paradox of the 'Afric Muse.'" *PMLA* 113, no. 1 (1998): 64–76.

Blockett, Kimberly. "Do You Have Any Skin in the Game?" *Legacy: A Journal of American Women Writers* 31, no. 1 (2014): 63–65.

Bowles, Gloria, M. Giulia Fabi, and Arlene R. Keizer, eds. *New Black Feminist Criticism, 1985–2000*, by Barbara Christian. Urbana: University of Illinois Press, 2007.

Boyd, Melba Joyce. *Discarded Legacy: Politics and Poetics in the Life of Frances E. W. Harper, 1825–1911.* Detroit: Wayne State University Press, 1994.

Boyd, Melba Joyce. *Wrestling with the Muse: Dudley Randall and the Broadside Press.* New York: Columbia University Press, 2003.

Braxton, Joanne M., and Andreé Nicola McLaughlin, eds. *Wild Women in the Whirlwind: Afra-American Culture and the Contemporary Literary Renaissance.* New Brunswick, NJ: Rutgers University Press, 1990.

Brooks, Joanna. "Our Phillis, Ourselves." *American Literature* 82, no. 1 (2010): 1–28.

Brown, Beth. Review of *In Search of Our Mothers' Gardens: Womanist Prose*, by Alice Walker. *CLA Journal* 27, no. 3 (1984): 348–52.

brown, drea. *dear girl: a reckoning.* Los Angeles: Gold Line, 2015.

Brown, Priscilla Ann. "What Saves Us: An Interview with Wanda Coleman." *Callaloo* 26, no. 3 (2003): 635–61.

Brown, Sterling A. *Outline for the Study of the Poetry of American Negroes.* New York: Harcourt, Brace and Company, 1931.

Burton, Nylah. "Alice Walker's Terrible Anti-Semitic Poem Felt Personal—to Her and to Me." *New York Magazine*, December 28, 2018.

Butler, Octavia E. "Black Feminism: Searching the Past." Review of *In Search of Our Mothers' Gardens: Womanist Prose*, by Alice Walker. *Washington Post*, October 17, 1983.

Bynum, Tara. "Phillis Wheatley on Friendship." *Legacy: A Journal of American Women Writers* 31, no. 1 (2014): 42–51.

Bynum, Tara. "Phillis Wheatley's Pleasures: Reading Good Feeling in Phillis Wheatley's Poems and Letters." *Common-place* 11, no. 1 (2010). www.commonplace.online/article/phillis-wheatleys-pleasures/.

Bynum, Tara A. *Reading Pleasures: Everyday Black Living in Early America.* Urbana: University of Illinois Press, 2023.

Bynum, Tara A., Brigitte Fielder, and Cassander L. Smith. "Special Issue Introduction: 'Dear Sister: Phillis Wheatley's Futures.'" *Early American Literature* 57, no. 3 (2022): 663–79.

Carby, Hazel V. Foreword to *Seraph on the Suwanee: A Novel* (1948), by Zora Neale Hurston, vii–xviii. New York: HarperPerennial, 1991.

Carretta, Vincent. *Phillis Wheatley: Biography of a Genius in Bondage.* Athens: University of Georgia Press, 2011.

Carretta, Vincent. *Phillis Wheatley Peters: Biography of a Genius in Bondage.* 2011. Reprint, Athens: University of Georgia Press, 2023. All references are to this most recent edition, unless otherwise noted.

Carretta, Vincent. "Phillis Wheatley's First Effort." *PMLA* 125, no. 3 (2010): 795–97.

Carretta, Vincent. Review of David Waldstreicher, *The Odyssey of Phillis Wheatley: A Poet's Journeys Through American Slavery and Independence. Early American Literature* 59, no. 1 (2024): 154–58.

Cavitch, Max. *American Elegy: The Poetry of Mourning from the Puritans to Whitman.* Minneapolis: University of Minnesota Press, 2007.

Cervenka, Exene, and Wanda Coleman. *Twin Sisters.* Freeway Records, 1985, vinyl.

Christian, Barbara. *Alice Walker's "The Color Purple" and Other Works: A Critical Commentary.* New York: Monarch, 1987.

Christian, Barbara. *Black Feminist Criticism: Perspectives on Black Women Writers.* New York: Pergamon, 1985.

Christian, Barbara. *Black Women Novelists: The Development of a Tradition, 1892–1976.* Westport, CT: Greenwood, 1980.

Christian, Barbara, ed. *"Everyday Use": Alice Walker.* New Brunswick, NJ: Rutgers University Press, 1994.

Christian, Barbara. *New Black Feminist Criticism, 1985–2000.* Edited by Gloria Bowles, M. Giulia Fabi, and Arlene R. Keizer. Urbana: University of Illinois Press, 2007.

Christian, Barbara. "The Race for Theory." *Cultural Critique*, no. 6 (1987): 51–63.

Christian, Barbara [T.]. "Ritualistic Process and the Structure of Paule Marshall's *Praisesong for the Widow." Callaloo*, no. 18 (1983): 74–84.

Christian, Barbara [T.]. *Teaching Guide to Accompany Black Foremothers: Three Lives by Dorothy Sterling.* Old Westbury, NY: Feminist Press, 1980.

Christian, Barbara. "Your Silence Will Not Protect You: A Tribute to Audre Lorde." *Berkeley Women's Law Journal* 8, no. 1 (1993): 1–5.

Chuong, Jennifer Y. "Engraving's 'Immoveable Veil': Phillis Wheatley's Portrait and the Politics of Technique." *Art Bulletin* 104, no. 2 (2022): 63–88.

Clarke, Allison. *Phillis*. Calgary: University of Calgary Press, 2020.

Coleman, Wanda. *Bathwater Wine*. Santa Rosa, CA: Black Sparrow, 1998.

Coleman, Wanda. "Imagining Phillis Wheatley: A Cross-Century Dialogue." Readings and Conversations. Poets House, New York City, November 16, 2001. https://poetshouse.org/audio/2001-wanda-coleman-on-phillis-wheatley-full-audio/.

Coleman, Wanda. *Mercurochrome: New Poems*. Santa Rosa, CA: Black Sparrow, 2001.

Coleman, Wanda. *The Riot Inside Me: More Trials and Tremors*. Boston: David R. Godine, 2005.

Coleman, Wanda. "Wanda Coleman: The TNB Self Interview." *Nervous Breakdown*, February 8, 2012. https://thenervousbreakdown.com/wcoleman/2012/02/wanda-coleman-the-tnb-self-interview/.

Coleman, Wanda. *Wicked Enchantment: Selected Poems*. Edited by Terrance Hayes. Boston: Black Sparrow, 2020.

Collins, Patricia Hill. *Black Feminist Thought: Knowledge, Consciousness, and the Politics of Empowerment*. 2000. Reprint, New York: Routledge, 2009.

Combahee River Collective. "Combahee River Collective Statement" (1977). In *How We Get Free: Black Feminism and the Combahee River Collective*, edited by Keeanga-Yamahtta Taylor, 15–27. Chicago: Haymarket Books, 2017.

Cooper, Brittney C. *Beyond Respectability: The Intellectual Thought of Race Women*. Urbana: University of Illinois Press, 2017.

Corral, Eduardo C. "To Robert Hayden." *Poetry* 199, no. 3 (2011): 264–66.

Crenshaw, Kimberlé. "Demarginalizing the Intersection of Race and Sex: A Black Feminist Critique of Antidiscrimination Doctrine, Feminist Theory and Antiracist Politics." *University of Chicago Legal Forum* (1989): 139–68.

Crenshaw, Kimberlé. "Mapping the Margins: Intersectionality, Identity Politics, and Violence Against Women of Color." *Stanford Law Review* 43, no. 6 (1991): 1241–99.

Dargan, Kyle. "Kyle Dargan (1980–)." In *Angles of Ascent: A Norton Anthology of Contemporary African American Poetry*, edited by Charles Henry Rowell, 434–38. New York: W. W. Norton, 2013.

Dargan, Kyle. *The Listening*. Athens: University of Georgia Press, 2004.

Davies, Carole Boyce. *Caribbean Spaces: Escapes from Twilight Zones*. Urbana: University of Illinois Press, 2013.

Dayton, Cornelia H. "Lost Years Recovered: John Peters and Phillis Wheatley Peters in Middleton." *New England Quarterly* 94, no. 3 (2021): 309–51.

Deane, Charles. *Letters of Phillis Wheatley, the Negro-Slave Poet of Boston.* Boston: John Wilson and Son, 1864.

De Veaux, Alexis. *Warrior Poet: A Biography of Audre Lorde.* New York: W. W. Norton, 2004.

Douglass, Frederick. *Narrative of the Life of Frederick Douglass, an American Slave, Written by Himself* (1845). In *The Portable Frederick Douglass*, edited by John Stauffer and Henry Louis Gates Jr., 3–100. New York: Penguin, 2016.

Dove, Rita. *Mother Love: Poems.* New York: W. W. Norton, 1995.

duCille, Ann. "Feminism, Black and Blue." In *True Confessions: Feminist Professors Tell Stories Out of School*, edited by Susan Gubar, 147–53. New York: W. W. Norton, 2011.

duCille, Ann. "The Occult of True Black Womanhood: Critical Demeanor and Black Feminist Studies." *Signs: Journal of Women in Culture and Society* 19, no. 3 (1994): 591–629.

duCille, Ann. "Tribute to Barbara T. Christian." *Meridians* 1, no. 1 (2000): xvi–xviii.

Dungy, Camille T., ed. *Black Nature: Four Centuries of African American Nature Poetry.* Athens: University of Georgia Press, 2009.

Dungy, Camille T. *Soil: The Story of a Black Mother's Garden.* New York: Simon & Schuster, 2023.

Ellis, George E., Charles Deane, Robert C. Winthrop, et al. "Special Meeting, December, 1889. Charles Deane." *Proceedings of the Massachusetts Historical Society* 5 (1889–90): 116–41.

Ellis, Nadia. *Territories of the Soul: Queered Belonging in the Black Diaspora.* Durham, NC: Duke University Press, 2015.

Ellison, Ralph. "Portrait of Inman Page: A Dedication Speech" (1979, 1980). In *Going to the Territory*, 113–19. 1986. Reprint, New York: Random House, 1995.

Ford, James Edward III. "An African Diasporic Critique of Violence." In *Systems of Life: Biopolitics, Economics, and Literature on the Cusp of Modernity*, edited by Richard A. Barney and Warren Montage, 56–81. New York: Fordham University Press, 2019.

Ford, James Edward, III. "The Difficult Miracle: Reading Phillis Wheatley against the Master's Discourse." *CR: The New Centennial Review* 18, no. 3 (2018): 181–224.

Foreman, P. Gabrielle. "A Riff, a Call, and a Response: Reframing the Problem That Led to Our Being Tokens in Ethnic and Gender Studies; or, Where Are We Going Anyway and with Whom Will We Travel?" *Legacy: A Journal of American Women Writers* 30, no. 2 (2013): 306–22.

Foster, Frances Smith, ed. *Love and Marriage in Early African America.* Lebanon, NH: University Press of New England, 2008.

Foster, Frances Smith. "The Personal Is Political, the Past Has Potential, and Other Thoughts on Studying Women's Literature: Then and Now." *Tulsa Studies in Women's Literature* 26, no. 1 (2007): 29–38.

Foster, Frances Smith. *Written by Herself: Literary Production by African American Women, 1746–1892.* Bloomington: Indiana University Press, 1993.

Frazier, S. [Susan] Elizabeth. "Some Afro-American Women of Mark." *African Methodist Episcopal Church Review* 8 (April 1892). Reprinted in *Women's Work: An Anthology of African-American Women's Historical Writings from Antebellum America to the Harlem Renaissance*, edited by Laurie F. Maffly-Kipp and Kathryn Lofton, 100–111. Oxford: Oxford University Press, 2010.

Gable, Mona. "Understanding the Impossible: Poet and Professor Sherley Anne Williams, Who Once Picked Cotton in Fresno, Has Become a Surprise Best-Selling Novelist." *Los Angeles Times*, December 7, 1986.

García Peña, Lorgia. *Community as Rebellion: A Syllabus for Surviving Academia as a Woman of Color.* Chicago: Haymarket Books, 2022.

Gates, Henry Louis, Jr. "In Her Own Write." Foreword to *The Collected Works of Phillis Wheatley*, edited by John C. Shields, vii–xxii. New York: Oxford University Press, 1988.

Gates, Henry Louis, Jr. *The Trials of Phillis Wheatley: America's First Black Poet and Her Encounters with the Founding Fathers.* New York: Basic Civitas Books, 2003.

Gates, Henry Louis, Jr., and Nellie Y. McKay, eds. *The Norton Anthology of African American Literature.* New York: W. W. Norton, 1997.

Georges, Danielle Legros, and Artress Bethany White, eds. *Wheatley at 250: Black Women Poets Re-imagine the Verse of Phillis Wheatley Peters: An Anthology.* Cambridge, MA: Pangyrus, 2023.

Gilmore, Ruth Wilson. *Golden Gulag: Prisons, Surplus, Crisis, and Opposition in Globalizing California.* Berkeley: University of California Press, 2007.

Giovanni, Nikki. *The Collected Poetry of Nikki Giovanni, 1968–1998.* New York: HarperPerennial, 2007.

Glatt, Carra. "'To Perpetuate Her Name': Appropriation and Autobiography in Margaretta Matilda Odell's Memoir of Phillis Wheatley." *Early American Literature* 55, no. 1 (2020): 145–76.

Glave, Thomas. "To Hell with the Goddess: In Celebration of the Human Person Audre Lorde." *Feminist Wire*, February 19, 2014.

Graham, Maryemma. *The House Where My Soul Lives: The Life of Margaret Walker.* New York: Oxford University Press, 2022.

Griffin, Farah Jasmine. "Conflict and Chorus: Reconsidering Toni Cade's *The Black Woman: An Anthology.*" In *Is It Nation Time? Contemporary*

Essays on Black Power and Black Nationalism, edited by Eddie S. Glaude Jr., 113–29. Chicago: University of Chicago Press, 2002.

Griffin, Farah Jasmine. *In Search of a Beautiful Freedom: New and Selected Essays*. New York: W. W. Norton, 2023.

Griffin, Farah Jasmine. "That the Mothers May Soar and the Daughters May Know Their Names: A Retrospective of Black Feminist Literary Criticism." *Signs: Journal of Women in Culture and Society* 32, no. 2 (2007): 483–507.

Gumbs, Alexis Pauline. *Dub: Finding Ceremony*. Durham, NC: Duke University Press, 2020.

Gumbs, Alexis Pauline. *M Archive: After the End of the World*. Durham, NC: Duke University Press, 2018.

Gumbs, Alexis Pauline. *Spill: Scenes of Black Feminist Fugitivity*. Durham, NC: Duke University Press, 2016.

Gumbs, Alexis Pauline. *Survival Is a Promise: The Eternal Life of Audre Lorde*. New York: Farrar, Straus and Giroux, 2024.

Gumbs, Alexis Pauline. "'We Can Learn to Mother Ourselves': The Queer Survival of Black Feminism, 1968–1996." PhD diss., Duke University, 2010, https://hdl.handle.net/10161/2398.

Hacker, Marilyn. "1999 Lenore Marshall Poetry Prize." *The Nation*, December 6, 1999.

Harney, Stefano, and Fred Moten. *The Undercommons: Fugitive Planning and Black Study*. Wivenhoe, UK: Minor Compositions, 2013.

Harris, Adam. "The Death of an Adjunct." *The Atlantic*, April 8, 2019.

Hartman, Saidiya. "The Dead Book Revisited." *History of the Present: A Journal of Critical History* 6, no. 2 (2016): 208–15.

Hartman, Saidiya. *Lose Your Mother: A Journey Along the Atlantic Slave Route*. New York: Farrar, Straus and Giroux, 2007.

Hartman, Saidiya. "Venus in Two Acts." *Small Axe* 12, no. 2 (2008): 1–14.

Hartman, Saidiya. *Wayward Lives, Beautiful Experiments: Intimate Histories of Riotous Black Girls, Troublesome Women, and Queer Radicals*. London: Serpent's Tail, 2021.

Hatcher, John. *From the Auroral Darkness: The Life and Poetry of Robert Hayden*. Oxford: George Ronald, 1984.

Hayden, Robert. *American Journal*. Taunton, MA: Effendi, 1978.

Hayden, Robert. *Collected Poems*, edited by Frederick Glaysher. 1985. Reprint, New York: Liveright, 2013.

Hayden, Robert, ed. *Kaleidoscope: Poems by American Negro Poets*. New York: Harcourt, Brace & World, 1967.

Hayden, Robert. "A Letter from Phillis Wheatley." *Massachusetts Review* 18, no. 4 (1977): 645–47.

Hayden, Robert. "Middle Passage." *Phylon* 6, no. 3 (1945): 247–53. Reprinted (revised version) in *A Ballad of Remembrance*. London: Paul Bremen, 1962.

Henderson, Mae Gwendolyn. "In Memory of Sherley Anne Williams: 'Some One Sweet Angel Chile' 1944–1999." *Callaloo* 22, no. 4 (1999): 763–67.

Higginbotham, Evelyn Brooks. *Righteous Discontent: The Women's Movement in the Black Baptist Church, 1880–1920.* Cambridge, MA: Harvard University Press, 1994.

Hine, Darlene Clark. "Rape and the Inner Lives of Black Women in the Middle West." *Signs* 14, no. 4 (1989): 912–20.

Holland, Sharon Patricia. "The Erotic." In *Keywords for Gender and Sexuality Studies*, edited by the Keywords Feminist Editorial Collective, 83–85. New York: New York University Press, 2021.

Holmes, Linda Janet. "Lessons in Boldness, 101." In *Savoring the Salt: The Legacy of Toni Cade Bambara*, edited by Linda Janet Holmes and Chery A. Wall, 154–59. Philadelphia: Temple University Press, 2007.

Holmes, Linda Janet. "Making Dreams Work." In *A Joyous Revolt: Toni Cade Bambara, Writer and Activist*, 97–120. Santa Barbara, CA: Praeger, 2014.

Hong, Grace Kyungwon. *Death Beyond Disavowal: The Impossible Politics of Difference.* Minneapolis: University of Minnesota Press, 2015.

Hopkins, Pauline E. "Famous Women of the Negro Race: IV. Some Literary Workers." *Colored American Magazine* 4, no. 4 (1902–3): 276–80.

Howe, Susan. *My Emily Dickinson.* 1985. Reprint, New York: New Directions, 2007.

Hull, Gloria T. *Color, Sex, and Poetry: Three Women Writers of the Harlem Renaissance.* Bloomington: Indiana University Press, 1987.

Hurston, Zora Neale. *Their Eyes Were Watching God.* 1937. Reprint, New York: Amistad, 2006.

Hutchins, Zachary McLeod. "'Add New Glory to Her Name': Phillis Wheatley Peters." *Early American Literature* 56, no. 3 (2021): 663–67.

Isani, Mukhtar Ali, and Phillis Wheatley. "'On the Death of General Wooster': An Unpublished Poem by Phillis Wheatley." *Modern Philology* 77, no. 3 (1980): 306–9.

Jackson, Virginia. *Before Modernism: Inventing American Lyric.* Princeton, NJ: Princeton University Press, 2023.

Jackson, Virginia. *Dickinson's Misery: A Theory of Lyric Reading.* Princeton, NJ: Princeton University Press, 2005.

James, Etta. *Time After Time.* RCA Victor, 1995, compact disc.

James, Etta, and David Ritz. *Rage to Survive: The Etta James Story.* 1995. Reprint, Cambridge, MA: Da Capo, 2003.

Jeffers, Honorée Fanonne. *The Age of Phillis.* Middletown, CT: Wesleyan University Press, 2020.

Jenkins, Candice M. *Private Lives, Proper Relations: Regulating Black Intimacy.* Minneapolis: University of Minnesota Press, 2007.

Johnson, E. Patrick, and Mae G. Henderson, eds. *Black Queer Studies: A Critical Anthology.* Durham, NC: Duke University Press, 2005.

Johnson, James Weldon, ed. *The Book of American Negro Poetry*. New York: Harcourt, Brace and Company, 1922.

Jones, Meta DuEwa. "Poetics." In *Keywords for African American Studies*, edited by Erica R. Edwards, Roderick A. Ferguson, and Jeffrey O. G. Ogbar, 147–51. New York: New York University Press, 2018.

Jordan, Jennifer. "Feminist Fantasies: Zora Neale Hurston's *Their Eyes Were Watching God*." *Tulsa Studies in Women's Literature* 7, no. 1 (1988): 105–17.

Jordan, June. *Civil Wars*. 1981. Reprint, New York: Touchstone, 1995.

Jordan, June. *Some of Us Did Not Die: New and Selected Essays of June Jordan*. New York: Basic/Civitas Books, 2002.

Keizer, Arlene R. "Black Feminist Criticism." In *A History of Feminist Literary Criticism*, edited by Gill Plain and Susan Sellers, 154–68. 2007. Reprint, Cambridge: Cambridge University Press, 2012.

Keizer, Arlene R. *Black Subjects: Identity Formation in the Contemporary Narrative of Slavery*. Ithaca, NY: Cornell University Press, 2004.

Lee, Kirsten. "Archives: 'Sister, Wasn't It Good': Archival Gestures, Mutual Witness, and the 1973 Phillis Wheatley Poetry Festival." *Early American Literature* 57, no. 3 (2022): 857–71.

Lootens, Tricia. *Lost Saints: Silence, Gender, and Victorian Literary Canonization*. Charlottesville: University Press of Virginia, 1996.

Lorde, Audre. *The Cancer Journals*. 1980. Reprint, New York: Penguin Books, 2020.

Lorde, Audre. *Sister Outsider*. 1984. Reprint, Berkeley: Crossing Press, 2007.

Magistrale, Tony, and Patricia Ferreira. "Sweet Mama Wanda Tells Fortunes: An Interview with Wanda Coleman." *Black American Literature Forum* 24, no. 3 (1990): 491–507.

Magloire, Marina. "Moving Towards Life." *Los Angeles Review of Books*, August 7, 2024.

Magloire, Marina. *We Pursue Our Magic: A Spiritual History of Black Feminism*. Chapel Hill: University of North Carolina Press, 2023.

Mason, Julian D., Jr., ed. *The Poems of Phillis Wheatley*. Chapel Hill: University of North Carolina Press, 1966. Enlarged ed., Chapel Hill: University of North Carolina Press, 1989.

McKay, Nellie. "Black Woman Professor—White University." *Women's Studies International Forum* 6, no. 2 (1983): 143–47.

McKay, Nellie Y. "Naming the Problem That Led to the Question 'Who Shall Teach African American Literature?'; or, Are We Ready to Disband the Wheatley Court?" *PMLA* 113, no. 3 (1998): 359–69.

McKay, Nellie Y., and Shanna Greene Benjamin. "Breaking the Whole Thing Open: An Interview with Nellie Y. McKay." *PMLA* 121, no. 5 (2006): 1678–81.

McKittrick, Katherine. *Demonic Grounds: Black Women and the Cartographies of Struggle*. Minneapolis: University of Minnesota Press, 2006.

Mock, Janet. *Redefining Realness: My Path to Womanhood, Identity, Love and So Much More*. New York: Atria Books, 2014.

Moody, Joycelyn, Frances Smith Foster, Nell Irvin Painter, et al. "In Memoriam: Professor Nellie Y. McKay (1930–2006)." *African American Review* 40, no. 1 (2006): 5–38.

Moonan, Wendy. "Slave Poet's 1776 Letter, 'New Discovery' Is for Sale." *New York Times*, November 11, 2005.

Morris, Susana M. *Close Kin and Distant Relatives: The Paradox of Respectability in Black Women's Literature*. Charlottesville: University of Virginia Press, 2014.

Morrison, Toni. *Beloved*. 1987. Reprint, New York: Vintage International, 2004.

Mossell, N. F. *The Work of the Afro-American Woman*. 1894. Reprint, New York: Oxford University Press, 1988.

Muller, Lauren, and the [Poetry for the People] Blueprint Collective, eds. *June Jordan's Poetry for the People: A Revolutionary Blueprint*. New York: Routledge, 1995.

Muñoz, José Esteban. *Cruising Utopia: The Then and There of Queer Futurity*. New York: New York University Press, 2009.

Murphy, Dana. "Imagining Black Steminist Care: Nnedi Okorafor's *Binti*." *Black Scholar: Journal of Black Studies and Research* 54, no. 2 (2024): 58–69.

Murphy, Dana. "Praisesong for Margaret Walker's *Jubilee* and the Phillis Wheatley Poetry Festival." *African American Review* 53, no. 4 (2020): 299–313.

Myers, Joshua. *Of Black Study*. Las Vegas: Pluto, 2023.

Nash, Jennifer C. *Black Feminism Reimagined: After Intersectionality*. Durham, NC: Duke University Press, 2019.

Nash, Jennifer C. *How We Write Now: Living with Black Feminist Theory*. Durham, NC: Duke University Press, 2024.

Newson, Adele S. *Zora Neale Hurston: A Reference Guide*. Boston: G. K. Hall & Co., 1987.

"November Meeting. Death of Lord Lyndhurst; Death of Hon. William Sturgis; Dr. Ephraim Eliot; Diary of Ezekiel Price; Letter of Count De Marbois; Phillis Wheatley; Letters of Phillis Wheatley." *Proceedings of the Massachusetts Historical Society* 7 (1863–64): 168–79.

Odell, Margaretta Matilda. *Memoir and Poems of Phillis Wheatley, a Native African and a Slave*. Boston: Geo. W. Light, 1834.

Okeowo, Alexis. "How Saidiya Hartman Retells the History of Black Life." *New Yorker*, October 19, 2020.

O'Neale, Sondra A. "Challenge to Wheatley's Critics: 'There Was No Other 'Game' in Town.'" *Journal of Negro Education* 54, no. 4 (1985): 500–511.

O'Neale, Sondra A. "A Slave's Subtle War: Phillis Wheatley's Use of Biblical Myth and Symbol." *Early American Literature* 21, no. 2 (1986): 144–65.

Ovid. *The Metamorphoses.* Translated by Mary M. Innes. New York: Penguin Books, 1955.

Ovid. *The Metamorphoses.* Translated by Horace Gregory. New York: Mentor, 1960.

Ovid. *The Metamorphoses.* Translated by Frank Justus Miller. Cambridge, MA: Harvard University Press, 1966.

Ovid. *The Metamorphoses.* Translated by William S. Anderson. Norman: University of Oklahoma Press, 1972.

Ovid. *Ovid's Metamorphoses in Fifteen Books.* Edited by Samuel Garth et al. London: Printed for Jacob Tonson, 1717.

Painter, Nell Irvin. *Sojourner Truth: A Life, a Symbol.* New York: W. W. Norton, 1996.

Parks, Carole A. "Report on a Poetry Festival: Phillis Wheatley Comes Home." *Black World* 23, no. 4 (1974): 92–97.

Philip, M. NourbeSe, as told to the author by Setaey Adamu Boateng. *Zong!* Middletown, CT: Wesleyan University Press, 2008.

Phillips, Rowan Ricardo. *When Blackness Rhymes with Blackness.* Champaign, IL: Dalkey Archive Scholarly, 2010.

Phillis [Wheatley]. *Complete Writings.* Edited by Vincent Carretta. New York: Penguin Books, 2001.

Phillis [Wheatley]. *Poems on Various Subjects, Religious and Moral.* London: Printed for A. Bell, 1773.

Phillis [Wheatley Peters]. *The Writings of Phillis Wheatley Peters.* Edited by Vincent Carretta. 2019. Reprint, Oxford: Oxford University Press, 2024. All my references to Phillis's writings are from this volume, unless otherwise noted.

Pinto, Samantha. *Infamous Bodies: Early Black Women's Celebrity and the Afterlives of Rights.* Durham, NC: Duke University Press, 2020.

Priest, Myisha. "Salvation Is the Issue." *Meridians* 8, no. 2 (2008): 116–22.

Prins, Yopie. *Victorian Sappho.* Princeton, NJ: Princeton University Press, 1999.

Prins, Yopie. "'What Is Historical Poetics?'" *Modern Language Quarterly* 77, no. 1 (2016): 13–40.

Quashie, Kevin. *Black Women, Identity, and Cultural Theory: (Un)Becoming the Subject.* New Brunswick, NJ: Rutgers University Press, 2004.

Quashie, Kevin. *The Sovereignty of Quiet: Beyond Resistance in Black Culture.* New Brunswick, NJ: Rutgers University Press, 2012.

Raboteau, Albert J. *Slave Religion: The "Invisible Institution" in the Antebellum South.* 1978. Reprint, Oxford: Oxford University Press, 2004.

Randall, Dudley, ed. *The Black Poets.* New York: Bantam Books, 1971.

Robinson, William Henry. *Phillis Wheatley and Her Writings.* New York: Garland Publishing, 1984.

Rowell, Charles H., and Jerry W. Ward. "Ancestral Memories: The Phillis Wheatley Poetry Festival." *Freedomways* 14, no. 2 (1974): 127–45.

Rutledge, Gregory, Kimberly Blockett, Alicia Kent, et al. "'The Nellie Tree,' or, Disbanding the Wheatley Court." *African American Review* 40, no. 1 (2006): 39–66.

Ryan, Jennifer. "The Transformative Poetics of Wanda Coleman's *American Sonnets*." *African American Review* 48, no. 4 (2015): 415–29.

Ryan, Jennifer, and Wanda Coleman. "'Come. Glory in My Wonder's Will': An Interview with Wanda Coleman." *MELUS* 40, no. 1 (2015): 195–205.

Santamarina, Xiomara. *Belabored Professions: Narratives of African American Working Womanhood*. Chapel Hill: University of North Carolina Press, 2005.

Savonick, Danica. *Open Admissions: The Poetics and Pedagogy of Toni Cade Bambara, June Jordan, Audre Lorde, and Adrienne Rich in the Era of Free College*. Durham, NC: Duke University Press, 2024.

Sesay, Chernoh, Jr. "Remembering Phillis Wheatley." June 26, 2016. *Black Perspectives*, African American Intellectual History Society, https://www.aaihs.org/remembering-phillis-wheatley/.

Shamasunder, Sriram. "June Jordan's Legacy of Solidarity and Love Remains Relevant." *YES!*, February 13, 2023. https://www.yesmagazine.org/opinion/2023/02/13/june-jordan-legacy.

Shockley, Evie. *a half-red sea*. Durham, NC: Carolina Wren, 2006.

Shockley, Evie. *the new black*. Middletown, CT: Wesleyan University Press, 2011.

Shockley, Evie. *Renegade Poetics: Black Aesthetics and Formal Innovation in African American Poetry*. Iowa City: University of Iowa Press, 2011.

Slauter, Eric. "Looking for Scipio Moorhead: An 'African Painter' in Revolutionary North America." In *Slave Portraiture in the Atlantic World*, edited by Agnes Lugo-Ortiz and Angela Rosenthal, 89–116. Cambridge: Cambridge University Press, 2013.

Slauter, Eric. "Neoclassical Culture in a Society with Slaves: Race and Rights in the Age of Wheatley." *Early American Studies* 2, no. 1 (2004): 81–122.

Smallwood, Stephanie E. "The Politics of the Archive and History's Accountability to the Enslaved." *History of the Present* 6, no. 2 (2016): 117–32.

Smallwood, Stephanie E. *Saltwater Slavery: A Middle Passage from Africa to American Diaspora*. Cambridge, MA: Harvard University Press, 2008.

Smith, Barbara, ed. *Home Girls: A Black Feminist Anthology*. 1983. Reprint, New Brunswick, NJ: Rutgers University Press, 2000.

Smith, Barbara. "The Souls of Black Women." *Ms.* 2, no. 8 (1974): 42–43, 78.

Smith, Barbara. "Toward a Black Feminist Criticism" (1977). *Radical Teacher*, no. 7 (1978): 20–27.

Smith, Cassander L. *Race and Respectability in an Early Black Atlantic*. Baton Rouge: Louisiana State University Press, 2023.

Smith, Derik. "Quarreling in the Movement: Robert Hayden's Black Arts Era." *Callaloo* 33, no. 2 (2010): 449–66.

Smith, Derik. *Robert Hayden in Verse: New Histories of African American Poetry and the Black Arts Era.* Ann Arbor: University of Michigan Press, 2018.

Smith, Eleanor. "Phillis Wheatley: A Black Perspective." *Journal of Negro Education* 43, no. 3 (1974): 401–7.

Springer, Kimberly. *Living for the Revolution: Black Feminist Organizations, 1968–1980.* Durham, NC: Duke University Press, 2005.

Stepto, Robert B. *From Behind the Veil: A Study of Afro-American Narrative.* Urbana: University of Illinois Press, 1979.

Sterling, Dorothy. *Black Foremothers: Three Lives.* 1977. Reprint, New York: Feminist Press, 1988.

Stetson, Erlene. "Studying Slavery: Some Literary and Pedagogical Considerations on the Black Female Slave." In *All the Women Are White, All the Blacks Are Men, But Some of Us Are Brave: Black Women's Studies,* edited by Akasha (Gloria T.) Hull, Patricia Bell-Scott, and Barbara Smith, 61–84. 1982. Reprint, New York: Feminist Press, 2015.

Stowe, Lyman Beecher. *Saints, Sinners and Beechers.* Indianapolis: Bobbs-Merrill, 1934.

Strongman, SaraEllen. "'Creating Justice Between Us': Audre Lorde's Theory of the Erotic as Coalitional Politics in the Women's Movement." *Feminist Theory* 19, no. 1 (2018): 41–59.

Sullivan, Mecca Jamilah. *The Poetics of Difference: Queer Feminist Forms in the African Diaspora.* Urbana: University of Illinois Press, 2021.

Tate, Claudia, ed. *Black Women Writers at Work.* 1983. Reprint, Chicago: Haymarket Books, 2023.

Taylor, Keeanga-Yamahtta, ed. *How We Get Free: Black Feminism and the Combahee River Collective.* Chicago: Haymarket Books, 2017.

Thomas, Claudia N. *Alexander Pope and His Eighteenth-Century Women Readers.* Carbondale: Southern Illinois University Press, 1994.

Thomas, Lorenzo. *Extraordinary Measures: Afrocentric Modernism and Twentieth-Century American Poetry.* Tuscaloosa: University of Alabama Press, 2000.

Thorn, Jennifer. "'All Beautiful in Woe': Gender, Nation, and Phillis Wheatley's 'Niobe.'" *Studies in Eighteenth-Century Culture* 37 (2008): 233–58.

Thorsson, Courtney. *The Sisterhood: How a Network of Black Women Writers Changed American Culture.* New York: Columbia University Press, 2023.

Tinsley, Omise'eke Natasha. *The Color Pynk: Black Femme Art for Survival.* Austin: University of Texas Press, 2022.

Truth, Sojourner. *Narrative of Sojourner Truth* (1850). Edited by Nell Irvin Painter. New York: Penguin Books, 1998.

Vigderman, Patricia. "From Rags to Rage to Art." Review of *In Search of Our Mothers' Gardens: Womanist Prose*, by Alice Walker. *The Nation*, December 17, 1983, 637.

Waldstreicher, David. *The Odyssey of Phillis Wheatley: A Poet's Journeys Through American Slavery and Independence*. New York: Farrar, Straus and Giroux, 2023.

Walker, Alice. *Gathering Blossoms Under Fire: The Journals of Alice Walker 1965–2000*. Edited by Valerie Boyd. New York: Simon & Schuster, 2022.

Walker, Alice. *In Search of Our Mothers' Gardens: Womanist Prose*. 1983. Reprint, Orlando: Harcourt, 2004.

Walker, Alice. "The Revenge of Hannah Kemhuff." In *In Love and Trouble: Stories of Black Women*, 60–80. 1973. Reprint, Boston: HarperOne, 2001.

Walker, Margaret. "How I Wrote *Jubilee*" (1972). In *How I Wrote Jubilee and Other Essays on Life and Literature*, edited by Maryemma Graham, 50–66. New York: Feminist Press, 1990.

Walker, Margaret. "Phillis Wheatley and Black Women Writers, 1773–1973" (1973). In *On Being Female, Black and Free: Essays by Margaret Walker, 1932–1992*, edited by Maryemma Graham, 35–40. Knoxville: University of Tennessee Press, 1997.

Walker, Rebecca. *Black, White, and Jewish: Autobiography of a Shifting Self*. 2001. Reprint, New York: Riverhead Books, 2002.

Washington, Mary Helen, ed. *Black-Eyed Susans/Midnight Birds: Stories by and About Black Women*. New York: Anchor Books, Doubleday, 1990.

Washington, Mary Helen. Foreword to *Their Eyes Were Watching God* (1937), by Zora Neale Hurston, vii–xiv. New York: Perennial Library, 1990.

Wheatley, Phillis. See Phillis.

White, Evelyn C. *Alice Walker: A Life*. New York: W. W. Norton, 2004.

White, Gillian. *Lyric Shame: The "Lyric" Subject of Contemporary American Poetry*. Cambridge, MA: Harvard University Press, 2014.

Williams, Delores S. *Sisters in the Wilderness: The Challenge of Womanist God-Talk*. Maryknoll, NY: Orbis Books, 1993.

Williams, Pontheolla T. *Robert Hayden: A Critical Analysis of His Poetry*. Urbana: University of Illinois Press, 1987.

Williams, Sherley Anne. *Dessa Rose*. 1986. Reprint, New York: Quill, 2018.

Williams, Sherley Anne. "From Meditations on History (1980)." *Callaloo* 22, no. 4 (1999): 768–70.

Williams, Sherley Anne. *Give Birth to Brightness: A Thematic Study in Neo-Black Literature*. New York: Dial, 1972.

Williams, Sherley [published as Shirley] Anne. *The Peacock Poems*. Middletown, CT: Wesleyan University Press, 1975.

Williams, Sherley Anne. "Remembering Prof. Sterling A. Brown, 1901–1989." *Black American Literature Forum* 23, no. 1 (1989): 106–8.

Williams, Sherley Anne. "Returning to the Blues: Esther Phillips and Contemporary Blues Culture." *Callaloo* 14, no. 4 (1991): 816–28.

Williams, Sherley Anne. "Some Implications of Womanist Theory." *Callaloo*, no. 27 (1986): 303–8.

Williamson, Terrion L. *Scandalize My Name: Black Feminist Practice and the Making of Black Social Life*. New York: Fordham University Press, 2017.

Wright, Richard. "Between Laughter and Tears." *New Masses*, October 5, 1937, 22, 25.

Wynter, Sylvia. "Beyond Miranda's Meanings: Un/Silencing the 'Demonic Ground' of Caliban's Women." In *Out of the Kumbla: Caribbean Women and Literature*, edited by Carole Boyce Davies and Elaine Savory Fido, 355–72. Trenton, NJ: Africa World Press, 1990.

Page numbers in italics refer to figures.

legibility, 7, 12, 34, 37, 53, 61, 77, 90, 96, 111, 146.
   See also audiences; legacy
Lenore Marshall Poetry Prize, 136, 202n115
lesbians, xi, 15, 37–38, 164n10, 168n72. *See also*
   queerness
letters. *See* correspondence
LGBTQ+ community, 7, 91. *See also* queerness
liberation, ix, xi, 3, 30, 35, 77, 84
"Liberty and Peace, a Poem" (Phillis), 84–85
Lorde, Audre, 39, 61, 99, 145, 164n13, 168n72,
   175n51, 175n54, 175–76nn56–57, 176nn60–62,
   179n102, 195–96n39, 196n46, 197–98n59,
   206n24; *The Cancer Journals*, 14, 168n64;
   death, 15, 56; ephemera, 40; papers, 39, 100;
   Sister Outsider, xi, 20, 38; "Uses of the Erotic,"
   16–17, 35–38, 175n46, 175n49
loss, 9, 12, 17, 34, 78, 86, 127, 141, 143, 147,
   169n76, 187n44, 201n93; archival, 5, 20, 24,
   27, 33, 46, 49–51, 54, 71–72, 128, 136, 153,
   177n79; death and, 14, 57, 124, 131, 135, 138,
   142, 197–98n59, 203n123, 203–4n134. *See also*
   cancer; death; elegy; Phillis, works, unpublished; unpublished works

manumission, xi, 21, 28–30, 34, 40, 42, 86,
   95, 128–29, 131, 173n31. *See also* freedom;
   freedwomen
maroonage, 120. *See also* fugitivity
marriage, 8–9, 45–46, 54–56, 68, 128, 166n30,
   166n34, 173–74n31, 178n84, 180n115
Massachusetts Historical Society (MHS), 42,
   45–49, 51–52, 54, 171n8, 178n87, 202n103
McDowell, Deborah, 199n69; "Negotiating
   Between Tenses," 62
McKay, Nellie Y., 8, 9, 65–66, 120, 145, 151–52,
   164n13, 183nn4–8, 184n20, 196n43; death,
   4, 56, 63–64, 121, 197–98n59–61; "Naming
   the Problem That Led to the Question," 4,
   63, 170n3, 182n1; *Norton Anthology of African
   American Literature*, 122, 124, 154, 156,
   199nn69–70, 202n120
McKittrick, Katherine, 186n40; *Demonic
   Grounds*, 77
memorialization, 4, 8, 15, 57–58, 61–62, 78,
   99–100, 102, 107, 125–26, 142, 162n18
mentorship, 2, 23–25, 61, 65, 69, 109, 146, 151–53,
   170n3, 177n77, 183nn4–5, 203n131
methodology, xv, 2–3, 10, 12, 21, 49, 70, 76–77,
   96, 107–8, 110–11, 118, 127, 145, 196n43;
   radical, 4, 56, 68, 87, 91; reparative, 112–13,
   115, 146

Middle Passage, 2, 9, 31, 78–79, 90, 95, 190n87.
   See also enslavement; transatlantic slavery
misreading, 31, 67, 109. *See also* legibility
Mock, Janet, 7, 165n21–22
Moorhead, Scipio. *See* Scipio
Morrison, Toni, 206n24; *Beloved*, 95, 174–75n45
Moten, Fred, 102, 120, 163n4, 200n78
motherhood, 10–11, 34–35, 59–60, 82–84,
   98, 105–7, 111–12, 114–15, 120, 135, 167n49,
   168n72, 169n76, 170n3, 187n44, 188n56,
   193nn12–13, 194n18, 196n41, 198n63, 202n116,
   204n135; single, 121, 181n129, 198n62,
   198–99n65
mourning, xv, 9, 14, 21–22, 56–58, 83, 86, 96,
   105, 109, 111–13, 117, 121–22, 124, 126, 130–31,
   142, 151–52, 169n76
multihyphenate figures, 15, 37, 59, 136, 168n72
muses, 57–58, 75–76, 81, 85, 132, 147–48
music, xii–xiv, 97–98, 100–101, 162n17, 162n19,
   199n75. *See also* blues; songs
Myers, Joshua: *Of Black Study*, 150, 165n26
myth, 85, 168n70; African diasporic, 39; benign
   slavery, 10, 42, 93; classical, 9, 57–58, 80–82,
   84, 87–88, 169n76

National Black Feminist Organization, 161–62n9,
   176n60, 194n20
nature, xii, 39–40, 59, 104–8, 116, 152, 206n33
neoliberal university, 125, 140, 151, 154. *See also*
   academic job market; adjunctification; tenure
networks, 6, 27–28, 30, 36, 39–40, 43, 61, 109,
   127, 132, 152, 170n3, 200n81
"Niobe in Distress" (Phillis), 80–89, 187–88nn51–62,
   188–89nn70–76
Norton Anthology of African American Literature,
   122–24, 154, 156, 199nn69–70, 202n120

Obour [Tanner], 20, 53, 171nn9–10, 173n23,
   173n27, 173n30, 175n46, 177n79, 180n117;
   bequest, 25–26, 39, 42–52, 54–56; correspondence, 27–36, 93–95, 172n11, 178n88, 179n92,
   190–91n101; death, 49, 171n7–8; name, 46,
   171n7, 178n84; piety, 46, 53–54; relationship
   with Phillis, 5, 9, 23, 39–41, 62, 71, 164n16,
   172n14, 172n17, 174–75n45
O'Neale, Sondra, 187n48; "A Slave's Subtle War,"
   79, 165n23
oral history, 17, 34, 98, 122, 174n34, 178n86,
   199n70
organizing, 23–24, 36, 38, 61, 68, 102, 145, 148,
   162n14, 176n60, 194n20, 200n85; events,

97–100; textual, 122, 144. *See also* activism;
individual organizations and groups
Ovid, *The Metamorphoses*, 80–82, 87–89, 187n51,
188n52, 188n56, 189nn80–81

pain, 23, 89–90, 110, 130, 137, 143, 150, 194n27,
204n136, 204n141. *See also* grief; hardship;
illness; loss; mourning
Painter, Nell Irvin, 174n44
painting, 80–82, 88, 167n57, 188n52, 196n41
participation, 20, 47, 71, 129, 198n61; cultural,
107, 162n14, 180n117; in print culture, 29, 36,
38; religious, 30, 173n27; scholarly, xii, xv, 43,
55, 63, 65–66, 79, 100, 155, 176n60; structural
power and, 94, 131, 135, 201n93
patronage, 41, 93–94, 191n110. *See also* Huntingdon,
Countess of
Paul Laurence Dunbar Centennial Celebration,
97, 100
pedagogy, 1, 34, 65, 109–10, 195n28
personal stakes, 5, 14, 21, 24, 37, 91, 104–6,
108–9, 134, 198n62
Peters, John, 8–9, 14, 46, 49, 54, 68, 71, 128,
166n30, 166n34, 172n16, 173n31
Philip, M. NourbeSe: *Zong!*, 8
Phillips, Esther, 118–19, 121, 135–36
Phillis [Wheatley]: care for, 11, 92; childhood,
166n30; correspondence of, 6, 20, 26–30,
33–34, 39–43, 46–47, 48–49, 50, 94–95,
128, 164n16, 172n11, 172n17, 178n88, 179n92;
death, xv, 10, 14, 28, 48–49, 85, 111, 132, 138,
151, 168n64; enslavement of, 2–3, 8–12, 32,
42–43, 53, 88, 93, 95, 112–14, 130–31, 145,
161n2, 166n30, 187n48, 195n34; images of,
12, 52–53, 114; legacy of, 3, 14, 19, 85–86,
96–97, 141, 172n12; name, 8, 10, 167n46;
papers, 71; trip to London, England, 10, 41,
53, 93–97
Phillis [Wheatley], works: "America," 84,
188n63; "On Being Brought from Africa to
America," 3, 31–33, 78–81, 87, 92, 96, 99, 130,
138, 147, 187n42, 187n45; "On the Death of a
Young Lady," 130; "On the Death of General
Wooster," 128–29, 132–33; "To His Excellency
General Washington," 84–85, 92, 188n63;
"Hymn to Humanity," 74–77, 186nn32–33,
186n38; "On Imagination," 104; "Liberty and
Peace, a Poem," 84–85; "Niobe in Distress,"
80–89, 187–88nn51–62, 188–89nn70–76;
"To the Right Honourable William, Earl of
Dartmouth," 92–93, 190nn94–95; "To the

University of Cambridge," 146–47, 149–50;
unpublished, 5, 14, 27, 49, 51, 71–72, 128–29,
131–33; "On Virtue," 138–39. See also *Poems on
Various Subjects, Religious and Moral* (Phillis)
Phillis (slave ship), 9–10
Phillis Wheatley Poetry Festival, 97–103,
192n133
photocopying, 21, 65–66, 68–69
Pinto, Samantha, 12
Poems on Various Subjects, Religious and Moral
(Phillis), x, 10, 20, 25, 28, 40, 42, 45, 70–72,
74–75, 79–81, 84, 86, 93, 96–97, 99, 126,
131–33, 135, 145, 147; sale of, 29–30, 49,
127–28, 134, 161n6, 173n28, 189n76
poetics, xv, 1, 3, 7, 10, 30, 49, 87–88, 122, 134, 141,
165n17, 177n79; Black feminist, 35, 143
Poetry Center (Stony Brook University), 148
Poetry for the People, 1
poetry readings, xii, 89–90, 102, 138–39, 176n57,
190n87
Poets House, 137
portraits, 52–53, 114–15, 195n35. *See also* painting
poverty, 10, 56, 106–7, 120, 136, 197n57
power, xii, 3, 5, 12, 22, 187–88n51, 188n56;
dynamics, 17, 25, 28, 34, 71, 81, 84, 107, 117,
135, 178n89, 195n30, 200n78, 201n93
praisesongs, xv, 57, 97, 144
Pratt Institute, 109
praxis, 2, 16, 64, 164n9
predominantly white spaces, xiii, 31, 42, 110,
126, 140
pregnancy, 11, 56, 180–81n119
preservation, 4, 11, 20–21, 45, 49, 52–53, 69, 83,
86, 93, 100, 117, 126
Priest, Myisha: "Salvation is the Issue,"
197–98n59
privacy, 27–28, 42, 44, 48, 55, 119–21, 127,
172n17, 198n60
publication, 37–38, 43–45, 55, 72, 76, 84–85, 90,
96, 111, 120–21, 132, 146, 154, 162n12; by subscription, 41, 46, 127–28, 133–34; out-of-print
texts, 21, 66, 183n10

Quashie, Kevin Everod, 17, 169n76, 206n22
queerness, 7, 9, 36, 54–55, 91, 93, 102, 113.
See also lesbians
queer studies, 7, 20, 61, 165n21, 182n138
quilting, 69, 115, 167n49, 194n18

Raboteau, Albert J.: *Slave Religion*, 31–34, 171n9,
174n34, 174n41